WOMEN AND PHILANTHROPY IN NINETEENTH-CENTURY IRELAND

MARIA LUDDY

Lecturer in History, Institute of Education, University of Warwick

CAMBRIDGE
UNIVERSITY PRESS

Published by the Press Syndicate of the University of Cambridge
The Pitt Building, Trumpington Street, Cambridge CB2 1RP
40 West 20th Street, New York, NY 10011–4211, USA
10 Stamford Road, Oakleigh, Melbourne 3166, Australia

First published 1995

Printed in Great Britain at the University Press, Cambridge

A catalogue record for this book is available from the British Library

Library of Congress cataloguing in publication data
Luddy, Maria.
Women and philanthropy in nineteenth-century Ireland/Maria Luddy.
p.   cm.
Includes bibliographical references and index.
ISBN 0 521 47433 7 (hardback)
1. Women philanthropists – Ireland – History – 19th century.
2. Women social reformers – Ireland – History – 19th century.
I. Title.
HV541.L83   1995
361.7′4′082 – dc20   94–30052–CIP

ISBN 0 521 47433 7 hardback
ISBN 0 521 48361 1 paperback

This book represents a new departure in Irish history providing the first comprehensive examination of the role of women in philanthropy in nineteenth-century Ireland. The author focuses on the impact of religion on the lives of women and argues that the development of convents in the nineteenth century inhibited the involvement of lay Catholic women in charity work. Sectarianism was a dominating feature of women's philanthropic activity and this is most clearly evident in women's work with children. The author also analyses the work of women in areas of moral concern such as prostitution, prison and temperance work. The book concludes by examining the links between philanthropy and politics arguing that non-conformist rather than Catholic women were to the fore in reformist organisations which sought social and political change in Irish Society. This study makes an important contribution both to Irish history and to our knowledge of women's lives and experiences in the nineteenth century.

WOMEN AND PHILANTHROPY IN NINETEENTH-CENTURY IRELAND

For my parents
Simon and Rose

Contents

Tables

Acknowledgements

This book could not have been completed without the assistance of a large number of people. Professor Tom Dunne, who supervised the original thesis, has my deepest gratitude for the help, encouragement and advice provided over a long number of years. Writing on such a broad topic allowed me to travel to various archives in Ireland and England. I would like to thank the staffs of the National Library, Dublin, the Public Records Office in Dublin and Belfast, the Royal Irish Academy, Dublin, the British Library and the Fawcett Library in London for their assistance in locating material. Mr David Sheehy of the Dublin Diocesan Archive provided valuable assistance in locating uncatalogued documents. During the course of my research I had occasion to visit a number of convents and was met at all times not only with abundant hospitality, but also unlimited access to archive material. I would like to thank the following in particular for their help: Sr Francis Brigid, RSC, Milltown; Sr Good Counsel of the Good Shepherd Convent in Limerick; Sr Magdalena of the Mercy Convent in Baggot St, Dublin; Sr Martina of the Good Shepherd Convent, Waterford; Sr Pierre of the Mercy Convent in Limerick. I also wish to express my thanks to the committee of the Cottage Home for Little Children in Dun Laoghaire for allowing access to their records. Mr Evan Hassell of the Harcourt Home provided me with introductions to the committees of many charitable societies. Miss N. Dwyer of Miss Carr's Children's Home and the committees of St John's House of Rest, Denny House, the Girls' Friendly Society and the Young Women's Christian Association were generous in providing material.

A number of individuals have read earlier drafts of this book either in its entirety or as single chapters. Professor Leslie Clarkson advised a number of alterations which he will recognise in this text. Mary Cullen and Margaret MacCurtain provided valuable comments. Dympna McLoughlin has always proved stimulating company for the discussion of the history of Irish women and has influenced aspects of this work. My very good friends, Dr Des Marnane and Dan Finnan have been there from the start, offering all kinds of encouragement. The anonymous readers for Cambridge University Press have also helped make this a better book. My thanks must also go to Warwick University which granted study leave that allowed me to finish this work.

My sister, Geraldine, spent long hours checking and rechecking figures and helped in all sorts of ways, as only a sister can. Virginia Crossman has read and reread these pages on more occasions than I am sure even she wishes to recall. Her comments have been invaluable and her continued support more than I deserve.

Abbreviations

CAI	Cork Archives Institute
DDA	Dublin Diocesan Archives
EWJ	*Englishwoman's Journal*
EWR	*Englishwoman's Review*
GSC	Good Shepherd Convent
HC	House of Commons Papers
MC	Mercy Convent
NLI	National Library of Ireland
PRO	Public Records Office
PRONI	Public Record Office, Northern Ireland
RCB	Representative Church Body Library
RCPI	Royal College of Physicians of Ireland
RSC	Religious Sisters of Charity
RSC/G	Religious Sisters of Charity, Generalate

Introduction

'The great and weighty business of life', preached the Rev. John Gregg in 1856, 'devolves on men, but important business belongs to women.' 'Women', he proclaimed, 'have the honourable employments of instructing childhood ... [their] labours may be in the sickroom, the chambers of affliction, in the haunts of misery [and] amongst the struggling poor.'[1] Few individuals, either Catholic or Protestant, would have disagreed with him. In fact, by mid-century it was widely agreed that women had played a major role in providing charity to the poor and outcast. The tradition of benevolence which middle and upper-class women had developed by mid-century became even more pervasive as the century progressed. Asserting their moral and spiritual right to engage in charitable work, women's social activism was to have a profound influence on Irish life in the nineteenth and twentieth centuries.

Although limited by society's expectations to the home in the early years of the century, middle-class Irish women increasingly made use of their given spiritual and moral influence to justify their entrance into society, especially through philanthropic work. They developed institutions and societies on a local and national scale, to deal with the problems of the poor, the outcast and deviant, and neglected and orphaned children. Their philanthropic work took many forms, from mere almsgiving, to the provision of employment for women and girls, the building of institutions to house the homeless and outcast, the initiation of schemes to make the poor less dependent on charity, the development of programmes to facilitate moral reform, work in public institutions such as workhouses, hospitals and prisons, and the provision of orphanages. By the end of the century women had played a major role in developing a com-

[1] Rev. John Gregg, *Women: A Lecture* (Dublin, 1856), pp. 4–5.

1

paratively humane and all-embracing welfare system and in the process had broadened their sphere of action and influence from the private to the public sphere.

The world of the nineteenth-century middle and upper-class woman was limited, it has been claimed, by the ideology of separate spheres which functioned to prescribe certain roles for both men and women.[2] Whether the dichotomy between the public and private worlds was as sharp as has been declared by historians is open to question.[3] The Irish case is particularly interesting in this respect. Irish women were reminded of their maternal and nurturing role through secular and religious teachings, and yet although the world of work was extremely limited for middle and upper-class women, their activities in the philanthropic sphere brought these women into the public world without any great tension.

The overwhelming importance of religion in the lives of nine-teenth-century Irish women cannot be overemphasised. Voluntary effort was the response of women to their Christian duty to help the deprived of society, but it was also, in many instances, an expression of the desire of philanthropists to control and reform the behaviour of those considered to be the outcasts of society, which essentially meant those who did not conform to ideas of middle-class respect-ability, such as prostitutes and others deemed to be moral degener-ates. The attempt to impose a middle-class sense of morality on the poor is one of the major elements in this study of charity work. The philanthropy of Irish women was also suffused with religious rhe-toric and imagery, particularly that of female religious. Religion decided the membership of philanthropic organisations, it targeted those who were considered most in need, it divided and separated women's organisations from each other.

[2] The 'cult of domesticity' and the 'separate sphere' theories have been used by American and British historians to describe the position of upper and middle-class women in nineteenth-century American and British societies. The ideologies developed from the removal of women as an economic power with the development of industrial society. To legitimise this removal women were urged to devote their energies to the family, the 'private sphere', and to cultivate the virtues of submissiveness, piety and domesticity. See Barbara Welter, 'The cult of true womanhood, 1820–1860', *American Quarterly*, 18 (1966); Nancy F. Cott, *The Bonds of Womanhood: Women's Sphere in New England, 1780–1835* (Yale University Press, 1977); Carroll-Smith Rosenberg, 'The female world of love and ritual: relations between women in nineteenth century America', *Signs*, 1:1 (1975), pp. 1–29.

[3] See, for example, Linda Kerber, 'Separate spheres, female worlds, woman's place: the rhetoric of women's history', *Journal of American History*, 75:1 (1988), pp. 9–39; Mary P. Ryan, *Women in Public* (Baltimore, 1990).

Without doubt women's involvement in philanthropy provided them with personal and group authority and power. Above all philanthropy was a business undertaking which required judicious use of resources, whether material or monetary, the keeping of accounts, in some instances the payment of individuals, and in many cases the maintenance of buildings. These practical functions and the power women wielded is often obscured in the trivial sentimentality of the annual reports which in some sense deny the very difficult and often arduous tasks that faced philanthropic women. Women's activities in the charitable sphere also added considerably to the welfare infrastructure of the country. The most lasting institutions were those established and maintained by female religious, seen in the myriad of hospitals, refuges, reformatories, industrial schools etc. that they managed. Women's charitable work and its suffusion with religious idealism also placed women in the vanguard of the fight for souls which was such an important part of formal religious consolidation by various denominations in the nineteenth century.

A tradition of philanthropy led a number of women to an understanding of the economic and social causes of poverty. This resulted in some women becoming politicised by their philanthropic involvement and organising reform societies to agitate for legislative changes to improve the condition of the poor and also the condition of women. Women involved in reform movements such as the Dublin Aid Committee (later the Irish Society for the Prevention of Cruelty to Children), and the Irish Workhouse Association, lobbied, successfully, for political action to be taken with regard to child protection and workhouse management. Many of these reformist women came to believe that it was only when women were granted the franchise, at local and national level, that they could properly influence government policy with regard to the poor. From the 1870s such women began to campaign for the right to vote.

While most philanthropic women, and particularly nuns, would never have judged their actions in political terms there is no doubt that their work had political implications. In determining the nature of 'respectability' philanthropic women were also tremendously influential. Their attempts to mould and often recreate the characters of individuals who entered their refuges (for example, prostitutes and ex-prisoners), helped to define what type of behaviour was acceptable in society. Their role in consolidating

church power, whether Catholic or Protestant, by evangelising on a
vast scale bolstered and strengthened those churches' positions
within society. The 'devotional revolution' identified by Emmet
Larkin as occurring in post-famine Ireland, where a more
entrenched Catholicism came to be practised by an apparently more
devout population, probably owed more to the influence of nuns
than has ever been acknowledged.[4] Philanthropic women thus had a
powerful and diverse impact on nineteenth-century Irish society.

   Much has been written in the area of women's philanthropy over
the last ten years and this study is informed by the findings of other
historians. F. K. Prochaska's pioneering work, *Women and Philan-*
thropy in Nineteenth-Century England,[5] covers all the major areas of
female philanthropy such as their financial importance to charity
work, their role in rescue work, visitation and public institutions.
What emerges from Prochaska's study is the pervasive nature of
women's charitable activities in England during this period, a fact
that is echoed in the Irish experience. The work of American
historians Mary P. Ryan, Nancy Hewitt, Anne Boylan and Lori D.
Ginzberg has also been influential.[6] All of these historians argue for
the relationship which existed between women's philanthropic
work, the development of middle-class culture and politics, and an
understanding and consolidation of gender identity amongst philanthropic women, particularly after the American civil war. What
emerges is a complex picture of women's benevolence which
spanned the entire political spectrum from conservative to radical,
where ideology differed amongst groups of women and where internal group dynamics was shaped by family ties, race and social class.
Boylan argues for three different types of organisational tradition
developing in America from the early years of the nineteenth
century, a benevolent, reformist and feminist tradition, and notes
that these traditions 'remained essentially separate'.[7]

   In contrast, the evidence which emerges from this study shows
that Irish women developed two strands in their philanthropic

----

[4] See the work of Emmet Larkin, 'The devotional revolution in Ireland, 1850–75', *American
   Historical Review*, 77:3 (1972), pp. 625–52.
[5] F. K. Prochaska, *Women and Philanthropy in Nineteenth-Century England* (Oxford, 1980).
[6] Anne M. Boylan, 'Women in groups: an analysis of women's benevolent organisations in
   New York and Boston, 1797–1840', *Journal of American History*, 71 (1984), pp. 497–523;
   Nancy A. Hewitt, *Women's Activism and Social Change: Rochester, New York, 1822–1872* (Ithaca,
   1984); Lori D. Ginzberg, *Women and the Work of Benevolence* (New Haven, 1990).
[7] Boylan, 'Women in groups', p. 514.

activity, and using Boylan's terms, these were a benevolent and reformist tradition. The dominant tradition was that of bene-volence. Voluntary benevolent institutions were expressions of a desire on the part of the majority of philanthropic women to do good within a specific organisation which limited both the scope and recipients of its charity. The second tradition, which developed in the latter half of the century, can be described as reformist. In a limited number of voluntary associations a minority of women attempted to improve the plight of the poor and outcast generally through public and political action. In membership, organisation and methods of operation both the benevolent and reform societies were quite distinct. It is also significant that women in reformist societies were most often to be found in organisations working alongside men to secure their desired ends. These latter organi-sations redefined the terms of benevolence to some extent. While still arguing for a greater sense of morality amongst the poor, they also developed scientific approaches to the problems of poverty. Whereas most benevolent organisations were separatist in the sense that women alone generally managed and worked for their own societies, reformist organisations were based on gender alliance.

There are obvious similarities between philanthropic organi-sations of the different countries, particularly in areas of fund-raising, structural organisation and the recipients of charity. There are always some women who are more concerned with political reform than with 'mere' acts of benevolence. There are also clear signs of development in women's philanthropic societies over the century and there is the obvious mushrooming of such organisations by the end of this period. However, for all the similarities that appear there are very obvious differences. In Ireland the impact of religion on women's charitable work is of major significance. The expansion of Catholic convent networks and their impact upon limiting the involvement of lay Catholic women in philanthropic work is a major area of concern within this study. It is an aspect which appears unique to the Irish situation and as yet no parallels have been revealed for other European countries. The sectarian nature of women's benevolence is also a feature which seems especially strong in Irish philanthropy and this is revealed most clearly in work carried out with children.

This study focuses on a number of specific issues. Chapter 1 outlines briefly the social and economic position of women in nineteenth-century Irish society. In chapter 2 the important role religion played in women's lives and its impact on the development of their philanthropic activity is examined. The work of female religious and the extent to which their involvement in charity work obviated the need for lay Catholic women to engage in philanthropic enterprises is examined. All charities were sectarian in the sense that they were established on a religious basis and many dealt only with the destitute of their own persuasion. Many did not intend to be so and were willing to help any who sought aid, but in practice the poor of the various denominations sought help from philanthropists of their own religious persuasion. Religion allowed women to exercise their maternal and moral skills in the service of the poor on a broad scale and religious support validated women's work in this area. Religious difference was also the main force which separated various philanthropic groups and prevented a critique of social institutions. Through their evangelical and philanthropic work women were a primary force in the consolidation of church power in the last century.

Chapter 3 examines the role women played in organising charitable societies to look after the needs of children. It is in the area of child care that the most determined and aggressive work of philanthropists took place. Here also is seen the extensive impact that religion had on such organisations. Enormous numbers of orphanages and poor schools were established to deal with destitute and orphaned children, and their regimes reflected women's attitudes towards the parental abilities and responsibilities of the poor and their concept of parenthood in general. It was also in work with children that religious tensions between voluntary organisations surfaced most frequently.

Chapter 4 outlines the work of women with prostitutes. The 'fallen woman' was the most feared outcast of society. Women pioneered work with prostitutes and attempted to reform and remould them in the image of the ideal wife and mother. In this chapter an attempt is made to examine the extent of prostitution in Irish society and to analyse how these outcast women used the institutions and societies set up for their reformation. Here we can see that the poor and outcast must not always be viewed as victims but could exercise some control over their own lives. The operation of the Magdalen asylums in reforming outcast women is particularly important for what it reveals about the women who ran them as well as those who were the focus of reforming zeal. While the work of reformation was generally undertaken by benevolent women the implementation of the Contagious Diseases Acts brought some of these women into the reformist fold. The involvement of Irish women in the campaign to repeal the Acts shows that some women actively questioned the existence of a sexual double standard. Chapter 5 continues on the theme of the 'fallen woman' by looking at the woman prisoner, the extent of female criminality and women's efforts to bring about reform not only in the prison system but also through the establishment of refuges and homes for these 'outcasts'.

In chapter 6 the general variety of women's charity work is examined to reveal that charity was selective and it was both class and gender biased. There were distinct differences between the charity allowed to the destitute poor, the 'respectable' poor and the 'genteel' poor. The provision of charity within rural communities is also examined and here a picture of personal and organised charity emerges. The development of women's reformist activities is considered against the background of almost a century's philanthropic work. The importance of the temperance movement and of a tradition of philanthropy in encouraging women to demand access to formal political power, and subsequent campaigns to enable women to become poor law guardians and to participate in local and national elections are the subjects which round off this study.

This work relies heavily on printed annual reports of various charitable organisations. For many of the societies studied even such material is incomplete and there is rarely a full sequence of consecutive reports. For those societies which are still in existence the source material is much more varied and the information in the annual reports can be supplemented by that in minute books and registers detailing receipts and expenditure and the number of people to whom relief was given. These also provide case histories of those helped. Annual reports, and even minute books, also give a very good picture of the perceptions of those who provided the charity but they tell us little or nothing about those who received it. However, there are some means available to gauge how the poor viewed the system of charity. By analysing the registers of the various Magdalen institutions, for example, we can arrive at some picture of the life of a prostitute and we can see them as people who often used the system for their own ends. Convent archives contain collections of annals, registers and other miscellaneous documents which are generally rich in detail and provide a fascinating insight into convent life of the nineteenth century. Diocesan archives proved to be a tremendously rich source of material. Here are letters from the poor seeking relief and favours from the bishops, a voluminous correspondence between various religious congregations and the bishops and most interesting of all copies of many of the annual reports of Protestant organisations, particularly those which were considered to be proselytising agencies.

The information gleaned from annual reports, minute books and registers has been supplemented by numerous articles penned by women in the newspapers and journals of the time. Both the *Englishwoman's Journal* and the *Englishwoman's Review* proved to be invaluable sources of information on nineteenth-century Irish women, with numerous articles about their philanthropic and political activism. There were also a number of contemporary journals which were concerned with the social issues of the day, the chief amongst these being the *Journal of the Statistical and Social Inquiry Society of Ireland* and the *Irish Quarterly Review*, the latter being especially informative about the provisions made for prisoners, juvenile delinquents and the outcast women of society, and the *Transactions of the National Association for the Promotion of Social Science*, which from mid-century debated major issues of social concern including various aspects of women's rights.

This study is in one sense a work of recovery, revealing the extent to which women shaped nineteenth-century Irish society. It is also a study of the moral power of middle and upper-class women and their attempts to use that power to define their own social and political base in Irish society.

CHAPTER 1

Women in Irish society: 1800–1900

The history of women in nineteenth-century Ireland is the history of millions of women of different classes, different opportunities and different expectations. During the nineteenth century population expansion and contraction, partial industrialisation, the over-whelming agricultural nature of the country, urbanisation, famine, emigration and political upheaval changed the structures of Irish society and affected the role of women in social, economic and political life. Women themselves acted individually and collectively throughout the century to bring about changes in their lives and in so doing were instrumental in shaping Irish society and its values, though the forms of individual and collective action were influenced by the economic circumstances in which women found themselves. This chapter provides a brief outline of the circumstances of women's lives in the last century. It considers, in particular, the issues of employment, education and poverty. The contraction of employment opportunities for women had a profound influence on the extent of female poverty. Such poverty was a problem that was of primary concern to women philanthropists.

WOMEN AND EMPLOYMENT

There is no reliable quantitative data on the employment patterns of women and men in the period 1800 to 1840. We must rely very much on contemporary evidence, often anecdotal, and on various surveys and reports to provide us with the detail necessary to build up a picture of women's economic activity. The evidence available makes it clear that women of the poorer classes contributed to the family economy in an essential way, both by performing unpaid work within the home and by providing additional sources of income, and their contribution often made the difference between survival and destitution. Mary E. Daly has noted that women's earnings in the pre-famine period were used to pay the rent or to purchase necessities and the employment opportunities of women, particularly in home industry, was a factor in allowing early marriage.[1] Contemporary evidence suggests the essential role women played in economic life. One investigation, conducted in 1818 and 1819, noted that 'at Skibereen females are employed in manufacturing flax . . . and are represented to contribute materially to the support of the family'.[2] At the same time in Cork city it was noted that women could find employment as 'workwomen [in] mantua making, and straw bonnet making; as fruit women, vegetable women, charwomen, and washer women, at the rate of 10d per day'.[3] Agricultural work also provided women with an income. In Ennis it was noted that they 'have little employment, except in the latter part of spring, in spreading potatoes, manure, and afterwards in weeding; during harvest time in binding corn and gathering potatoes'.[4] The loss of income from any of these sources could plunge a single woman or family into destitution. For Irish women homes were places of work where spinning and weaving, amongst other occupations, were carried out and were vital for the support of the family. The decline of the linen, cotton and woollen industries, experienced from the 1830s, caused hardship to families who depended on the supplementary income this employment brought.

Further evidence from the Poor Law Inquiry of the 1830s adds to the picture of the continual labour of the peasant woman. The evidence collected by the commissioners, from all strata of society, paints a vivid portrait of work, destitution and poverty. In County Mayo, for example, the Rev. Peter Ward informed the commissioners that women 'occasionally assist during the spring and harvest, there being no employment for them since the destruction of the linen trade. I have minutely inquired as to what a woman could earn at spinning linen or woollen, and find that the most an attentive spinster could earn would not exceed 4d per day; a female servant will, when so fortunate as to get service, obtain wages, sometimes 5s per quarter, sometimes 6s.'[5] In County Cork, the Rev.

[1] Mary E. Daly, 'Women in the Irish workforce from preindustrial to modern times', *Saothar*, 7 (1981), pp. 74–82.
[2] *First Report of the General Board of Health in the City of Dublin* (Dublin, 1822), p. 64.
[3] Ibid., p. 65.
[4] Ibid., p. 69.   [5] *Poor Inquiry* (Ireland), appendix D, HC 1836 [36], xxxi.

Patrick Quinlan noted that 'the labouring women and children are employed at the selling of potatoes, binding of corn, and picking potatoes; their usual hire with diet is from 3d to 4d per day'.[6] Women in urban areas tended to work at occupations connected with textiles, retailing and provisioning and also of course, they shared the labour in their husbands' trades or businesses. The majority of the population, in pre-famine Ireland, lived at subsistence level, dependent on small agricultural holdings and seasonal employment in order to survive.

The Great Famine of 1845–50, rather than being a watershed in Irish economic and social history, may have accelerated changes already occurring in the economic and social life of the country. The most dramatic and immediate effect of the famine was to reduce the population by 1.5–2 million. The population of the country continued to decline from 6.5 million in 1851 to 4.39 million by 1911.[7] A high emigration rate and a low birth rate ensured this continued population decline. The famine had consequences also for women's work. Changing patterns of land holding and land usage, alterations in marriage and inheritance systems, the low level of industrialisation, changing expectations amongst families regarding women's function and a high level of emigration played their part in altering women's work patterns in Ireland.[8]

The traditional fields of employment for women were domestic work, agricultural work and textile work. The poor level of industrialisation in Ireland meant that factory work was not widely available to women.[9] The exception was the northern part of the country where Belfast and Derry had become the textile centres of the country. Domestic service remained the greatest employer of women, an occupation considered by many to be ideally suited to single women.[10] While preparing to marry and organise her own home she could acquire all the necessary skills in the home of an employer. While the census figures do not detail the exact level of employment engaged in by women they reveal some general trends in women's employment. With the exceptions of the professional

[6] Ibid.
[7] Mary Daly, *A Social and Economic History of Ireland Since 1800* (Dublin, 1981), chapter 5.
[8] L. Kennedy and L. A. Clarkson, 'Birth, death and exile: Irish population history, 1700–1921' in B.J. Graham and L.J. Proudfoot (eds.), *An Historical Geography of Ireland* (London, 1993), pp. 158–84.
[9] *Census of Ireland*, 1881.   [10] Ibid.

and commercial classes, all classes of female employment experienced a decline.[11] In 1881, for example, 48 per cent of the female
workforce were to be found in the domestic class, by 1901 that class
made up 35.2 per cent of the female workforce. In 1881 the
percentage of female agricultural workers was 12, but by 1911 that
percentage had fallen to 3.2.[12] It was the middle classes which
benefited most from the increases in professional employment. The
numbers of women engaged as teachers, nurses, shop assistants,
female religious, doctors, clerks and journalists had increased significantly over the period and by 1901 made up almost 6 per cent of
adult female employment.[13] This increase also reflected the beneficial effects of secondary and higher education for women.
Throughout the century women's earnings were generally much
lower than those of men. On average, women earned one to
two-thirds less than men for work of comparable value. In the second
decade of the century women workers earned £1 10s to 2 guineas for
six months work as farm servants where male servants, working
under the same conditions earned from 3 to 4 guineas. Weekly wages
for women in the Belfast linen mills averaged 11s in 1875 rising to 12s
by 1906.[14]

Though Ireland was to remain an agricultural economy, by the
end of the century many more Irish men and women lived in urban
areas and were employed in non-agricultural occupations than had
previously been the case. The extent of urbanisation was, by
European standards, relatively limited. By 1901, however, 31 per
cent of Irish people lived in towns and cities with a population of
over 2,000.[15] There was no great transformation in the work
available to women as a result of urbanisation. It is clear that
women, of necessity, worked whenever and wherever they could find
employment. Throughout the century women engaged in 'respectable' employments such as weaving, spinning, agricultural and
industrial labour but women also earned an income through the less
respectable occupations of begging, huxtering and prostitution.

Another aspect of post-famine Irish society was the high level of
emigration amongst Irishwomen. Emigration from Ireland had been
a reality since the eighteenth century and between 800,000 and

---

[11] *Census of Ireland*, 1911.   [12] Ibid.   [13] *Census of Ireland*, 1901.
[14] Daly, *Social and Economic History*, pp. 105–7.
[15] S.A. Royle, 'Industrialization, urbanisation and urban society in post-famine Ireland
c.1850–1921', in Graham and Proudfoot, *Historical Geography of Ireland*, pp. 258–92.

1,000,000 people left the country in the period 1815 to 1845.[16] Between 1851 and 1900, 1,941,618 men and 1,789,133 women emigrated and in the last decade of the nineteenth century the emigration of Irish women exceeded that of men by 30,386.[17] In the pre-famine period emigrants tended to be either single males or family groups, many coming from the northern counties. In the post-famine period women began to make up a larger proportion of emigrants than previously. For many women the shores of America, and other countries, were more appealing than those of Ireland.

One of the more striking demographic trends in Ireland in the post-famine period was the growing number of single women. In 1871, 43 per cent of all women aged between 15 and 45 were married, by 1911 that had dropped to 36 per cent.[18] Just over 8 per cent of the adult female population over the age of 35 were single in 1901. At the same time just over 9 per cent of the adult female population were widows. By 1911 celibacy levels for women had doubled and the average age at marriage for Irishwomen was 28.[19] The possibility of marriage and whatever degree of financial security went with that state was a less likely life choice for a significant number of Irish women as the century progressed. Contracting employment opportunities, the lack of economic independence, the real possibility of spinsterhood and increased emigration were amongst the forces shaping women's experience in the nineteenth century.

A combination of circumstances made women more vulnerable to economic hardship than men. Lack of employment opportunities, poor pay, lack of skills, various life crises such as desertion by a spouse, the incapacity of a spouse, pregnancy, the number of dependent children and age all influenced women's ability to support themselves or their families. Since women's work was generally irregular or seasonal, their capacity to remain economically independent was limited. Women, for example, were much more likely to enter state institutions of relief, such as the workhouse, than men. Women were also to be found in greater numbers in both religious and lay run philanthropic institutions.

[16] David Fitzpatrick, *Irish Emigration 1801–1921* (Dundalk, 1984).
[17] W.E. Vaughan and A.J. Fitzpatrick (eds.), *Irish Historical Statistics, Population 1821–1971* (Dublin, 1978), pp. 261–3.
[18] Daly, *Social and Economic History*, p. 92.
[19] Kennedy and Clarkson, 'Birth, death and exile'.

STATE PROVISION FOR THE POOR

The historian Oliver MacDonagh has noted the extent to which the state became involved in welfare provision in nineteenth-century Ireland.[20] There was, for example, an extensive dispensary system which catered for the poor in operation from 1805 and a state supported hospital system which was well in place by the 1840s. This was in contrast to the situation which prevailed in England. The introduction of the poor law system in 1838, based on the English model, was another step in the attempt to contain Irish poverty. Government was concerned by the extent of Irish poverty and by the fact that many Irish paupers made their way to England to search for work and often became a burden on the poor law there. The Irish poor law divided the country into 130 administrative areas, designated unions. Each union was to erect its own workhouse which was to be administered by a local board of guardians, drawn principally from the local landed gentry. The workhouses were to be made as unattractive as possible to inmates to deter all but the most desperate cases from seeking relief. Within the workhouses families were split up, though children under two could stay with their mothers. Despite the rules and regulations which were intended to govern the workhouse and to control the lives of those within its walls, many of the inmates were able to use the system for their own ends. Dympna McLoughlin has shown, for example, how female paupers used assisted emigration schemes organised by some boards of guardians to make their way to America and other countries.[21]

During the period of the famine the workhouses became overcrowded and could not deal with the level of distress which had arisen in the country. In an attempt to deal with the disaster the government instituted relief committees throughout the country. By July 1846 almost 700 such committees had been instituted, offering employment and food to the people. In March of 1847 the government introduced soup kitchens, and during the summer of that year almost 3 million people a day were receiving relief in the form of soup. The soup kitchens lasted until September 1847. During the

---

[20] Oliver MacDonagh, *Ireland: The Union and its Aftermath* (London, 1977).
[21] Dympna McLoughlin, 'Workhouses and Irish female paupers, 1840–70', in Maria Luddy and Cliona Murphy (eds.), *Women Surviving: Studies in Irish Women's History in the 19th and 20th Centuries* (Dublin, 1990), pp. 117–47.

famine the number of workhouses was increased to 163.[22] The
workhouses were so full that by the winter of 1847–8 the poor law
commissioners authorised outdoor relief to the able-bodied. In July
1849 the workhouses housed over 200,000, with another 800,000 on
outdoor relief.[23] In 1848 a total of 417,139 persons were relieved in
the workhouse, rising to 932,284 in 1849. At the same time 1,433,042
were in receipt of outdoor relief, a figure that fell to 1,210,482 in
1849.[24] Although placed under great stress during the period of the
famine the workhouses remained the principal state system of relief
for paupers to the end of the century.

From the 1850s women were to be found in workhouses in greater
numbers than men. The entrance of women into workhouses tended
to be seasonal and coincided with employment opportunities available, for example, in agriculture. Table 1.1 reveals the number of
inmates in Irish workhouses between 1871 and 1901. Women were
also more likely to be found in charitable institutions, such as homes
for the aged, sick and infirm, than men. The number of women in
such institutions increased throughout the latter half of the century
revealing not only a willingness amongst women to seek aid outside
the institution of the workhouse, but also the desire of philanthropists, who were most often female, to cater to their needs.[25]

The most vulnerable sections of the community were children and
single women. As noted, occupations open to women were limited
and single women and widows, particularly if they had dependant
children, were more prone to destitution than married women.
Widows appear to have been especially at risk throughout the
century. They made up, on average, 10 per cent of the adult female
population throughout the century and received particular attention from philanthropists with a large number of widows'
almshouses operating in all parts of the country. There were at least
ninety-nine almshouses and widows' homes operating in Ireland in
the nineteenth century. Twenty-nine of these were either mixed or
catered for men, while the remainder looked after the needs of
women.[26] The extent to which women were susceptible to poverty

---

22 Cormac Ó Gráda, *The Great Irish Famine* (London, 1989), p. 45; Mary E. Daly, *The Famine in Ireland* (Dublin, 1986), p. 93.
23 Ibid.   24 Ó Gráda, *Irish Famine*, p. 46; Daly, *Famine*, p. 94.
25 See Maria Luddy, 'Women and Philanthropy in 19th Century Ireland' (Ph. D., University College Cork, 1989), appendix 2.
26 Ibid., appendix 1, for a list of the widow's almshouses operating in Ireland.

Table 1.1. *Inmates of workhouses, 1871–1901*

Year	Males	Females
1871	21,491	27,435
1881	26,314	29,516
1891	19,998	22,350
1901	21,343	21,700

Source: Census, Ireland, 1881, 1891, 1901

Table 1.2. *Permanent residents of charitable institutions in Ireland, 1851–1881*

Year	Males	Females
1851	569	1,702
1861	456	1,631
1871	629	2,500
1881	858	2,953

Source: Census, Ireland, 1881

can be demonstrated by examining admissions of women to charitable institutions. Table 1.2 shows that women were more likely than men to be found in charitable institutions, such as homes for the aged, infirm or sick.

According to the 1881 census there were 148 hospitals, asylums and almshouses which provided a permanent residence for those who were ill or distressed. The total number of places available within these institutions was 5,575 and more than 72 per cent of these places were taken up by women. It is interesting to note that the numbers of girls in orphanages and industrial schools considerably outnumbered boys. In 1871, for example, 5,174 girls and 2,908 boys were catered for in these institutions. In 1901 more than 62 per cent of the inmates of these institutions were girls.[27] There are also other indicators of poverty amongst women. In the census figures available regarding beggars, females of all ages numbered 10,444 as against 2,586 males in 1861. Female vagrants numbered 8,394 as against 2,269 males in 1871.[28] Women philanthropists responded to the extent of poverty in Ireland by instituting various types

[27] *Census of Ireland*, 1871, 1901.   [28] *Census of Ireland, General Report*, 1861, 1871.

of charitable organisations which catered for the poor at all levels.

While the state pioneered many innovations in the provision of welfare, such as the dispensary system, the work of female and male philanthropists was significant and far-reaching. As the century progressed the organisation of welfare services fell more directly into the hands of philanthropists, either lay or religious. For example, the reformatory and industrial schools established by the government in the 1850s and 1860s would not have been feasible without the already existing network of religious and lay run institutions which took over, or in many instances expanded, the care received by destitute children.[29] The variety of charitable institutions organised by philanthropists also reduced the burden of financial support the government had to make for the poorest sections of the population.

EDUCATION

One of the major changes to occur in women's lives in the nineteenth century was the expansion of secondary and higher education. The establishment of the National Board of Education in 1831 attempted to introduce a non-denominational educational system into the country. Its subsequent history proved that such an ideal was unworkable and in reality the majority of schools under the national system were run by and for Catholics. By 1900 there were over 8,684 national schools in operation throughout the country.[30] For the majority of pupils the three Rs provided the basic curriculum with an emphasis on domestic skills being imparted to girls.

The most dramatic change in girls' education in the nineteenth century came about in the secondary and third levels. The establishment of the Ladies' Collegiate School (later Victoria College) in Belfast in 1859 and the Queen's Institute (1861) and Alexandra College (1866), both in Dublin, heralded new directions in the education of middle-class girls. The pioneers of these schools and colleges, individuals such as Margaret Byers, Isabella Tod and Ann Jellicoe, also organised campaigns to ensure that girls would benefit from any changes brought about in education through legislation. The passing of the Intermediate Education Act in 1878 was an important development in making higher education available to women and Tod and Byers campaigned to ensure that girls would

---

[29] Jane Barnes, *Irish Industrial Schools, 1868–1908* (Dublin, 1989).
[30] Daly, *Social and Economic History*, p. 116.

benefit from the changes proposed. The Act of 1878 was concerned
with second level education. It opened up intermediate examinations to boys and girls and provided government grants to both
male and female students on an equal basis.[31]

Writing in 1874, Isabella Tod summed up the prevailing attitudes amongst the middle classes to their daughters. Middle-class
parents, she wrote, looked forward to 'all their daughters marrying,
to all these marriages being satisfactory, and to the husbands being
always able and willing to take the active management of every-
thing . . . We shall not stop to discuss whether such a state of things
is even desirable. It is sufficient to point out that it does not and
cannot exist.'[32] Tod was arguing for the extension of educational
opportunities for middle-class women which would enable them to
engage in suitable employment. That a debate about women's education and employment could take place in the 1870s showed how
much Irish society had changed for women. Women of the middle
classes were beginning to demand greater educational opportunities
and were also seeking access to formal political power in the shape
of the franchise at local and national level. The recognition that
marriage could not ensure women's financial survival, that the
possibility of marriage for many women did not, in fact, exist,
altered middle-class women's relationship to the world of education
and work.

The Royal University of Ireland Act of 1879 opened up university examinations to women. The Protestant colleges, such as
Victoria and Alexandra did well in these examinations and convents began to offer their students advanced opportunities from
1882. In that year the Dominican convent in Eccles Street in
Dublin offered higher education for Catholic women. By 1895,
Loreto College, also in Dublin, was established for the higher education of women and all of these colleges, together with establishments in the north of Ireland, played a vital role in opening up
higher education to women.[33] The changes brought about in
women's education by the end of the century led to women playing
an important role in the political, cultural and social life of the

---

[31] See the articles in Mary Cullen (ed.), *Girls Don't Do Honours: Irishwomen in Education in the 19th and 20th Centuries* (Dublin, 1987).
[32] I.M.S. Tod, *On the education of girls of the middle-classes*, pamphlet (London, 1874), pp. 9–10.
[33] On the higher education of women in Ireland see Eibhlín Breathnach, 'Women and higher education in Ireland, 1879–1914', *The Crane Bag*, 4 (1980), pp. 47–54.

country. Many of the changes brought about had been fought for by women who had their activist roots in the philanthropic organisations of the nineteenth century.

WOMEN AND POLITICS

Historians tend to view women's involvement in nineteenth-century politics as being limited to their quest for the vote and their role in the land war through the work of the Ladies' Land League. Women were, in fact, an active force in the political life of the country on a formal and informal basis. Throughout the century women played their part in riots, election mobs, agrarian secret societies and faction fights.[34] Many of their concerns were rooted in local political and economic circumstances with issues relating to land holding or representation being the most important. Though women, and indeed most men, did not have a formal political role as electors they influenced the outcome of elections in a multitude of ways, through, for example, rioting, intimidation and bribery. The range of women's political activity is too great to go into here in any detail but informal activity remained part of women's political repertoire throughout the century. During the land war, for instance, many commentators noted the extent to which women played a key role in intimidating process servers.[35]

From the 1860s women also began to play an important public role in formal political life. Many of women's political concerns, as will become apparent from this study, developed from their philanthropic interests. Women became involved in the fight to repeal the Contagious Diseases Acts and fought successfully for the poor law and local government franchises. At the same time women campaigned for improved educational opportunities for women, agitated for alterations in the married women's property laws, and fought, successfully, for state intervention in issues concerned with the welfare of the poor and destitute. Those women most involved in formal politics were from the middle classes, and the majority had their roots in philanthropic organisations. Women and children throughout the nineteenth century were the primary recipients of charity which came increasingly to be provided by other women,

---

[34] K.T. Hoppen, *Elections, Politics and Society in Ireland, 1832–1885* (Oxford, 1984), pp. 406–8.
[35] See, for example, Janet K. TeBrake, 'Irish peasant women in revolt: the land league years', *Irish Historical Studies*, 28:109 (May 1992), pp. 63–80.

either lay or religious. At the same time philanthropic activism was to have profound social and political consequences not only on the beneficiaries of charity, but also on the women who provided that aid.

CHAPTER 2

Women, religion and philanthropy

The Rev. Bernard O'Reilly, in his book, *The Mirror of True Womanhood*, noted in the 1870s that Catholic female religious were, 'guided by the divine instinct ... [they] seek each other's society to encourage each other to live godly lives ... as well as to plan means for relieving the poor, providing for the needs of a church in debt, or from saving from want, temptation and ruin the youthful and destitute of their own sex'.[1] Throughout the nineteenth century Irish middle-class women of all religious persuasions developed an enduring tradition of establishing voluntary agencies and societies which catered for the needs of the destitute of their own sex and for children. Without doubt, however, the greatest power and control over philanthropic endeavours exercised by women was that of Catholic female religious. One result of their pre-eminence in the philanthropic field is revealed by the almost complete absence, most noticeably from the 1850s onwards, of independent charitable societies organised by lay Catholic women. From the early years of the nineteenth century Catholic women's contribution to charity work became vested in religious congregations, a move which was encouraged and often initiated by both clerics and lay individuals. This obviously had important consequences for the extent to which lay women became involved in voluntary effort and it also defined the structure and limits of the societies they organised.

The majority of charitable societies founded, or managed, by lay Catholic women in the period prior to the 1850s were refuges.[2] These catered for the needs of women who were elderly and incap-

---

[1] Rev. Bernard O'Reilly, *The Mirror of True Womanhood* (Dublin, n.d.), pp. 337–8. This book was an advice manual for Catholic women. It had originally been published in America in 1877 and went through at least thirteen editions.

[2] See Luddy, 'Women and philanthropy', appendices 1 and 2, for lists of charitable enterprises.

able of looking after themselves, the unemployed, and those who were considered outcast, either as prostitutes or as ex-prisoners. Throughout the late eighteenth and nineteenth centuries prostitution was a considerable problem in Irish cities[3] and the regime imposed in these refuges attempted to reform and rehabilitate 'fallen' women. Such work was considered to be ideally suited to women because they were thereby seen to be helping the most 'misfortunate' of their own sex. For example, the Magdalen asylum in Galway city was founded in 1832 by a Miss Lynch who returned from France to undertake the work. She died in 1847 but by then had ensured that the Sisters of Mercy would take over the refuge. A note in the annals of the convent observed that 'she spent her best years and the greatest part of her income in the service of the poorest, the most abandoned and the most wretched of earth's erring creatures'.[4] Little is known about the operations of these early asylums since this type of charity work was carried on out of the public eye and the refuges managed by Catholic women published no annual reports. Many other charitable institutions taken over by nuns had previously been operated by lay women. The Refuge in Ashe Street had been run as a home for destitute women from 1811 when it was handed over to the Sisters of Charity by the lay women's committee in 1815.[5] A number of the Catholic Magdalen asylums had been managed originally by clerical and lay committees before eventually being handed over to various religious congregations.[6]

From the evidence available it appears that Catholic clerics offered support to the women who managed these asylums, principally by recommending suitable cases for reform, by raising funds and attending to the religious needs of the inmates. In some instances also there is clear evidence that some Catholic clerics exerted a degree of control over lay women philanthropists which is not to be found amongst clerics of other persuasions. The Magdalen asylum in Limerick was established in 1824 by a Miss Reddan and operated by her until 1848 when the Sisters of the Good Shepherd were invited from France to take over its management. Little is known of Reddan's background but her motivation for establishing the refuge was certainly inspired by religious idealism. She was involved in other charitable work in Limerick and nursed cholera

---

[3] See chapter 4.   [4] Personal correspondence with the Mercy convent, Galway.
[5] S[arah] A[tkinson], *Mary Aikenhead: Her Life, Her Work and Her Friends* (Dublin, 1879), p. 499.
[6] See chapter 4.

patients in the epidemic of 1832. She was anxious to join a religious community, the Mercy congregation being her preference, but was not allowed to do so by the local bishop, Dr Ryan, until she could guarantee that the refuge would continue. When she invited the Good Shepherd Sisters to Ireland her way was again barred as the bishop thought that she should join that congregation and it was only after an unsuccessful noviciate with those sisters that she was allowed to join the Mercy nuns.[7] The refusal by Ryan to allow Reddan to join the Mercy congregation is an example of the authority and power exercised by Catholic clerics over lay women's philanthropic work; an authority and power which became more pervasive as the century progressed.

Religion gave middle-class women the excuse to organise voluntarily, to enter the public domain and engage in work which was considered socially useful. While Protestant and Quaker women developed an independent and secular tradition of philanthropic involvement which removed itself, within the first three decades of the century, from clerical influence Catholic women did not do so. In societies organised by Catholics the clergy exerted a powerful control over the direction taken by women philanthropists, seen particularly in the formation of female religious congregations, and the impact of such influence shaped the conservative nature of Catholic social action among both lay and religious.

FEMALE RELIGIOUS AND CHARITY WORK

Communities of Catholic female religious expanded dramatically during the last century. In 1800 there were 120 nuns in Ireland; by 1851 that number had risen to 1,500 and to over 8,000 by 1901.[8] By this time nuns made up more than a quarter of the professional adult women workers enumerated in the census returns. A study by Caitriona Clear has charted this expansion and analysed the general function of convents in Irish society.[9] My intention is to focus on nuns as groups of philanthropic women who were bound by relig-

---

[7] For some information on Reddan see M.C. Normoyle, *A Tree is Planted: the Life and Times of Edmund Rice* (Dublin, c. 1976, printed for private circulation), p. 259; MS, Synopsis of the annals (GSC, Limerick); Catriona Clear, *Nuns in Nineteenth-Century Ireland* (Dublin, 1987), p. 62.
[8] Tony Fahey, 'Nuns in the Catholic church in Ireland in the nineteenth century', in Cullen (ed.), *Girls Don't Do Honours*, p. 7.
[9] Clear, *Nuns*.

ious vows and to assess their role in the provision of services to the
needy in Irish society. The expansion of female religious communities during the last century accomplished a number of things, but
basically it provided relatively wealthy single women with the
opportunity of engaging in socially active work in a society which
denied that right to most middle-class women. It also answered the
obligations of the church to respond to the vast amount of poverty
and distress which existed within the country.

The founders of the native Irish congregations were women of
independent wealth and all of them had engaged in charitable work
prior to establishing religious communities. Nano Nagle, for
example, founder of the Presentation Order, operated poor schools
in Cork city, using her own financial resources, from 1755.[10] Mary
Aikenhead, founder of the Sisters of Charity, Frances Ball, founder
of the Loreto congregation, and Margaret Aylward, founder of the
Sisters of the Holy Faith, had all spent a long number of years
engaged in philanthropic work.[11] The primary motivation for the
charitable work of these women arose from strong and deeply held
religious convictions and all of them, with the exception of Catherine McAuley, were interested in entering the communal religious
life. The motivation to establish convents came, no doubt, from their
religious beliefs but it would also have been very difficult for these
women to continue their charitable work or to extend its scale
without organising on a communal basis. This had to take the form
of a religious community because it was the only collective grouping
of philanthropic women which was acceptable to Catholic church
authorities.

Catherine McAuley, for example, did not originally intend to
establish a religious community along the lines of that organised by
Mary Aikenhead. McAuley had been left a fortune of £28,000 by

---

[10] T. J. Walsh, *Nano Nagle and the Presentation Sisters* (Dublin, 1959), pp. 55–87. Nagle was, of
course, providing Catholics with education during the period when the penal laws were
still in existence. There were fears amongst the Catholics in Cork that Nagle's disregard for
the penal laws would provoke repressive action from the Protestant authorities (p. 52).
The Presentation Order was canonically erected in 1805 and the aspiration of Nagle that
they would operate among the people was altered by the taking of solemn vows and a rule
of enclosure which confined them to their convents. See Walsh, pp. 44–181; Clear, *Nuns*,
p. 49.

[11] See Member of the Congregation, *Life and Work of Mary Aikenhead* (London, 1925),
pp. 12–19; *Mary Aikenhead*, pp. 71–223; H.J. Coleridge, *The Life of Mother Frances Mary
Teresa Ball* (Dublin, 1881), pp. 34–6; and Margaret Gibbons, *The Life of Margaret Aylward*
(London, 1928) for details about these founders.

her adoptive father, William Callaghan, in 1822. Having worked in a poor school in Dublin she decided to set up an institution which would provide shelter and training to young girls. The home opened in Baggot Street, Dublin in September 1827. When McAuley took up permanent residence in Baggot Street in 1828 the home had a student population of 500 and was also taking in women for the refuge. McAuley's helpers, one of whom was her cousin, another the daughter of Daniel O'Connell, lived in a community bound by both their charitable work and by religious vows which they had taken privately. There was much opposition to these ventures from the inhabitants of the neighbourhood, who feared an influx of poor women into their fashionable street, and there was also a measure of hostility from the Catholic clergy to their work. Because of its structure this community of women, though established on a religious basis, remained outside the control of the church hierarchy. A public appeal for funds for the work of the women opened the way for attack. In 1829 one priest berated McAuley for attempting to usurp male prerogatives and deemed it inappropriate for women to engage in finance, philanthropy or business.[12] A Canon Kelly accused McAuley of encroaching on the work of the Sisters of Charity, previously established in 1815. By 1830 Kelly suggested to McAuley that Archbishop Murray intended handing over the work to the Sisters of Charity, with McAuley being allowed to remain within the convent as a lay woman. This, in fact, forced her to accede to the clergy's wishes. 'I never intended', she stated later in life, 'founding a religious congregation, all I wanted was to serve the poor since that seemed to be what God expected of me.'[13] The inability of McAuley to continue in her work outside the structure of a formal religious congregation underlines the power which the Catholic clergy exerted over groups of philanthropic women. Although her case may be an exception it is significant that the few groups of Catholic lay women who did organise outside that structure always sought the support of clerics and do not appear to have organised without their approval. Some women, like Mary Aikenhead for example, believed that more than individual philanthropy

---

[12] Sr M. Angela Bolster, *Catherine McAuley In Her Own Words* (Dublin, 1978), pp. 17–30.

[13] Quoted in Bolster, *McAuley*, p. 30; for the entire episode regarding McAuley's work see pp. 28–35: Bolster, *Catherine McAuley: Venerable for Mercy* (Dublin, 1990), pp. 21–36; Sr M. Bertrand Degnan, *Mercy Unto Thousands* (Dublin, 1958), pp. 49–143.

was necessary in order to overcome the poverty of the people and the only acceptable form of communal activity for them was to form a religious congregation.

Recent work by Mary Peckham credits the expansion of the conventual movement in Ireland in the early nineteenth century to the 'wealth, drive, and personal goals of women'.[14] She also argues that it was aided by the kinship and friendship ties which existed between female religious and their lay and clerical supporters. Without doubt close personal friendships and family relationships lay at the heart of female philanthropic networks throughout the century and this is particularly evident when one examines the ties that existed between Catholic lay women and female religious. Male support, however, was also essential in establishing religious communities of women and all founders of convents had to ensure clerical support to aid their survival. When reading the biographies of founders, the official histories of convent establishments, or the original documents which lie in convent archives, it is clear that the language of these works often tends to obscure the reality of the impact of the founders on their own establishments. The rhetoric of convent life, the language of communication between the nuns and the public and between the nuns and the clergy hides the very direct impact which these women had on the work they were determined to carry out. In histories of communities we are told that nuns were 'invited' to establish branch convents in various dioceses. We are constantly reminded of the humility, self-sacrifice and sanctity expressed by convent founders. We are told that the women who founded the new congregations felt keenly that they lacked the abilities or experience to carry out the functions of their position. Mary Aikenhead, we are informed, constantly questioned her own abilities and received much support from Dr Murray and two priests who acted as her spiritual advisors.[15] Frances Ball is presented by one of her biographers as a confident woman. Lest we imagine her to be too confident, and perhaps unwomanly, the same biographer noted that lessons in humility were taught to her by Dr Murray, who pointed out her defects to her and the biographer notes that later in life Ball 'related instances of how the archbishop

---

[14] Mary L. Peckham, 'Re-emergence and early development of women's religious orders in Ireland, 1770–1850', *Women's History Working Papers*, 3 (1990), University of Wisconsin Madison, p. 5.

[15] Member of the Congregation, *Life and Work*, pp. 15–51.

had mortified her in little things, and it was obvious that she was grateful to him'.[16]

Such anecdotes mask the strong personalities of these founders. The originators of the native religious congregations were essentially non-conformist. Those women joining communities, particularly those established in the first decades of the last century, displayed unconventional behaviour. For instance, it was not usual for women to live together removed from direct male control, it was not customary to conduct poor schools or engage in house visitation and the care of the sick on a vast scale. These women were overcoming social prescriptions and the impact of their work, together with their personal struggles to establish and maintain their communities, led to innovations in how women could experience their lives in nineteenth-century Ireland. Their seeming obsequiousness to bishops or members of the clergy is often a strategy of compromise which allows them to develop their work without undue interference.[17] The lack of confidence attributed to these women in the initial stages seems at odds with their undoubted success in running efficient communities and philanthropic enterprises. It also reveals how unprecedented and remarkable was their work. Nuns describe, and have described, their motivation for entering convents as a 'vocation' but this rhetoric, which conjures images of otherworldly ideals, should not blind us to the expectations which nuns, as women, had for convent life.

The case for clerical control over religious foundations made in the first half of the century should not be overestimated but it is true that the clergy exerted a degree of control which became more powerful as the century progressed. An English visitor to Cork in 1835 enquired about the work of the Sisters of Charity of Bishop Murphy. Dr Murphy told him that there were six of the sisters in the city at that time, 'always ready to obey his [the bishop's] call in ministering to the sick, but quite subservient to his authority'.[18] Control was also exerted in other ways. Dr Slattery of Thurles, it was noted by the Presentation convent annalist, was adamant that the expenditure of the convent should not exceed its income. 'So particular was he', the annalist continues, 'that with the exception of diet and clothing, he

---

[16] Quoted in Loreto Sister, *Joyful Mother of Children: Mother Frances Mary Teresa Ball* (Dublin, 1961), p. 55.
[17] Peckham, 'Re-emergence', passim.
[18] G.F.G. Mathieson, *Journal of a Tour in Ireland in 1835* (London, 1836), p. 6.

forbade the smallest outlay without his special leave'.[19] Bishops had
the ultimate power to grant dispensations of religious vows. Nuns
who felt disgruntled or aggrieved at their treatment within a community often wrote to the local bishop to intervene on their behalf in
convent affairs. By the end of the century official clerical visitation
was a regular feature of convent life.[20] After mid-century clerics
gradually gained ultimate control over convents, they had the
power to interfere as much or as little as they desired in convent
management.

Entry, noviciate and profession were formalised rituals which
functioned to separate the woman psychologically from the world
and to bind her more firmly to the community.

To Jesus Christ as their God, their saviour and their spouse, have these
virgins dedicated their lives, consecrated their bodies, sacrificed their
property; thus detached from all worldly charge and solicitude, they prefer
to spend the remainder of their mortal pilgrimage in the service of the sick
and wretched poor, for His greater love and reverence.[21]

The profession of a nun followed the ritual of a wedding ceremony
which united the nun with her spouse, Christ. Through their work
and prayers nuns were pursuing both their own salvation and also
the salvation of their charges. Nuns, in taking vows, made a 'holo-
caust of [her] being to God'.[22] Total abnegation of self was one of
the ideals of religious life. 'Our daily examen', wrote Mary
Aikenhead,

and our consideration of our interior state will show each the deficiencies in
her own self; and by fervent prayer, and devout reception of the Holy
Sacraments, we shall conquer self and the enemy who is actively engaged in

---

[19] MS annals (Presentation Convent, Thurles). For other examples of clerical control see the
following small sample of letters, all in the DDA; Sr M. Joseph Pearson to Archbishop
Cullen, 17 January 1853, wherein she complains about the prioress and asks Cullen to
come 'out and make the promised [sic] regulations which we trusted would promote our
peace and happiness', Cullen Papers 325/8/171 (Nuns). Similarly, when the Mercy nuns in
Naas were asked to take over the workhouse hospital in that town they wrote and asked
Cullen's permission, see, Sr M. Mathews to Cardinal Cullen, 2 April 1876, Cullen Papers
322/6/14 (Nuns, 1876). Sr M. Vincent Whitty wrote to Cullen in October 1850 seeking
permission to open a convent in Drogheda, Cullen Papers, miscellaneous 1850. For the
control of financial accounts see, for example, Sr M. Gertrude White to Cullen looking for
permission to take more than £50 from the bank, 22 September 1852, Cullen Papers
325/1/231 (Nuns, 1852) (DDA).
[20] See, for example, accounts of convent visitation in box marked Nuns (DDA).
[21] Sermon of Fr Kenny at the first public clothing ceremony of the Sisters of Charity on 24
September, 1817; MS copy of the sermon RSC/G, 1/C/40 (Milltown). For the process of
becoming a nun see Clear, *Nuns*, pp. 69–80.
[22] Kenny, Sermon.

raising obstacles to our perfection. We must be watchful and active to oppose our enemies (for assuredly self is the worst enemy).[23]

By her example of charity and of pious living a nun not only aided people in their physical needs but also encouraged them to emulate her activities and thus win them to God. 'Persons consecrated to God in an Order which labours for the salvation of souls ought to be the most attractive people in the world ... they may be so many magnets to attract to Jesus Christ all with whom they come in contact', Catherine McAuley stated.[24] Religious superiors expected, though they did not always get, total obedience from members of the community and male church authorities in turn demanded ultimate obedience in matters of policy and discipline. In the Rules for the Sisters of Charity obedience is cited as the most necessary requirement for the success of the institute. The Sisters were enjoined to obey 'not only exteriorly, with exactness, promptness, courage and due humility, in the execution of whatever is commanded, without excuse or murmur but must also endeavour to have interior resignation and mortification of their own will and judgement'.[25] This insistence on obedience was traditional and experienced by women generally in society with regard to a range of male authority figures. Female religious did not develop an autonomous style of female leadership, it was outside their experience or expectations as women to develop such styles. By the end of the century whatever independence they had in their initial years of operation had been overtaken by obedience to clerics in the restructured hierarchical church.

A convent was, and had to be, a homogenous community in order to survive and function efficiently. Not all women who wished to devote their life to a community were acceptable. Of the 1,348 entrants to the Sisters of Charity for the period 1812 to 1900 a total of 535 women were either dismissed or left the congregation (see table 2.1). The term dismissed was used in the official records and related to all women who left the congregation and does not necessarily mean they were expelled. A number of them fell into bad health and were forced to leave for this reason. The harsh regime imposed on the novices also led to some leaving and it is obvious that the expectations of others regarding community life were not ful-

---

23 P. M. MacSweeney (ed.), *Letters of Mary Aikenhead* (Dublin, 1914), p. 397.
24 Quoted in Bolster, *McAuley*, p. 84.
25 *Rules of the Religious Sisters of Charity* (Dublin, 1941), p. 29.

Table 2.1 *Number of entrants to the Sisters of Charity, 1812–1900*

1812–30	1830–40	1840–50	1850–60	1860–70	1870–80	1880–90	1890–1900
80	85	121	126	191	195	289	261

Total   1,348
Total classified as Domestic Sisters   384 (28.48%)
Total number of Domestic Sisters dismissed   176 (32.89%)
Total number of Choir Sisters dismissed   359 (37.08%)
Total number dismissed   535 (39.68%)

Average age of entry

27.95	26.2	24.04	24.56	24.07	24.34	23.95	24.28

Source: MS alphabetical catalogue of entrants 1812–1900 (RSC/G, Milltown).

filled by the reality of devotion to hard work and prayer which was demanded. It was not enough that a woman wished to devote her life to the objects of a community, a sincere 'vocation' was of primary importance. Mary Aikenhead, although anxious for novices, advised her sisters to 'pray that no one may come to us who has not a true supernatural vocation, and is likely to persevere'.[26] 'Vocation' seems not only to have a religious connotation but also implies a strong will to successfully engage in the work of the convent.

One of the most significant aspects in the growth of convents in the nineteenth century is that most entrants chose to join active congregations. Women were making choices about their lives. Motivation for entering convents varied and not all women joined through a sense of religious idealism. One of the Sisters of Mercy wrote to Archbishop Cullen in 1861 requesting to be dispensed of her vows. She admitted that she entered the convent in Baggot Street a month after leaving school and did not properly consider if she had a vocation or not. Likewise she stated that since her entrance she had neglected her religious duties and the work she did

---

[26] MacSweeney (ed.), *Letters*, p. 160. Similarly writing in 1841 she states 'the care of that department (noviceship) is truly a weighty affair, and all ought to pray for its inmates, who are exposed to great temptations and illusions, that not one, who has received a true vocation, may ever leave the congregation; also for superiors, that they may have a right understanding in training up the young members, and in steadily requiring all who refuse to correction of their faults to retire', pp. 396–7.

in the convent was not done for God 'but for creatures, one of my great faults is human respect, always thinking what people say or think of me'. She found herself 'very much attached to my superior which I fear was a great inducement to me to remain in religion . . . I have never known what it was really to subdue myself . . . I feel I will never be a good nun.'[27] The all too human weaknesses felt by this woman were probably echoed by other nuns who found convent life too much for them.[28]

Those entering a community also had to agree with its objectives. One incident, dealt with in the annals of the Sisters of Charity, shows how a clash about objectives could seriously damage a community. Between 1834 and 1837 an effort was made on the part of some members of this congregation to alter the aims of the community by withdrawing sisters from personal service to the poor in hospitals and home visitation and diverting their activities into a more intellectual channel. Eliza Bodenham, an Englishwoman of wealthy family and a novelist of some popularity, was accepted as a postulant in Stanhope Street convent in 1827 by Mary Aikenhead. In 1833 Bodenham was sent to Paris, with another sister, to study the latest methods of hospital nursing for the proposed opening by Aikenhead of St Vincent's Hospital in Dublin. Bodenham was not particularly keen on this work but in 1834 she was appointed mistress of novices and rectress of Stanhope Street convent. In 1835 she had arranged a clothing ceremony which was out of the usual routine and this was stopped by Aikenhead. The latter investigated the state of affairs in Stanhope Street and discovered that Bodenham had influenced many of the novices into thinking that in devoting their lives to serving the sick they were squandering intellectual gifts which could be used to greater advantage in educating the daughters of wealthy Catholics. Bodenham had also made arrangements, unknown to Aikenhead, to establish a convent in England and to transfer novices from Stanhope Street there. It appears also that she had raised doubts about the legality of Aikenhead's superiorship.

---

[27] Letter of Sister Mary Stanislaus McCann to Archbishop Cullen, undated, Cullen Papers, File 11, Sisters of Mercy, c. 1860, 333/6/8 (DDA).

[28] Other women were better suited and remained extremely content with convent life. Lucy Sherlock, of Waterford, corresponded regularly with Dr Murray's secretary, the Rev. Dean Hamilton, about her vocation and on entering St Mary's convent in Waterford expressed her delight with convent life. See Letters of Lucy Sherlock to Rev. Dean Hamilton, 2/11/1842; 10/2/1843; 12/5/1843, Hamilton Papers, Nuns, 1843, Files 36/6/39; 36/6/40; 36/6/45 (DDA).

Archbishop Murray, on being informed of the matter, deprived
Bodenham of her two offices and she was sent to Sandymount as an
ordinary community member. She caused trouble there also and
finally in 1839 she was dismissed from the convent. The impact of
her dismissal was felt in the community for some time and a number
of sisters considered she had been harshly treated. The outcome of
the whole episode involved thirteen novices leaving the convent.
One of these, Margaret Aylward, was later to found the Sisters of the
Holy Faith.[29]

A solid religious vocation and sympathy with the ideals of a
community were essential elements in ensuring a successful life
within a house. However, social homogeneity was also an important
factor contributing to the success of a community. Clear shows in
her study that internal convent structures and social organisation
mirrored the social divisions which existed in society at large. In her
analysis of the social backgrounds of convent entrants she reveals
two distinct social groupings within the convent itself. The choir
nun, usually from a privileged background, carried out the public
work for which the convent had been established. The lay sister,
generally from a lower social class and less well educated, carried
out the domestic tasks within the convent.[30] These distinctions were
also maintained within the Sisters of Charity, a congregation not
covered by Clear in her study. There was a specific hierarchy in
operation within this body. In the rule for precedence within the
convent, superiority was clearly laid out: 'The head superior ranks
first under all circumstances, next to her the assistants of the congregation and admonitress of head superior ... next to them professed
sisters of the first class whether they be formed or not, after these
novices and postulants of the first class and lastly domestic sisters
whether they be professed or not.'[31]

Although it cannot be clearly established for the whole period,
the available evidence suggests that for the earlier years of the

29 Bodenham was accepted as a novice in a French convent which she soon left. She was later
   released from her vows by Dr Murray. She lived in Tours as a lay woman until her death in
   1859. For an account of the entire incident, although from a not disinterested source, see
   Annals, RSC/G, 1/C/11 (Milltown); Member of the Congregation, *Life and Work*,
   pp. 171–93; Atkinson, *Mary Aikenhead*, pp. 306–17; Gibbons, *The Life*, pp. 34–65.
30 Clear, *Nuns*, pp. 86–99. See also Clear, 'Walls within walls: nuns in nineteenth-century
   Ireland' in Chris Curtin, Pauline Jackson, Barbara O'Connor (eds.), *Gender in Irish Society*
   (Galway, 1987), pp. 134–51.
31 MS, bound notebook, General customs of the pious congregation of the Religious Sisters of
   Charity, RSC/G, 1/C/18 (Milltown).

foundation's existence those designated choir sisters did bring substantial dowries to this congregation. For example, Frances Sweetman, who entered in 1819, brought £1,000. Two sisters, Alicia and Catherine Clinch, both of whom entered in 1815, brought £600 each with them. Between 1815 and 1834 dowries for choir sisters, ranged, on average, from £200 to £400.[32] As Clear notes, the absence of a dowry did not mean that a woman would not be accepted in a convent.[33] In general, poorer women could only become lay sisters and played no part in the public life or leadership of the congregation, though the Sisters of the Holy Faith were exceptional in this regard.[34] They did not insist on a dowry and the lack of one did not relegate a woman to the kitchen of the convent. Generally the necessity of some sort of dowry to become a choir sister may have discouraged many women of insufficient means from joining a community, particularly if they did not wish to become lay sisters.

The growth and expansion of female religious communities during the last century shows that they were popular among those middle-class women who had a religious commitment and a desire to do something worthwhile with their lives. The Presentation Order, for example, though following rules of enclosure, expanded significantly during the century and by 1874, 947 women were active in that community engaged mostly in providing education for poorer children.[35] Convents provided various services and thus allowed their members to engage in a variety of work. If a woman was a member of the Sisters of Mercy, for example, she could engage in teaching, nursing or undertake the care of various outcast groups in society such as prostitutes or ex-prisoners. The women who chose convent life were making a rational decision based on choice, and the variety of occupations offered by convents no doubt encouraged women to join.

Although age of entry varied from sixteen to fifty most women

---

[32] MS notebook, Income from sisters and expenditure to 1834, RSC/G, 1/C/25 (Milltown). Correlating this evidence with the list of entrants, which is found in the alphabetical catalogue of entrants 1812 1900, RSC/G (Milltown), none of those who supplied these substantial dowries were entered as domestic (lay) sisters. There is no evidence of what amounts, if any, were required from the domestic sisters.

[33] Clear, *Nuns*, pp. 86–99.

[34] Jacinta Prunty, 'Margaret Louisa Aylward, 1810–1889', unpublished paper, pp. 70–2. By the end of the century the Sisters of the Holy Faith did look for dowries from their entrants.

[35] William Hutch, *Nano Nagle: Her Life and Labour* (Dublin, 1875), appendix.

appear to have joined convents while in their twenties, when, as lay women, they would have been expected to marry. In the Sisters of Charity entrants' ages averaged twenty-four years, slightly higher than the averages revealed for other convents in Clear's sample.[36] In many of the early foundations women were quite a bit older when they entered religious communities.[37] Recent studies have shown that a large proportion of Irishwomen could not expect to marry in post-famine Ireland. Their options were then emigration or spinsterhood. The convent provided another alternative. Since the provision of a dowry appears to have been an important part in ensuring marriage, and those who entered the convents as choir nuns brought substantial monies with them, it would seem that certain women were choosing between marriage and convent life and found the latter a more satisfying alternative. This may not have been true for the poorer lay sisters who may have seen convent life more as an escape from dependence and economic instability. Convent life may have been appealing because it allowed women to give expression to their intellectual and vocational aspirations. Once within a convent many women used the religious life as a vehicle for self-advancement and self-expression. Within a community women attained levels of power, as religious superiors, bursars, novice mistresses, etc., which were unavailable to their lay peers.

Convents as institutions preserved internally traditional and conservative social and class values. Although anxious and willing to extend the scope of their work, convents and their founders were above all pragmatic and their institutions had to be run as businesses. Hence we see clusters of convents in relatively prosperous parts of the country while those rural areas suffering from poverty were least likely to be able to avail of the services offered by religious communities.[38] A number of factors inhibited the establishment of convents. Local clerical support for a foundation was one factor of considerable importance, but in order to survive convents had to have a guaranteed source of income. Some of the income came from dowries and bequests, but funds, particularly for the foundation of a community, usually came from outside the convent itself. Peckham

---

[36] Clear, *Nuns*, pp. 86–99.
[37] Ibid., pp. 53–5. In the four convents studied by Clear the average age of entrants was 22.1 years. For other examples see Maria Luddy, 'Presentation convents in county Tipperary, 1806–1900', *Tipperary Historical Journal* (1992), pp. 84–95.
[38] Clear, *Nuns*, pp. 36–44.

has estimated that of fifty-six native foundations made by 1846 just over 57 per cent were funded by women.[39] The availability of funds for convent establishment or use reveals an intense and complex network of friendship and kinship ties between female religious and the donating public.

CATHOLIC LAY WOMEN AND PHILANTHROPY

After 1830 few Catholic lay women involved themselves publicly in the provision of charity. The charitable work of nuns became the public face of private philanthropic enterprise and the funds secured for them, particularly by lay women, allowed them to expand their range of enterprises while relegating these lay women to the subordinate role of fund-raisers. Many charitable societies which had been formed by lay Catholics early in the century were also given over to the care of nuns, a pattern which repeated itself for the few organisations established by lay women after mid-century. Lay Catholic women did not in fact create enduring secular independent societies as their Protestant or Quaker counterparts did. In the Catholic case it was often a very wise decision to hand over the work of a lay committee. In many instances, through either financial or managerial neglect, the particular charity would have disappeared quickly without the intervention of the religious congregations. For example, the Magdalen asylum in Cork was established in 1809 and managed by male trustees and a female committee until 1845. The asylum, in those years, catered for about ten to twenty women and conditions within the refuge steadily deteriorated. By 1845 the committee were 'finding it impossible to discharge efficiently in their own persons the duties of guardianship and superintendence towards this important institution'[40] and asked the Sisters of Charity to take over the refuge, which by this time was almost in ruins. Although there are less dramatic examples of neglect it was often a very wise decision to bring in the nuns, who had the personnel, commitment, time and financial resources to revitalise the societies. In some instances it is quite clear that clerics preferred such institutions to be given over to nuns. One priest, writing in 1890, believed

---

[39] Peckham, 'Re-emergence', p. 23.
[40] Leaflet dated 2 April 1845, Cork, U140/D (CAI). For conditions in the refuge see letter from Mary Chantal to Mother M. Aikenhead dated 14 June 1846, File 1/13/97 SC (Milltown).

that all lay Magdalen asylums were 'terrible failures from a complete want of discipline and moralising influences' and that 'fallen women' could not be reformed 'through *lay* or *amateur* agencies alone'.[41]

The evidence shows that Catholic charities were much more likely to survive if they were taken over by nuns. The Victoria Asylum, for example, established in 1838 to look after female ex-prisoners, and managed by a committee of lay women, did not survive beyond 1847.[42] On the face of it there is no apparent reason why it should have closed considering that a similar refuge, organised by Protestant and Quaker women and founded in 1821, lasted, at least, to 1870.[43] It is significant that of all the charities established by lay Catholic women this was one of the few not given over to the care of nuns, a factor which probably led to its demise. Nuns always expanded the facilities of the societies they took over and catered for larger numbers of individuals than any of the lay societies which engaged in similar work. The expansion of convent networks did not mean that lay Catholic women ceased to function in the charitable sphere, but they did so in a much less public fashion than women of other denominations. The most prominent lay Catholic philanthropists were intimately associated with religious congregations and other Catholic women who engaged in charity work were firmly controlled by clerics.

Among the lay women who played an important function in Catholic philanthropy was Anna Maria Ball (1785–1871). She came from a wealthy background and had been educated at the Bar Convent in York, England, a convent which operated as a noviciate for a number of founders of religious congregations in Ireland.[44] Ball married John O'Brien, a wealthy Catholic merchant, in 1805 and although she had no children of her own cared for the three children of a younger brother after his death. With a few friends, she established an orphanage for destitute girls in Dublin in the first decade of the nineteenth century and then purchased a house in Harold's

---

[41] Letter dated July 1890, signed Archdeacon P., Murray Papers, File 31/7–9 Ordinary (DDA). Stressed in the original.

[42] Leaflet advertising the Victoria Asylum for Female Penitents (Dublin, 1839). This refuge was listed in *Thom's Directory* until 1847.

[43] See chapter 5.

[44] It was in this convent that Mary Aikenhead, Frances Teresa Ball and Catherine McAuley conducted their noviciates. It appears that many Irish Catholic girls were educated there.

Cross to which the orphanage was removed and given over to the care of the Poor Clares.[45] Mrs O'Brien, along with some other lay women, also established a House of Refuge in Ashe Street, Dublin, in 1809. This was transferred to Stanhope Street in 1814 and handed over to the Sisters of Charity, on their foundation, in 1815. She invited Mary Aikenhead, founder of the Sisters of Charity, to Dublin and the two women engaged in the visitation of the poor in the city. O'Brien was also a close friend of Archbishop Murray and the sister of Frances Teresa Ball, founder of the Loreto congregation in Ireland. Her close friendship with Archbishop Murray was of fundamental importance in aiding the establishment of religious congregations in Ireland. It was she who introduced Mary Aikenhead to the archbishop, and it was through her that Murray first encouraged the ambitions of Aikenhead and Ball to form religious communities. O'Brien worked closely with the Sisters of Charity after their foundation and donated funds to many of their projects.[46]

Another lay woman closely associated with charity work and with female religious was Ellen Woodlock (1811–84). She too was from a wealthy background, had married in 1830, but was widowed in 1834 before the birth of her only son. She appears to have spent some years engaged in charity work in her native city of Cork but by 1843 she was living as a Sister of St Louis in the convent at Juilly in France, her son being close at hand in a boarding school operated by the sisters. She eventually decided that a life in active charity work rather than teaching was more suited to her. By the summer of 1851 she had been dispensed from her vows and on her return to Ireland she established some form of industrial school in Cork. She remained in contact with the Sisters of St Louis, and was instrumental in bringing them to Monaghan in 1859.[47] Ellen Woodlock was primarily concerned with the care of children and had established St Joseph's Industrial Institute in Dublin in 1855. Although her school was small she was obviously highly thought of and was the only woman called to give evidence at a House of Commons Select Committee on Poor Relief in Ireland in 1861. Hers was a strong

45 Loreto Sister, *Joyful Mother*, p. 43.
46 Ibid., passim; R Bayley Butler and Sr Katherine Butler, 'Mrs John O'Brien, her life, her work and her friends', *Dublin Historical Record*, 33 (December 1979–September 1980), pp. 141–56.
47 For Woodlock, see Sr M. Pauline, *God Wills It! The Centenary Story of the Sisters of St Louis* (Dublin, 1959), passim; Matthew Russell, 'Mrs Ellen Woodlock, an admirable Irishwoman of the last century', *The Irish Monthly*, 36 (1908), pp. 171–6.

voice in the reformatory and industrial school movement in Ireland. Mrs Woodlock saw her homes as models to be followed by other women interested in the rescue of destitute girls. In the early 1860s she attempted, and failed, to have the Sisters of St Louis take over St Josephs.[48] Woodlock also helped to establish Temple Street Hospital for Children, which opened in 1873; it was handed over to the care of the Sisters of Charity in 1876.[49]

Sarah Atkinson (1823–93), writer and biographer of Mary Aikenhead, the wife of George Atkinson, a medical doctor and joint proprietor of the *Freeman's Journal*, was also involved in the provision of charity and was again closely associated with nuns. Atkinson was a close friend of Ellen Woodlock and helped her establish St Joseph's Industrial Institute. She also started a school for girls in Drumcondra, sometime in the 1850s, but this was closed later due to lack of funding and the girls handed over to the care of the Sisters of Charity. With Woodlock she also founded the Children's Hospital in Temple Street. Two of her sisters were members of the Sisters of Charity and one of these, Anna, was sister in charge of the Hospice, to which Atkinson donated funds. Atkinson and Woodlock were credited with gaining access to the North and South Dublin Unions for women visitors in the 1860s and it would seem likely that they acted as visitors themselves.[50]

The close links which existed between religious communities and lay Catholic women are best exemplified in the case of Margaret Aylward (1810–89). Aylward, born in Waterford, again came from a wealthy merchant family. She had engaged in some charitable work in the city but in 1834 joined the Sisters of Charity, her sister already being a member of that congregation. During her noviciate there was some internal trouble within the convent and she left in 1836. She returned to Waterford and continued in her charity work. She appears to have been quite an unhappy figure wrestling with

[48] Ellen Woodlock to Archbishop Cullen, 27 August 1862, Cullen Papers, 340/6/19 (Laity July–December 1862) (DDA).
[49] Atkinson, *Mary Aikenhead*, p. 505.
[50] Matthew Russell, 'A few more notes on Mrs Atkinson', *The Irish Monthly*, 22 (1894), pp. 179–88. For accounts of Atkinson's life and work see Russell, 'In memory of a noble Irishwoman', ibid., 21 (1893), pp. 464–9; 'Mrs Sarah Atkinson, a few notes in remembrance', ibid., 21 (1893), pp. 601–11; Bessie R. Belloc, 'My acquaintance with Ireland and Mrs Atkinson', ibid., 23 (January, 1895), pp. 22–5; K. Woodnutt, 'Sarah Atkinson as a social worker', *Dublin Historical Record*, vol. 21: 4 (1967), pp. 132–8; Sr Katherine Butler, *We Help Them Home: The Story of Our Lady's Hospice, Harold's Cross, 1879–1979* (Dublin, 1980), pp. 17–21.

the idea of joining another religious community. She entered the Ursuline noviciate in Waterford in 1846 but remained only two months.[51] By 1851 she had revitalised the Ladies' Association of Charity of St Vincent de Paul in Dublin. This association had previously been founded in Dun Laoghaire in 1843, by a priest, but it had remained a small body. It gained new life under Aylward's management and had as its purpose the temporal as well as the spiritual relief of the sick poor in Dublin. Members, through their work, believed they had succeeded in 'tackling the ignorant, rescuing the poor from proselytisers, protecting widows, sending children to school, procuring employment and places for the destitute [and] bringing absentees to their duty'.[52]

This association also opened an orphanage in 1856 called St Brigid's, an anti-proselytising agency rescuing children from Protestant agencies. 'It was God', a report stated, 'who urged us on, through His love for His faithful Irish church, to save the little ones from the dreadful calamity of heresy and perdition.'[53] The establishment of St Brigid's reveals the extent of the influence of religion on women's charitable work. Aylward, at this stage in the 1850s, was not concerned with the establishment of a religious congregation, but, as she wrote in 1854 'the more nearly we approach to a religious community the more successful shall we be'.[54] She wished, rather, to live in a community of women who were united by their religious convictions but did not necessarily desire to take formal religious vows.

Saving children from 'Protestant perversion' was the chief aim of Aylward and her helpers. It even led to Aylward spending six months in jail in 1860 on a contempt of court charge over the infamous Mary Mathews case.[55] On leaving prison Aylward continued her work with the orphanage. Like Catherine McAuley before her, she was encouraged to organise her band of women helpers into a religious congregation by Archbishop Cullen in order that they could continue their work and to achieve public respectability. Aylward was not too keen on this idea, particularly with two failed noviciates and the notoriety of a prison sentence behind her.

[51] Information on Aylward's life can be found in Gibbons, *Margaret Aylward*. This is the official biography.
[52] Ladies' Association of Charity, annual report, 1857, p. 9.   [53] Ibid., p. 16.
[54] Quoted in Gibbons, *Margaret Aylward*, pp. 205–6.
[55] Ibid., pp. 163–87. See also chapter 3.

Eventually, however, she established the Sisters of the Holy Faith which was canonically approved in 1869.[56] Interestingly Aylward maintained her personal independence by not wearing the religious style clothing which identified members of her community, nor did she end her travels to England and Europe.[57]

A number of common threads link these Catholic women who were active philanthropists throughout the century, the most obvious being that they were all connected in some way with members of religious congregations or the work of such congregations. It is clear that these women were deeply religious and a number had contemplated entering the religious life. They were also women of wealth and independence who had the financial resources not alone to engage in philanthropy but to channel their resources into areas which were of most concern to them. Thus we can witness Woodlock's disenchantment with the vocational aspirations of the Sisters of St Louis to educate Catholic girls, when she much preferred to help the destitute girls in the workhouse and had the financial means to do so. Not only are there links of friendship between these lay Catholic women, seen particularly in the case of Woodlock and Atkinson, but it is quite clear that friendship and kinship ties bound them to religious congregations. Unlike many philanthropists of other denominations, who generally limited themselves to one project, these Catholic philanthropists engaged in a variety of work, seen for example by Atkinson's visitation of the poor, her establishment of a school for poor girls, her involvement in St Joseph's Institute, her work with the Children of Mary and Temple Street Hospital and her visitations to the South Dublin Union. The fact that they eventually handed over many of their projects to nuns probably allowed them the time to engage in such a variety of work. Protestant and Quaker women usually had to confine their activities in order to ensure the success of their organisations.

There is no doubt that these lay women were of enormous benefit to religious congregations. They not only provided the funding for many projects but also broadened the direction of the various congregations' work by initiating projects which they later handed over to them. In handing over their enterprises, they were of course guaranteeing their continuity and expansion but they were also, to a

---

[56] Gibbons, *Margaret Aylward*, pp. 205–6.   [57] Prunty, 'Margaret-Louisa Aylward', p. 78.

certain extent, placing the responsibility for charity work in the hands of religious and removing the possibility from lay Catholics of contributing, other than financially, to active social work. Once in the hands of religious congregations philanthropic bodies were no longer answerable to the lay Catholic community. It is interesting to note that charitable societies managed by nuns rarely published any accounts, such as annual reports, of their work, in marked contrast to all the organisations managed by women of other religious denominations. The publication of such reports signifies a degree of accountability for the work being done. Nuns, it seems, were answerable only to the Catholic hierarchy to whom they did furnish financial and other returns of their enterprises.[58]

Undoubtedly, many Catholic lay women, other than those mentioned above, lent their support either financially or personally, to voluntary charitable organisations. Convents did of course receive enormous financial support from lay women and men. For example, Mrs Ryan, a niece of Archbishop Troy's, who had been in charge of the Magdalen asylum in Dublin, provided the Sisters of Charity with £1,500 to buy Donnybrook Castle and take over the care of the refuge in 1837.[59] In Cork the same congregation was funded by the sum of £3,150 by a Miss Mahony and her sister, who were, incidentally, aunts to Ellen Woodlock.[60] Lay women sometimes worked with nuns, particularly in the early years of a foundation's existence. A Mrs Dennis Bullen, for example, established an infant school in Dublin in 1837 to counteract the influence of local Protestant schools. She employed a teacher and requested the Sisters of Charity to visit the school whose management she oversaw.[61]

There were other societies established where lay women engaged in charity work, though their work in these societies is poorly documented. In Dublin, a Ladies' Clothing Society was founded in 1849. This society was established under the 'special patronage' of Archbishop Murray and while the women did the work of the society they appear to have been guided, and their functions strictly limited, by clerics and members of the St Vincent de Paul Society,

[58] See, for example, Accounts of St Joseph's Asylum, 1874 in Cullen Papers, 342/5/2 (Laity January–June 1874); Accounts of St Mary's parochial schools for 1864 in Cullen Papers 320/7/1, 1864; Accounts of St Clare's Orphanage, Cullen Papers, 322/6/1 (Nuns 1876) all in DDA.
[59] Member of the Congregation, *Life and Work*, p. 194.
[60] Typescript annals, vol. 2, pp. 35–6 (RSC, Milltown).
[61] Ibid.

previously established in 1846. The Dublin Ladies' Clothing Society provided free or cheap clothing to the poor. In order to acquire clothing the recipients had to produce tickets which were handed out by the male members of the Society of St Vincent de Paul in their home visitations. The women's primary function was to give out the clothing and they had no say in who would receive it; their second declared function was to raise and donate funds to the society.[62] Further hints of lay Catholic women's charitable work appear in another society which was again dominated by men. In either 1843 or 1844 the Association of Charity for the Relief of the Sick Poor of Rathmines, Harold's Cross and Ranelagh was established. Members of this society, both male and female, visited the sick poor in their own homes. One of the purposes of this society was to counteract the proselytising influences of Protestant agencies and the visitors ensured, as far as possible, that children went to Catholic schools. The one annual report which is available for this society has little to say on the work carried out by its women members and it is only in a passing reference that any idea of the extent of their involvement can be noted when it was reported that 'the ladies of the society made 1,989 visits during the year'.[63]

Some of the societies founded by lay Catholic women in the latter part of the century arose from attempts to counteract the perceived proselytising zeal of Protestant charitable societies and Catholic women were encouraged by clerics to organise and combat the work of such groups. An article published in the *Freeman's Journal* in 1883 entitled 'Save the Child' was a vitriolic attack on Protestant orphanages and schools. The author urged subscribers to donate to a 'Save the Child Fund'. The fund was administered by a group of Catholic lay women who worked closely with Aylward's St Brigid's Orphanage.[64] Similarly the Association for Visiting Hospitals, established in Dublin in 1873, under the patronage of Archbishop Cullen, and made up of women who visited eight hospitals in the city, had been initiated, by clerics, specifically to 'counteract the intrusive zeal of a host of Protestant visitors who enjoyed, naturally

---

[62] First report of the Dublin ladies' clothing society, 1849 (Dublin, 1850). See also the letter from the committee of this society to Cullen 1856, Cullen Papers 339/3/56 (Laity July–December 1856).

[63] Ninth annual report of the association of charity for the relief of the sick poor of Rathmines, Harold's Cross and Ranelagh, 1851–2 (Dublin, 1853).

[64] Anon., 'Save the child', reprinted as a pamphlet from the *Freeman's Journal*, 1 March 1883.

enough, free access to the wards in hospitals, of which their husbands, fathers [and] brothers were governors'. The women visited patients twice a week and their visitations were stated to have shielded them from the 'unwelcome attentions of Protestant patrons'.[65] Another society organised by Catholic lay women, was the Dublin Discharged Roman Catholic Female Prisoners' Aid Society, formed in 1881. It had been inspired by the work of the Prison Gate Mission, managed by Protestant and Quaker women, which had been established in the city in 1876. As one contemporary writer stated, 'it is certainly high time that we Catholics should imitate their [the Protestant] example'.[66] The function of this society was to cater for the needs of Catholic female ex-prisoners and no doubt to provide alternative accommodation to that available in the Protestant refuges of the city. The women who ran this society were aided in their work by the Sisters of Charity of St Vincent de Paul and in 1905, when the committee opened a second refuge in the city, they handed it over to these sisters.[67] The establishment of a Catholic crèche in Dublin in 1884 also copied the initiative taken by Protestant women as early as 1879. Again it was Catholic clergymen and male visitors of the St Vincent de Paul Society who urged these women to organise, though this crèche is one of the few organisations which was apparently managed completely independently by lay women.[68]

One woman, writing in 1878, noted that lay Catholic women were often reproached, as a group, for their lack of involvement in charitable enterprises. The reasons given for this were that women of charitable intent had joined convents. Catholic women, it was claimed, also had less money than Protestants to donate to charity; the education provided for Catholic girls did not include the acquisition of those skills needed to organise a charitable society, and finally it was said that Catholic women did not have the leisure time to engage in such work on any large scale.[69] The author accepted that there was a certain degree of truth in these excuses but argued that more lay Catholic women should involve themselves in phil-

---

[65] Anon., 'The association for visiting hospitals', *The Irish Monthly*, 15 (1887), p. 80.

[66] Anon., 'St Martha's home', *The Irish Monthly*, 10 (1882), p. 160.

[67] See the annual reports of the Dublin discharged Roman Catholic female prisoners aid society, 1886, 1905–7.

[68] The crèche or day nursery, report for the year 1888.

[69] Anon., 'About visiting the poor', *The Irish Monthly*, 6 (1878), pp. 336–7.

anthropic work because it was 'the sure infallible means not to be discontented and unhappy ... but ... which will satisfy and interest both heart and mind'.[70] Women of other religious denominations however, were not inhibited from forming societies though they too would have suffered from lack of funding and experience in organisational methods. What essentially inhibited lay Catholic women's involvement was the extent to which nuns had been allowed to develop charitable institutes.

From the 1850s only a handful of organisations were formed by lay Catholic women. These were the already mentioned St Joseph's Industrial Institute (1855), Our Lady's Association of Charity of St Vincent de Paul, reorganised by Aylward in 1853, the Association for Visiting Hospitals (1873), the Dublin Discharged Roman Catholic Female Prisoners' Aid Society (1881) and the Crèche (1884); of these only three organisations, St Joseph's, the Association for Visiting Hospitals and the Crèche were not eventually given over to the care of nuns, and it is likely that the first two societies did not last longer than ten years. Lay women could, of course, aspire to act as nuns did, and they were encouraged to do so but it appeared that to engage in the variety of work allowed nuns was only possible if they became nuns. It was nuns who symbolised the perfect response of women to charity. The Rev. Thomas Burke, writing in the 1870s, stated that: 'amongst the "consecrated daughters of loveliness" whom Christ has engaged as the spouses of His church – we find the golden garment of an organised charity. We find the highest, the best, and the purest, devoted to its service and to its cause.'[71]

That the church preferred women to stay out of public view was reiterated by Dr McCabe in a pastoral letter, which while ostensibly denouncing the Ladies' Land League also said much about clerical beliefs in women's place being firmly in the home:

the daughters of our Catholic people, be they matrons or virgins, are called forth under the flimsy pretext of charity to take their stand in the noisy streets of life. The pretext of charity is merely assumed; for already we have holy associations of men and women, who with the full blessing of religion, do the works of mercy, corporal and spiritual for the poor and afflicted ...

---

[70] Ibid., p. 340.
[71] The Rev. Thomas Burke, *Ireland's Vindication: Refutation of Froude and Other Lectures, Historical and Religious* (London, n.d.), p. 21.

In aiding the Land League, he continued, women are being asked to 'forget the modesty of their sex and the high dignity of their womanhood'. He further requested that clerics deny these women access to 'sodalities' because they are characters 'unworthy of a child of Mary'.[72]

The insistence of the Catholic hierarchy on collective philanthropy by women being organised through religious congregations denied lay Catholic women the opportunity of establishing voluntary societies on an independent basis, and consequently, of developing any critique of the social origins of poverty and destitution. Women of other denominations were much more involved in organisations which could be considered reformist, such as the Ladies' National Association which sought to repeal the Contagious Diseases Acts, the Philanthropic Reform Society, the Irish Workhouse Association and the National Society for the Prevention of Cruelty to Children, all of which broadened the definition of benevolence to include some form of political and public action to initiate legislative and social change.[73] A tradition of independent, philanthropic work by these women had encouraged them to organise for such ends and it is significant that Catholic women, who did not have a similar tradition, do not appear to have involved themselves in a reformist society.

CARE OF THE POOR AND INSTITUTIONAL WORK

The educational work undertaken by nuns in Ireland has been better treated by historians than have other aspects of their work,[74] such as the provision of facilities and care for the poor, destitute and outcast, which will be analysed here. Investigation of the records of any convent reveals a tremendous amount of charitable activity. Most of this work remains unrecorded in official public sources and nuns themselves rarely published reports on any of the institutions they ran. A year after the foundation of the Sisters of Charity in 1815 the nuns in North William Street, Dublin, began their visitation of

---

[72] *Freeman's Journal*, 12 March 1881.   [73] See chapters 4 and 6.

[74] See Fahey, 'Nuns' in Cullen (ed.), *Girls Don't Do Honours*, pp. 17–26; Clear, *Nuns*, pp. 112–25; Anne V. O'Connor, 'Influences affecting girls' secondary education in Ireland, 1860–1910', *Archivium Hibernicum*, 41 (1986), pp. 83–98; O'Connor, 'The revolution in girls' secondary education in Ireland, 1860–1910' in Cullen (ed.), *Girls Don't Do Honours*, pp. 31–54; Sr M. de Lourdes Fahy, *Education in the Dioceses of Kilmacduagh in the Nineteenth Century* (Gort, 1973).

the sick poor in their own homes. In 1818 Mother Catherine observed in her diary, 'during the winter and spring we have witnessed great misery among the poor; poverty seems for the most part the cause of most of their sufferings. That is the general cause of their sickness.'[75] It is difficult to quantify the welfare provided by most communities of nuns. Some small measure of their work can be seen, for example, in the relief provided by the Sisters of Charity in Gardiner Street, Dublin, in 1860. During that year the nuns attended to 494 sick cases at least twice a week, provided 13,000 breakfasts to children, attended to 30 to 40 families at least four times per week, and gave casual assistance in the form of money to at least 30 people per week. The Sisters of Mercy also undertook the visitation of the sick from all their convents. In Limerick from 1838 to 1844 they visited 3,161 individuals and from January 1845 to May 1850, during the famine years, attended to 4,737 people.[76] No doubt the formal and casual assistance provided by convents became a part of the survival strategy for many destitute individuals and families throughout the century.

As part of their work amongst the poor, nuns also engaged in religious evangelism. The Sisters of Charity visited Jervis Street Hospital, before it was taken over by the Sisters of Mercy, to attend to the spiritual needs of the patients. In all the institutions they ran nuns hoped to impress upon their charges the importance of a spiritual life. Women in nineteenth-century Ireland were the primary transmitters of religious belief, through their work in the home and through their philanthropic work amongst the poor. Nuns continued this function on a much broader scale bringing institutional religion into the homes and lives of all the people with whom they came in contact. Nuns were to the forefront in re-establishing the power of the Catholic church in Ireland and it was they who were the real force in implementing the 'devotional revolution'. In convents nuns established sodalities and prayer groups which were attended by their charges. In pursuing their own religious life, which involved charity work, nuns were agents of missionary activity. Indeed the only societies to which many poorer and working-class women had any access were religious ones and the function of such societies was to cater for both individual and collective salvation.

[75] MS Diary of Mother Catherine, 2/6/1812–29/8/1825, RSC/G (Milltown).
[76] Sisters of Charity, Cullen Papers, File 333/6/22 (DDA); MS Sick visitation book, 2 vols., 1838–47, 1847–50, MC (Limerick).

The nuns by their own example were the living embodiments of the ideal Christian woman and they tried to instil the same moral and religious standards in the women they helped. Nuns, or at least choir nuns, were from generally privileged backgrounds and though they worked with the poor and seem to have understood their problems, they remained, and considered themselves to be, both socially and morally superior to them. Nuns, like almost all philanthropists of the last century, did not publicly advocate social justice and taught the poor those skills which would enable them to function within their own level of society. Although they do not appear ever to have refused charity to anyone, the social divisions which, we have seen, were maintained in the convent, were sometimes carried over into their work. The Sisters of Mercy, for example, operated a night shelter for homeless women and children in Dublin from 1861. Huge numbers of women entered this night shelter annually and in one week in March 1867, 651 found refuge there.[77] The building which housed the shelter consisted of three floors, and, as one observer noted:

the first floor of the refuge contains the very poorest class who apply for admission, the homeless and the starving ... the beds consist simply of a matrass [sic] and rug laid in a sort of open wooden box, one close to the other ... on the second floor ... are iron bedsteads, not so close together, and a greater air of comfort is apparent; it is meant for the bettermost poor who may be reduced to utter penury...[78]

Of course nuns' perception of the poor was influenced by the prevailing philosophy of the 'deserving poor'. The distinctions revealed in the above extract regarding the poor may have been made to pander to public opinion. The general public, on whom the nuns relied, would not have considered indiscriminate almsgiving a laudable virtue. Further examples of elitism can be seen in the work of nuns in the sphere of education. They ran both poor and pay schools and the nature of the education provided depended to some degree on whether the clients paid for it or not.[79]

The work of the nuns flourished because they met the material

---

[77] Fanny Taylor, *Irish Homes and Irish Hearths* (London, 1867), p. 107. Like most charitable enterprises in which religious were involved no annual reports were published for this refuge. An investigation into the plight of the homeless poor in Dublin, carried out by the Statistical and Social Inquiry Society in 1876, stated that the shelter had room for 200 inmates. See Reports of the Charity Organisation Committee of the Statistical and Social Inquiry Society as to the Houseless Poor (Dublin, 1876), p. 4.

[78] Taylor, *Irish Homes*, p. 105.   [79] See n 74 above.

needs of the poor, they had the support of the Catholic population, and also because they personally derived great satisfaction from the work they were doing. Nuns also made a tremendous impact on public institutions. The visitation of the sick, undertaken by the nuns on their own initiative, paved the way for their entrance into the public nursing field. When cholera broke out in Ireland in 1832 nuns looked after the sick in both makeshift and public hospitals. In Dublin, Grangegorman Penitentiary was turned into a temporary hospital and the Sisters of Charity nursed there. Mary Aikenhead advised the nursing sisters, 'that by our attendance at the hospital we should tranquillise minds suffering from the effects . . . of agonising disease . . . [this] will be most effectively met by perfect composure both of countenance and manner while treating the poor sufferer and also by great simplicity in the manner of instruction'.[80]

Kinship and friendship ties were important in gaining Catherine McAuley admittance to Sir Patrick Duns Hospital as a visitor.[81] The Sisters of Mercy in Limerick were requested, in 1849, to deal with an outbreak of famine fever and took up temporary residence in St John's and Barrington's hospitals.[82] Nuns also did a tremendous amount of work for the poor during the famine period. In Cork the Mercy nuns:

from an early hour of the day until evening . . . were in attendance on the sick in their houses, in the hospitals and in the workhouse. The community prepared and distributed food and all the means of relief within their reach to the crowds of destitute people who flocked to the convent . . . ten sisters were stricken with famine fever in the early months of 1847; out of this number two died . . .[83]

With the opening of St Vincent's Hospital in 1834 Mary Aikenhead consolidated the acceptance of nuns as nurses in hospitals. To prepare for the opening of St Vincent's, Aikenhead had sent three of her sisters to France to learn the skills of nursing and hospital management.[84] The Sisters of Mercy opened the Mercy Hospital in

---

[80] Quoted in Member of the Congregation, *Life and Work*, pp. 127–8.
[81] Rev. Dominick Murphy, *Sketches of Irish Nunneries* (Dublin, 1865), p. 141; Bolster, *Venerable for Mercy*, p. 29.
[82] Annals, vol. 1, MC (Limerick).
[83] Quoted from the annals of the Mercy convent, Cork in Sr M. Angela Bolster, *Mercy in Cork 1837–1987* (Cork, 1987), p. 7. For the work of the Presentation sisters in Thurles during the famine see Anon., *Records and Memories.*, p. 12. For the work of the Sisters of Charity see Member of the Congregation, *Life and Work*, pp. 274–9.
[84] Members of the Congregation, *Life and Work*, pp. 146–70; Atkinson, *Mary Aikenhead*, pp. 227–43.

Table 2.2 *No. of nuns engaged in workhouses in 1873*

Workhouse	Number of nuns	Payment per annum (total) (£)	Congregation
Ballinasloe	2	£37	Mercy
Cork	8	£240	Mercy
Galway	3	£60	Mercy
Killarney	4	£50	Mercy
Kilmacthomas	1	£46	St John of God
Limerick	8 to 10	£60	Mercy
Tullamore	3	£60	Mercy
Wexford	2	£52	St John of God

Return of all the workhouses in Ireland in which nuns are engaged as nurses, HC 1873 (246), lv, 865

Cork in 1857 and the Mater in Dublin in 1861.[85] Within workhouse hospitals nuns made profound advances. In 1873 there were eight workhouse hospitals under the care of nuns, by 1895 that number had risen to sixty-three; by 1898 it was seventy-three and in 1903 eighty-four.[86]

Entrance and permission to nurse in these institutions was not gained without difficulty. In Limerick in 1860 the Mercy nuns expressed interest in taking over the nursing duties of the workhouse hospital. Problems arose regarding the superintendence of the nuns in the hospital and their relationship to the matron and master. Fears were also voiced regarding the impact of a group of religious women catering for patients of all denominations. After much correspondence between the local board of guardians and the poor law commissioners the latter finally allowed the local board to hire the nuns as nurses and they took up duty in 1861.[87] Nursing was to become closely linked with female religious and indeed with an element of religious commitment. Nuns often worked for nominal salaries within these hospitals and may inadvertently have damaged the monetary value of women's work generally in nursing by doing this. For example, the Cashel poor law guardians, debating whether

[85] Bolster, *Mercy in Cork*, pp. 24–5.
[86] *Workhouse infirmaries in Ireland in which nuns were employed in any capacity in 1903* [C. 1694], HC 1903, lix.
[87] Helen Burke, *The People and the Poor Law in 19th Century Ireland* (Dublin, 1987), pp. 262–72. Burke quotes extensively from the correspondence initiated by the poor law guardians and the poor law commissioners office in Dublin regarding these problems.

the Sisters of Mercy should nurse in their workhouse, were told by a J.J. Guiry that the nuns 'if appointed, only expect as much as will support them'. The clerk of Castlecomer Union outlined the pay and conditions of the nuns in that workhouse in 1877 'two choir sisters receive £20 per annum and rations, and a lay sister, who takes charge of the hospital kitchen and acts as servant to the choir sisters, receives £4 and rations'.[88] Nuns in essence were supporting the existence of a cheap welfare system.

Nuns themselves were not formally trained as nurses and they learned the profession through experience. Lay women appear to have been more concerned with training and a number of training institutes were established from the 1840s on.[89] It was not until the end of the century that nuns acquired formal training. In 1897 the Sisters of Mercy in Limerick, on the recommendation of Lady Monteagle, invited a Miss Pringle, a Nightingale nurse, to provide classes for them. She gave lectures in the convent and went on the wards with the sisters. How effective or acceptable her methods were to the nuns is open to question as a cryptic comment in the convent's Annals suggests: 'though very well trained she knew more theory than practice'.[90] Nuns were also limited by their own rules in terms of the amount of care they could provide, for example they could not, in deference to modesty, nurse male patients or attend births.[91] In spite of these limitations nuns undoubtedly set new standards of cleanliness, care and order in hospitals.

Apart from that done by nuns the major part of nursing was undertaken, for much of the century, by poor women, who had no training and generally carried out such work in return for maintenance within the institution. In 1872, Jeremiah Dowling, MD, stated that 'they [the nurses] were generally taken from the lowest class, restrained by no sense either of decency or religion, loud voiced, quarrelsome and abusive – they are sometimes removed from the hospital to the gaol'.[92] These women did not engage in the work because of a sense of vocation but because it offered them shelter and support in a time of need. In spite of the extent to which nuns nursed in workhouse hospitals the impetus for the reform of nursing came from outside agencies, like the Irish Medical Associ-

---

[88] *Clonmel Chronicle and Tipperary Examiner and Advertiser*, 3 February 1877.
[89] See chapter 6.
[90] Annals, vol. iv, 1882–97, pp. 398–441, MC (Limerick).   [91] Clear, *Nuns*, pp. 125–34.
[92] Jeremiah Dowling, MD, *The Irish Poor Law and Poor Houses* (Dublin, 1872), p. 86.

ation and the Irish Workhouse Association, rather than from the nuns.[93] In 1881 there was a call from the *Medical Press and Circular* that probationary nurses be trained in workhouses, and from the 1890s members of the Irish Medical Association were also calling for reform. The Irish Workhouse Association, formed in 1896, had the reform of workhouse management and nursing as part of its aims. The standard expected of nurses was taken to be that practised by the nuns. Nuns in workhouses, it was declared, 'breathe insensibly a higher tone and a different standard'.[94] Nursing became increasingly linked with religious commitment and developed a strong altruistic dimension.

Like all female philanthropic groups in the last century nuns concentrated their charitable efforts on women and children. It would have been unacceptable to society and indeed to the nuns' own rule to engage in helping groups of destitute men on a large or organised scale. That work remained the preserve of male philanthropists. Nuns, because of their standards, authority and otherworldly commitment, had greater access to all public institutions than any groups of lay women. They visited prisons, instituted orphanages, homes for the aged, Magdalen asylums and after midcentury ran the majority of reformatory and industrial schools;[95] 70 per cent of orphanages, for example, were under the care of the Sisters of Mercy after 1850.[96] Within these institutions inmates were invariably taught skills in domestic duties. In the Ennis industrial school, operated by the Mercy Sisters, one observer noted with approval that 'the sisters are most anxious to train the children in habits of thrift and neatness and to fit them either for domestic service or to manage their own homes'.[97] In Spark's Lake reformatory in Monaghan, run by the Sisters of St Louis, a report from 1861 states that 'we attach more importance to the religious and industrial training of these poor children than to mere book learning'. The report continues, ' a mere course of school instruction proves a real misfortune, in many cases a curse, to those of our girls who are

[93] Patricia Kelly, 'From workhouse to hospital: the role of the Irish workhouse in medical relief to 1921' (MA, UCG, 1972), pp. 126–93.
[94] Lord Monteagle, 'The Irish workhouse system' *New Ireland Review*, 6 (November, 1896), p. 130.
[95] Jane Barnes, *Irish Industrial Schools*.
[96] Sister of Mercy, History of the Mercy Order in Ireland (unpublished typescript, Convent of Mercy, Baggot Street), n.d.
[97] K.S. Knox, 'A visit to an industrial school', *The Irish Monthly*, 22 (1894), p. 303.

thrown on the battle of life'. One of the chief causes of mischief amongst young girls was seen by these nuns to arise from the reading of novels. 'The result of this [novel] reading varies with different dispositions, but in all cases, the mind becomes occupied with ideal notions of life.' The delusions created by novel reading, according to this report, led inevitably to criminality.[98] It was only by the use of needle, thimble and scissors, that the rescue of these girls could be contemplated, a practical education which would fit them for their future needs.

In the Houses of Mercy operated by the Sisters of Mercy the acquisition of domestic skills was considered to be of the utmost importance. In Limerick, for example, over 80 per cent of the inmates of the refuge were placed in domestic service.[99] Of course the range of occupations open to women was very limited, and nuns, in their pragmatic way, taught those skills which could be used by their pupils. Female religious were innovative in many instances and provided occupations for women outside the domestic sphere. Mother Mary Arsenius, a Sister of Charity, opened a woollen factory in Foxford in 1892 with some financial aid from the Congested Districts Board.[100] The mill employed fifty workers, male and female, and Arsenius, in her attempts to revive the Foxford area initiated other schemes, one of which involved teaching the local farmers how to raise a variety of crops. For the local girls classes in cooking and domestic work were initiated 'since their domestic happiness demanded not only cleanliness of apparel and of home, but a varied knowledge of cookery'.[101] Other enterprises to provide employment for girls were begun in a number of convents. The Presentation nuns in Youghal started a lace-making industry in the convent in 1847 to provide employment for girls pauperised by the famine. The industry was still operating in 1900 and at one stage employed 120 women. Other enterprises which included lace-making, knitting, crochet work and weaving were organised in other convents. In Ballaghadereen, for example, the Sisters of Charity engaged 130 girls in a hosiery, shirt-making, needlework and

---

[98] Report of Spark's Lake Reformatory School for Girls, 1861, pp. 7–9.
[99] MS Register of the House of Mercy, Limerick (MC, Limerick).
[100] Rev. Dennis Gildea, *Mother Mary Arsenius of Foxford* (Dublin, 1936), pp. 91–123; Rev. M.O'Riordan, *Catholicity and Progress in Ireland* (St Louis, 1905), pp. 406–9.
[101] Gildea, *Mother Mary Arsenius*, p. 111.

laundry enterprise.[102] Like other philanthropists the provision of employment by nuns was an attempt to make individuals responsible for their own welfare. Overall it is evident that convents engaged in industrial employment on a relatively large scale, with their lace, knitting and linen businesses and the laundries that were attached to their various asylums. It is not clear what conditions were like in these workplaces, and laundries, for example, which were run by convents were excluded for many years from factory inspection. The sisters of the Good Shepherd in Limerick drafted a letter to parliament requesting to be omitted from inspection. Their charitable work, they claimed, was enough to allow them to control their own laundries and inspection would 'be a violation of the religious feelings and home privacy . . .' of the convents.[103] Hilda Martindale, the resident factory inspector in Ireland, was not always pleased with the working conditions she found in these institutions and through her investigations and reports succeeded in having them officially inspected from 1907.[104]

Nuns' sense of self had been shaped by the prevailing philosophy regarding the attributes of the ideal woman. They themselves personified this ideal state through self-abnegation, committed work and religious vocation. It was their religious commitment to charity work which enhanced their position and removed them from the ordinary sphere of lay women. They worked quietly and efficiently and did not threaten the status quo. They were successful in their work and the result of that success was to socialise their charges, principally other women, into traditional occupations and submission to authority. Lay Catholic societies could not compete with the resources, commitment, sense of authority and religious spirit shown by the nuns. These were the qualities which allowed nuns to gain access to institutions which often remained closed to lay women. One of the results of the advancement of female religious in Ireland was to remove, almost totally, the lay Catholic woman from engaging in public philanthropy.

---

[102] Joseph A. Glynn, 'Irish convent industries', *New Ireland Review*, 1 (1894), pp. 236–44; O'Riordan, *Catholicity*, pp. 405–19; Rosa Mullholland, 'Linen-weaving in Skibbereen', *The Irish Monthly*, 18 (1890), pp. 145–8.
[103] Draft letter to 'The honourable the commoners of Great Britain and Ireland in parliament assembled' from the Sisters of the Good Shepherd in Ireland, GSC, Limerick.
[104] Mary Drake McFeely, *Lady Inspectors: The Campaign for a Better Workplace 1893–1921* (Oxford, 1988), pp. 100–1.

PROTESTANT WOMEN AND PHILANTHROPY

While Catholic philanthropy, vested in female religious, developed on a broad scale over the century the charitable work of women of other denominations also extended its boundaries. In the earlier part of the century some Protestant women organised themselves into groups which functioned as auxiliaries to male-run Bible societies. The principal Irish Bible societies were branches of organisations established in England and from the start of their work in Ireland encouraged female participation. The Hibernian Church Missionary Society (established in 1799), the Irish Evangelical Society and the Hibernian Bible Society (established in 1806) were amongst the largest of such organisations. The purpose of an auxiliary was strictly limited in the first decade of the century and women were encouraged only to subscribe and collect funds for the parent body. As one clergyman wrote:

> to collect such sums, is peculiarly the task of your sex, prevented by nature and by education from the active and busy employments which engage the attention of men, your privileges extend to the domestic walks of life, your influence is felt and acknowledged, even where it escapes the careful observer. To impress the youthful mind, to direct the genial current of Christian feeling, to nurture, and under God to try to effect the Christian principle is your high duty.[105]

Women joined these auxiliaries in large numbers, despite the limitations set on their actual participation in the work of the society. In 1816, for example, the Dublin Female Association established in 1814, which acted as an auxiliary to both the Irish Evangelical Society and the London Missionary Society, had a total of 377 subscribers of whom 308 or 82 per cent were women.[106] By 1825 the Hibernian Missionary Society had at least thirty-five auxiliary associations, all of which were run by women.[107] F.K.

---

[105] *Address from the Dublin Ladies' Association, Auxiliary to the Hibernian Church Missionary Society, to the Female Friends of the Mission* (n.p., c. 1820), p. 3.

[106] Dublin Female Association, annual report, 1816, subscription lists.

[107] In Dublin these auxiliaries included the Dublin Female Association, a Ladies' Union Society and the Salem Chapel Female Association. There was also a Bedford Row Auxiliary Missionary Society operated by women in Limerick, a Londonderry Female Association and a Mallow Ladies' Association, among others. See Report of the Committee of the Hibernian Missionary Society, Auxiliary to the London Missionary Society, 1825, p. 56. Similarly the Church Missionary Association instituted women's auxiliaries for the collection of funds in places such as Dublin, Lisburn, Kinsale and Kilkenny.

Prochaska, who has analysed the extent of women's auxiliaries in late eighteenth and early nineteenth-century England, perceives their function to have been mostly the raising of funds and concedes their subservience to the male run parent societies.[108] Auxiliaries were encouraged because they swelled the coffers but women soon used their auxiliary roles to engage in other public charitable work. In 1819 the Ladies' Bible Association initiated visitation of the poor in the parishes of St Thomas and St George in Dublin. The primary purpose of the visitation was to spread the gospel by distributing Bibles. The philosophy of the society expressed the belief that lack of knowledge of the Bible played a role in determining poverty: 'the destitute state of this metropolis [Dublin] with respect to the Holy Scriptures and the consequent ignorance and depravity of the lower ranks of its population, had excited on their behalf the strongest feelings of commiseration in the mind of every sincere friend of society'.[109]

The women who engaged in visitation were a little apprehensive about their work and requested two male members of the Dublin Auxiliary Bible Society to attend and oversee their monthly meetings. For some of the women visitation opened up new vistas of action and they stated 'that the day spent in visiting the poor was to them the happiest day of the week'.[110] This work was reported to have resulted in parents sending their children to Sunday School, awakening interest in the Bible and consequently improved the 'cleanliness' of the homes visited.[111]

Women were eventually encouraged to institute new Bible societies and in 1825 it was acknowledged that they were the 'life of such associations'.[112] In the pamphlet which made this acknowledgement, the anonymous author defended such women from criticisms, current at the time, that distributing Bibles and tracts took them away from their proper concerns of home and family and brought them into contact with a world which coarsened their gentility.

Church Missionary Association in aid of the Hibernian Auxiliary to the Church Missionary Society, annual report, 1816.

108 F.K. Prochaska, 'Women in English philanthropy, 1790–1830', *International Review of Social History*, 19 (1974), pp. 426–45; Prochaska, *Women and Philanthropy in 19th Century England*, pp. 21–34.

109 Ladies' Bible Association for the Seventh District of the City of Dublin, annual report, 1820, p. 8.

110 Ibid., p. 15.   111 Ibid., p. 14.

112 Anon., *Address to Ladies of Bible Associations* (Dublin, 1825), p. 4.

Society in general and women in particular were encouraged to look on this work as of vital importance. This writer argued that the task only took a couple of hours a week to perform and thus could not interfere with her duties to her family. The women themselves, it was noted, considered it 'a privilege to be employed in conveying the Word of everlasting life to her neighbours'.[113] The primary motivation for women engaged in this work was evangelical but there was an obvious sense of fulfilment evident in this work as well and women continued to organise in such societies throughout the century. The spread of women's involvement in Bible associations also had practical implications for the Protestant churches. As Hempton and Hill observe, 'women's auxiliaries were used to establish a base in Ireland, getting round the barriers imposed by the church on male dominated societies which were regarded, especially in Anglican circles, as a threat to Episcopal authority'.[114] Women's financial support was also essential, either in terms of personal donations or through their activities as fundraisers.

Two main types of religious organisation for women appear, therefore, to have existed among Bible societies during the century. One, like the Ladies' Bible Association, established in 1821, for promoting the religious instruction of the Irish people, was operated by women but their only function was to collect and forward funds to a parent body.[115] There were numerous societies with this function. The other, which involved direct missionary activity, is of more interest here as it allowed women to expand their social role through charitable work and to make an impact on secular life. Before examining these latter societies some mention must be made of the Sunday School. The first Sunday Schools were established in

---

113 Ibid.
114 David Hempton and Myrtle Hill, *Evangelical Protestantism in Ulster Society, 1740–1890* (London, 1992), p. 139.
115 See reports of the Ladies' Irish Association, 1887, 1897, 1899; Yearly Statement of Progress in the Irish Islands, annual report, 1840. This society had women's auxiliaries who supplied money and clothing to the mission. Committee of the Hibernian Church Missionary Society, Auxiliary to the Church Missionary Society for Africa and the East, annual report, 1816. Again this society had women's auxiliaries who collected funds. Hibernian Bible Society, annual report, 1887; Report of the Irish Branch of the Society for Irish Church Missions for the year 1884; Report of the Committee of the Hibernian Society for Aiding the Translation of the Holy Scriptures into Foreign Languages, 1824; Naas Ladies' Association, annual report, 1848; Reports of the General Irish Reformation Society for the Restoration in Ireland of her Primitive Religion and the Necessary Protection of Converts, 1886, 1889.

Ireland in County Down in 1770, and in Dublin in 1786.[116] The Hibernian Sunday School Society was formed in 1809 and this society changed its name to the Sunday School Society in 1815.[117] By 1818 a ladies association in connection with the society had been established in Dublin, again with the purpose of raising funds for the parent society.[118] Very little research has been done on the Sunday School movement in Ireland and no clear picture of the role of women in organising or teaching in these schools emerges from the available material although it must have been significant since by 1836 at least one-third of the teachers were women.[119]

In attempting to translate religious belief into practice the more important societies were the Dublin Visiting Mission, established in 1849; the Belfast Female Mission founded in 1859, the Dublin Bible Woman Mission established in 1861; the Young Women's Christian Association which began in 1855; and the Girls' Friendly Society, which operated in Ireland from 1877. These missions and associations brought into being a whole network of philanthropic agencies, generally with evangelical purposes, under the direction of women. The Dublin Visiting Mission was organised by the Irish Church Missions from Townsend Street. In 1885 the treasurer and secretaries of the Mission were women. It employed scripture readers to visit the homes of the poor. The Mission also ran Sunday Schools, prayer meetings and Gospel meetings.[120] One of the women intimately associated with it was Mrs Ellen Smyly, who, as we will discover later, was instrumental in establishing homes and schools for destitute children. Her primary source of motivation was evangelical and she employed women to look after her homes. The homes were conducted along the lines of a traditional family group and the women engaged in their management united both their maternal and spiritual mission to play a redemptive role.[121]

Protestant women, like their Catholic counterparts, provided charity mainly to women and children and received public support

---

116 Helen Ruth Clayton, 'Societies formed to educate the poor in Ireland in the late 18th and early 19th centuries' (M. Litt., TCD, 1981), p. 68.
117 Ibid., p. 70.   118 Ibid., p. 78.
119 Ibid., p. 159. In 1824 a training school for Sunday School mistresses was opened in Dublin. By 1831, 1,908 masters and 482 mistresses had been trained; by the end of 1836 1,975 men and 597 women had received training.
120 The only annual reports available for this Mission are for 1886, 1889–90 and 1895 and a pamphlet from 1871 which describes the work of the Mission.
121 See chapter 3.

because they did not exceed what were considered the limits of women's activities. Even the Bible Woman Mission, which operated in Dublin, concerned itself particularly with women and children. The aim of this mission was clearly stated in a report from 1877: 'to endeavour, by means of Bible women, mother's meetings, trained nurses, district visiting, temperance associations and similar agencies to make use of women's work for the promotion of and the temporal welfare of the poor in Dublin'.[122] The Mission worked under the direction of Church of Ireland ministers but its everyday activities were conducted by women. Here was women's redemptive mission clearly put into action. For too long, one report recorded, women's work and power had been neglected in bringing comfort to the poor.[123] Bible women, by their own admission, did not wish to encroach on those areas in which male ministers worked.[124] Women's role was defined and confined by traditional assumptions regarding women's proper sphere of influence and the women working in these societies were quite willing to work within these limits. They saw themselves as the agents through whom the poor were brought back to religion. In 1877 the Mission employed four Bible women who visited the poor and it was through this visitation that a scheme was developed to provide nurses for the sick. A training home for this purpose was opened in 1878. The Female Mission in Belfast, established in 1859, engaged in similar work with Bible classes being held for mill girls and visitations and prayer meetings being a constant feature of the work. An extra dimension of this Mission's work was to send suitable cases to reform institutions. In 1862 the Mission workers had made over 8,000 visitations.[125] Thus religious activities developed wider social roles and the religious motivation which gave rise to such societies allowed women to influence secular life. Sewing classes, savings clubs, cookery classes and mother's meetings also became part of this work. The Mission engaged women on both a voluntary and salaried basis, the Bible women and nurses being paid for their work.

The foundation of charity for these women was the example of Christ and its purpose was to provide the poor with the means of taking responsibility for their own lives. They did not provide alms

---

[122] Report and Statement of Accounts of the Dublin Bible Woman Mission, 1877, p. 4 (hereafter DBM).

[123] Ibid., p. 5.　　　[124] Ibid., p. 6.

[125] *Northern Whig*, 6 January 1870, 20 January 1894; *Banner of Ulster*, 8 January 1863.

indiscriminately but attempted to teach the poor thrift and religion; lack of knowledge in these areas was for them the cause of poverty and they did not question the structures of society. The evangelical mission of these Protestant women was similar in function to that of Catholic nuns. It was women who were the chief workers in the missionary field and it was they who were most successful in spreading the message of their various denominations. The type of self-help society which was such a common feature of Protestant philanthropy was echoed in the establishment of both the Young Women's Christian Association and the Girl's Friendly Society.

YOUNG WOMEN'S CHRISTIAN ASSOCIATION AND THE GIRLS' FRIENDLY SOCIETY

The YWCA was founded in England in 1855 and the first Irish branch opened in Dublin in 1866. It operated under the auspices of the Church of Ireland and was run by a ladies' committee and clergymen. The purpose of the association was to befriend young Protestant women and to promote their welfare.[126] Four classes of membership existed ranging from ordinary members and associates, both consisting of young women who were helped by the association, to working members and honorary associates, who were expected to operate the association. The members of these latter two groups had to pay a fixed subscription of not less than 2s 6d and 5s respectively and appear to have been of the middle and upper classes.[127] All the women connected with the association were bound by its primary objective, 'winning souls to the Lord Jesus Christ'.[128] There are no details on the actual numbers who joined the association but by 1900 it operated homes in eight Irish towns and cities.[129] The provision of homes in large centres of population was a deliberate strategy on the part of the YWCA. In Dublin and Belfast employment agencies for girls engaged in domestic service were opened and the homes provided cheap accommodation for members who awaited domestic or nursing situations.

---

[126] Barrett, *Guide*, part iii, pp. 59–60.

[127] Young Women's Christian Association, annual report, 1887, p. 8 (hereafter YWCA).

[128] Ibid., p. 16.

[129] YWCA, annual report, 1900, p. 4. Homes were operating in Armagh, Belfast, Cork, Limerick, Lisburn, Lurgan, Waterford and there were five homes in and around Dublin.

Within the homes the matrons substituted for parents and instilled a specific religious influence within the context of a Christian home.

The YWCA conducted both a moral and a spiritual mission. It placed signs in railway and boat stations which indicated where girls could obtain respectable lodgings. It was feared that girls coming to the cities looking for employment could easily be led astray and fall into bad company and bad habits.[130] The superintendents of the homes were urged to act as mothers to the girls residing there and these homes were to be a mirror of the ideal Christian home which offered comfort, protection and religious training to their occupants. Women were the instruments with which evil was to be overcome in the world, through the YWCA the work of women was to regenerate society by first of all protecting girls from the dangers of irreligion and then through them improving the moral and religious tone of society at large.[131] Amongst its other work the association promoted temperance and in 1887 claimed that 3,000 of its members were total abstainers. Members of the association also acted as visitors to the Prison Gate Mission in Dublin and held Bible classes in some of the Dublin hospitals thus uniting their religious outlook with a desire to effect moral change through their public actions.[132]

The work of the YWCA was complemented by the establishment of the Girls' Friendly Society in Ireland in 1877, though both organisations remained distinct from each other. The GFS was originally founded in England by Mrs Townsend in 1874.[133] Like the YWCA its aim was to protect young Protestant girls by training them in religious principles and domestic duty. Its internal organisation was similar to that of the YWCA with associates, members and candidates. In 1881 it had 15 branches throughout Ireland; by 1900 it had 157 branches operating in 512 parishes with a total membership of 14,962.[134] Within the GFS several different areas of work were carried out and there were separate 'departments' for each section. Among these departments was the emigration department which looked after girls travelling from Ireland to situations abroad, a department for members in service which operated a registry of girls available for domestic service for potential employers and an

---

130 YWCA, annual report 1887, p. 31.
131 *Go Forward* (YWCA monthly journal), 100 (May 1895), pp. 119–22.
132 YWCA, annual report, 1890, pp. 23, 35.
133 Mary Heath Stubbs, *Friendship's Highway* (London, 1935), chapter 1.
134 Girls' Friendly Society, annual report, 1881, pp. 18–30; 1900, p. 5 (hereafter GFS).

industrial department which provided classes in dress-making and cookery for its members throughout the country. The basic characteristics of a GFS girl were expected to be 'purity of life and friendship'. By instituting a society for single women the GFS's expressed aim was to 'raise the moral tone of all classes'.[135]

Both the YWCA and the GFS were interested in turning out devout girls who would create domestic happiness in their future family lives. Here we can see the dynamic of maternalism in action. Both societies in their tiered system of organisation, brought the socially superior upper and middle-class woman into contact with working girls of the 'lower orders' and attempted through religion and friendship to create a bond between them. The majority of girls who belonged to these societies ended up as domestic servants and the friendliness expressed towards them on the part of the societies' organisers was not intended to breach the walls of the class system. Mutual co-operation between the members of these societies was encouraged. They were in effect extending women's role into the public sphere but that extension was essentially a domestic one. Women in the GFS who were encouraged to visit members in their workplaces always sought the permission of the girl's employer. Throughout, there was a respect instilled in both workers and visitors for formal authority. Neither group advocated any form of political action and in 1893 when the Irish branch of the GFS advocated signing a petition to protest against the Home Rule Bill the resulting circular caused upset in the ranks of the managing council.[136] Like most religiously inspired philanthropic groups of the last century both organisations were socially conservative and inactive in areas which urged legislation regarding the working and social conditions of the poor in society. Both organisations also reinforced the view that women were essentially only temporary workers in the public workplace and their ideal position was in the home. Neither organisation, though heavily involved in attempts to find domestic situations for their members attempted to challenge or investigate the conditions under which their members worked. A more immediate function of the homes provided by the YWCA and the GFS was to control the sexual morality of the young women who came to the large towns and cities looking for employment. By the

[135] GFS, annual report, 1883, p. 5.
[136] MS Minute book, 17 March 1893 (GFS, Leeson Street, Dublin).

1870s and 1880s the problem of sexual morality had become a public issue in Ireland due to the campaigns which surrounded the Contagious Diseases Acts. The organising members of the YWCA and the GFS were obviously ambivalent about the changing role of women in society, exemplified in their eyes by the numbers of single women searching for jobs in the metropolis far away from the constraints of family life. In the late nineteenth and early twentieth century thousands of Irish women used these 'homes' and indeed life there offered opportunities for friendship, protection and economic benefit. Maternalism was the watchword of both organisations and the imitation of family life was the strong cohesive ideal which bound these societies together.

Women of Protestant denominations appear to have been more independent of clerical authority in their philanthropic work than their Catholic counterparts. These women did, however, work closely with male clerics and had them on advisory committees. Throughout the century almost all women's voluntary societies had male committee members and clerical members added authority and status to these societies and legitimated their purposes. Catholic women, as we have noted, rarely undertook organised charity work on an independent personal basis. There is strong evidence to suggest that Protestant women did so, and on a broad scale.

Miss Mary Meredith Carr began the Stanhope Mission, on her own initiative, around 1885. This Mission, eventually based in Dun Laoghaire, survived until her death in 1916. Carr, along with two other women, went onto the streets and invited women they met to attend the Mission. Carr, who wrote the annual reports of the Mission herself, stated that her purpose was 'to bring the word of God to all'.[137] Through the Mission she organised sewing classes for poor women, distributed Bibles, engaged in house to house visitation, opened a shelter for destitute men and women and tried to secure employment for them. She also ran a Sunday School, which, it was reported, had an average attendance of sixty people every week.[138] For Carr the religious element of the work was of primary importance and the ultimate purpose was to convert those who attended the Mission to the Church of Ireland. In 1893 six such conversions, from Catholicism, were claimed.[139] Her work did not

---

[137] Stanhope Mission, annual report, 1890, p. 3 (hereafter SM).
[138] SM, annual report, 1892, pp. 3–4.
[139] SM, annual report, 1894, p. 5.

always meet with support and an attempt by her to initiate a sewing class in Dalkey in 1895 had to be abandoned as the women 'were afraid to come'.[140] She did not wish to have her work made publicly known and for this reason was hesitant in publishing any annual reports. The fact that these reports were not for public consumption suggests that Carr was unwilling to allow individuals, possibly the Catholic clergy, to become too familiar with the work she was doing. Essentially she was engaged in an evangelical mission which was anathema to Catholics at this period. Although the numbers attending the Mission never appear to have been large Carr obviously derived great satisfaction from it and her life work was to instil her religious beliefs in those who came under her influence.

Independence can also be seen in the numbers of foreign mission societies established by women throughout the century. For example, the Female Association for Promoting Christianity Among the Women of the East, established in 1873, sent out female missionaries. A Miss Hassard took over the management of the female staff in the Dublin University Mission in India, without payment, in December of 1891. She was an experienced worker in a Dublin parish and had spent twelve years as a missionary in South Africa.[141] In December 1879 we find a missionary conference being held in Alexandra College, Dublin which was a 'women only' event. By 1889 the Alexandra College Dublin Missionary Society had been formed. Drawing room meetings, the staple form of fund-raising and publicity used by women in the nineteenth century, were used in 1874 to establish a Mission to Lepers in India. By the second year of its operation the fund-raisers accumulated £800 for this cause.[142] The life of Irish women missionaries needs more extensive examination than can be afforded here. These women were bringing to foreign parts that religious message which their fund-raisers and supporters already saw in action, although on a different scale, in Ireland.

QUAKER WOMEN AND PHILANTHROPY

The philanthropic work of Quaker women took many forms including the initiation of refuges, schools and crèches and it is for their

---

140 SM, annual report, 1895, p. 5.
141 D.M. McFarlan, *Lift thy Banner: Church of Ireland Scenes 1870–1900* (Dundalk, 1990), pp. 92–100.
142 Ibid., p. 72.

work during the famine that they are best remembered. Quaker philanthropy belonged more to the realms of reformist movements like the anti-slavery and anti-war movements than that of other denominations. Quaker women played a major role in initiating the suffrage movement and were to be found in the most progressive reformist organisations of the day, the Philanthropic Reform Association, the National Society for the Prevention of Cruelty to Children and the Irish Workhouse Association. All of these societies differed from other charitable organisations in the level of public and political action which women were willing to undertake to initiate social change. The operation of gender equality and the concern with social issues which formed part of the Quaker tradition probably goes some way to explain Quaker women's involvement in reformist societies. Their sense of individual responsibility was highly developed and Quaker women received a great deal of support from their own families and within their own community for their activities. In the reformist societies they organised or joined, Quaker women were supported by some of their Protestant sisters but from the evidence available Catholic women appear to have offered little if any, practical support. Quaker women's philanthropic work is often bound up with overt political concerns and this can be seen most clearly in their involvement and initiation of anti-slavery societies and a brief look at their work in this area underlines the pioneering reformist spirit which is evident in all of their philanthropic dealings.

ANTI-SLAVERY SOCIETIES

The information available on anti-slavery societies is quite scant. The earliest such society found is the Hibernian Ladies' Negroes' Friend Society which operated in the 1830s. Another society, dating from that period, was the Dublin Ladies' Association. A Dublin Ladies' Anti-Slavery Society existed from the 1850s and survived until at least 1861. In 1856 an Irish Ladies' Anti-Slavery Society began operating and it too appears to have lasted until the 1860s. Also in the years 1845–7 a Cork Ladies' Anti-Slavery Society, whose members included individuals from Cork city, Youghal, Bandon and Tralee, did its share to promote the anti-slavery cause.[143] The

---

[143] See Richard S. Harrison, *Irish Anti-War Movements, 1824–1974* (Dublin, 1986), for an account of the Quakers' involvement in peace movements. Report of the Hibernian Ladies' Negroes' Friend Society, 1833; Catherine Elizabeth Alma, *An Appeal from the*

committees of these societies were composed entirely of women with the exception of one man who served on the Cork Ladies' Anti-Slavery Society committee. Although it is impossible to ascertain with any degree of certainty the religious affiliations of the committee members it appears from the membership lists of the DLASS that the majority of committee members were Quakers.[144]

These anti-slavery societies were quite small. For example, the total number of subscribers to the DLASS in 1858 was just 33, 18 of these were women and the rest men; in 1860 there were 40 subscribers, again with 18 women and 22 men.[145] Members of the same family also appear to have been subscribers, with, for example, eight members of the Webb family, who were Quakers, subscribing to the DLASS in 1860.[146] From the subscription lists available Quakers appear to have been the major source of financial support for these societies. Given the narrow base of their operation there were practical limits to the amount of support such societies could offer to their American and British counterparts and indeed the women who organised these societies were well aware of their limits. Their primary objective was to raise the consciousness of the Irish people as to the horrors of slavery. To this end the DLASS annually distributed thousands of copies of a leaflet entitled 'Address to Emigrants' to emigrant offices in Dublin, Belfast, Cork and Derry. The dubious effect of such a paper blitz was noted in an annual report of 1860 when the committee admitted that 'we regret to acknowledge that hitherto our Irish emigrants have done small credit to the land of their birth and have generally thrown their influence into the pro-slavery side'.[147]

In 1859 the same society facilitated a lecture tour by a Miss Sarah Parker Redmond 'a coloured lady from Salem' who spoke at meetings in Dublin, Waterford, Clonmel and Cork. In 1860 they invited George Thompson, an eminent American anti-slavery activist, to lecture in Dublin. The society also contributed small sums of money to the Philadelphia Vigilance Committee and an average of £20 was forwarded annually to aid 'the fugitive department' which allowed slaves to escape from plantations and make their way to

Dublin Ladies' Association (Dublin, 1837); annual reports of the Dublin Ladies' Anti-Slavery Society 1859–61; annual reports of the Cork Ladies' Anti-Slavery Society, 1845–7.

144 Annual reports of the Dublin Ladies' Anti-Slavery Society, 1859–61.
145 Ibid., 1861. See also annual report, Hibernian Ladies' Negroes' Friend Society, 1833.
146 Annual report, DLASS, 1861.   147 Ibid., 1860, p. 5.

Canada.[148] This committee also received the latest anti-slavery literature from America and recommended such reading matter to their subscribers. The Irish Ladies' Anti-Slavery Society was much more limited in its aims and its sole purpose appears to have been to encourage Irishwomen to donate articles and needlework which would be auctioned at the Rochester [New York] Anti-Slavery Society's annual bazaar.[149] The Cork Ladies' Anti-Slavery Society also raised funds which it forwarded to the Boston Female Anti-Slavery Society and it published extracts from American newspapers dealing with the horrors of slavery.[150] An anti-slavery petition was presented to Queen Victoria in 1838 which was signed by 75,000 Irishwomen.[151]

As in most organisations established by women the committees of these societies sought support for their cause primarily by appealing to other women. They accepted the status of wife and mother as a universal bond uniting all women and they used this to harness sympathy for their cause. In an appeal from the Dublin Ladies' Association, published in 1837, Irish women, it was declared, as wives and mothers free from slavery, must empathise with their slave bound sisters who as a 'wife may be torn from the husband of her choice forever', or as a mother have no 'right of maternal property in her offspring'.[152] The belief in the innate moral superiority of women was also revealed, a sentiment expressed again and again by all the voluntary organisations of the nineteenth century. 'Let us not', the appeal continued, 'be deterred because we are women – but let us remember that oft times God uses the weak things of the world to confound the things that are mighty.'[153] The information available on these Irish women's societies is limited. However, their existence reveals that the reformist instinct was strong among Quaker women from the early years of the century and it was an instinct which they brought to bear on all their philanthropic work. Evidence of this reformist spirit will be seen more clearly in their campaign against the Contagious Diseases Acts and their involvement in prison reform which will be discussed later.

[148] Ibid., p. 6; 1861, p. 5.
[149] Ibid., p. 7. See also 'To philanthropists who "remember them that are in bonds"', which appears to have been published by the Irish Ladies' Anti-Slavery Society. Dowden Collection, U. 140 (CAI).
[150] Annual report, Cork Ladies' Anti-Slavery Society, 1846.
[151] Richard S. Harrison, 'Irish Quaker perspectives on the anti-slavery movement', *The Journal of the Friends' Historical Society*, 56: 2 (1991), p. 115.
[152] Alma, *Appeal*.   [153] Ibid.

Throughout the nineteenth century there were, therefore, a number of patterns to be observed in women's philanthropic work. The expanding congregations of female religious engaged in the most widespread charity work, and associated with them were the lay Catholic women confined in their activities by their acceptance of nuns as the ideal providers of Catholic relief. There were also groups of Protestant women who engaged independently in pastoral and philanthropic work. Within the formal church structure there were also a number of Bible women. Women were undoubtedly the means of evangelical action in nineteenth-century Ireland and this was as true of Catholic women as it was for women of Protestant denominations.

Protestant women had more flexibility with regard to organising societies and they were allowed much greater leeway in the work they did. While generally under the nominal control of clerics they appear to have operated their societies according to their own wishes. The minority position of Protestants in Irish society allowed a sense of community to develop among these philanthropic women and there was a greater degree of cross class involvement in their charitable societies as witnessed by the Young Women's Christian Association and the Girls' Friendly Society. Protestant women unlike their Catholic counterparts did become involved in reformist societies and were generally more aware of the need for social change, although of a limited kind, than their Catholic sisters. While religion acted as unifying force for Protestant and Catholic women within their own communities it also allowed for great disharmony between women of different denominations and this can be seen most clearly in women's work with children.

CHAPTER 3

Saving the child

Like a number of other Catholic ladies in Dublin in the last century, Maria Murray was in the habit of roaming poor areas of the city to ascertain how many Catholic children attended Protestant schools. Her purpose, she wrote to Cullen in 1864, was to take 'as many children from the proselytising parties as I can snatch'. She also explained that it was not the government which supported these institutions but that it was 'the Protestant ladies of Dublin who are doing the mischief'.[1] Murray suggested to Cullen that one way to counteract this problem was to establish an alternative Catholic run home to look after any children who were in danger of falling into Protestant hands. Murray's school does not appear to have become a reality but other Catholic women established orphanages and homes to counteract what they saw as the proselytising zeal of Protestants. Throughout most of the nineteenth century state involvement in the provision of institutional services, such as schools and workhouses, created much heated debate regarding religious issues. It was from the 1850s that the Catholic church reacted most vigorously to proselytism.[2] To the forefront of that fight, particularly for the 'souls of children', were Catholic female religious. Of all aspects of philanthropic endeavour in the nineteenth century it was women's work with children which most empowered them. It was also the work which most divided women philanthropists from each other.

---

[1] Maria Murray to Archbishop Cullen, 17 March 1864, Cullen Papers, File 320/4/48 (Laity 1864). See also the report of the anti-proselytising committee, Cullen Papers, File 339/2/36 (1856); a paper on proselytising schools in Murray Papers, File 33/15/6 (Education, undated); and letter from Sarah Corr to Cullen 15 January 1872, Cullen Papers File 335/2/11 (Laity 1872) (DDA).

[2] There are few works which deal adequately with the issue of proselytism. See Desmond Bowen, *Souperism: Myth or Reality – a study of Catholics and Protestants during the Great Famine*

The maternal role attributed to women allowed them greater access to institutions which dealt with children, and individual women established numerous orphanages and homes to look after the needs of various groups, whether orphans, deserted children or those who lived on the streets. Writing in 1862 one male writer observed that women had a special role in caring for the young. While men could provide patronage and funding for an institution it was the duty of women to provide 'the peculiar training, the required knowledge, but above all, the sympathy, the encouragement, the practical friendship, the example of purity, reserve, modesty, self-control – all these so necessary if the poor girl is to grow up a blessing, not a curse to the community'.[3] The fruits of philanthropists' activities, both male and female, in the area of childcare can be seen by looking at Dublin which had over 120 educational institutions, orphanages and refuges operating in 1884.[4] Outside the private philanthropic sphere children were also catered for in institutions such as workhouses and gaols. Traditionally workhouses and orphanages were the principal institutions which catered for the destitute child, but by mid-century the establishment of 'ragged schools', and from the late 1850s and 1860s industrial and reformatory schools, principally under the care of female religious, further increased the facilities available to destitute, pauper and criminal children.

Most orphanages and homes, whether run by male, female or mixed committees, had women as matrons who oversaw the running of the institution. The matron, in essence, was the symbolic 'mother' of the institution and carried out the nurturing functions of motherhood, along with organising the practical details of running the 'home'. The involvement of so many women philanthropists with such homes should come as no surprise. Within these institutions they were fulfilling their 'natural' role. They modelled such institutions upon their own ideals of what family life should constitute and since these philanthropists were from the middle classes their ideal revolved around middle-class mores. A female presence was essential

(Cork, 1970); Bowen, *The Protestant Crusade in Ireland, 1800–1870* (Naas, 1978); Robins, *Lost Children*, chapter 6.

3 Mark O'Shaughnessy, 'Some remarks upon Mrs Hannah Archer's scheme for befriending orphan pauper girls', *Journal of the Statistical and Social Inquiry Society of Ireland* (April 1862), p. 144.

4 Barrett, *Guide*, part ii, pp. 1–59.

to nurture the children. Education and training, both religious and vocational, were provided to prepare the children for their proper role in the world, idleness was discouraged and children were not left to roam the streets. These philanthropists particularly wanted to save children from the dangers and corruption of the streets and from what they considered to be the inherent depravity of the workhouse, and provide them instead with the safety and security considered one of the virtues of middle-class family life.

Given the strength of the religious convictions of many philanthropists it is not surprising to see the majority of orphanages and homes established on a denominational and sectarian basis. For the women involved, looking after the physical needs of the children was often only a beginning; far more important were their attempts to inculcate a certain moral, spiritual and social outlook in their charges. This was extended into the public sphere when, from mid-century, women played an important role in humanising the conditions under which the workhouse child was maintained. Also by the end of the century women collaborated with men in attempts to protect children by improving their legislative position. The history of the child in Irish society has yet to be written and in the absence of such a history some facts about the level of destitution among the child population will show how important were the changes which were brought about for their care by the end of the century.

In the eighteenth century foundling hospitals were established in Cork and Dublin to deal with abandoned infants. Conditions were horrendous and the mortality rate very high. Between 1735 and 1743, 3,972 foundlings were admitted to the Dublin Foundling Hospital and 2,754 died.[5] In the late eighteenth and early nineteenth centuries many orphanages were opened but destitute children were also to be found in large numbers in the houses of industry and prisons. Robins, in his study of the charity child, observes that many who ended up in prison did so, not due to criminal activity, but because there was nowhere else for them to go.[6] In the 1851 census

---

[5] Robins, *Lost Children*, p. 17. This is a fine study of the institutional care provided for destitute children. The work concentrates principally on the role of the workhouse and changing attitudes to the care of children within that system. It does not cover the area of private philanthropic enterprise regarding children or indeed the role of women in the care of children. The whole question of the economic function of children within the family unit and indeed the attitudes and perceptions of both middle-class and working-class parents towards their children needs to be investigated.

[6] Ibid., p. 117.

returns 10,554 persons, under the age of fifteen, were returned as beggars.[7] In 1852 the number of boys, under the age of fifteen, committed to the Richmond Bridewell under the vagrancy laws was 1,540.[8] In her study of late nineteenth and early-twentieth-century Dublin, Mary Daly has calculated that approximately 16 per cent of the inmates of the South Dublin Union, in the years 1875 to 1904, were children under the age of fourteen.[9] By 1900 there were approximately 104 industrial schools, reformatories and voluntary orphanages operating throughout the country which had the capacity to cater for over 11,200 children.[10]

The children of the poor often played an important role in the family economy, a function which often went unacknowledged by philanthropists. The case history of one child, who spent some time in the William Henry Elliott Home for Waifs and Strays attests to the fact that children often worked, not to support themselves alone but often to support their parents. Jinny O'D— had been brought to the home by her mother; both were in rags and without shelter. Jinny had provided for herself and her mother by selling matches and newspapers on the street. The mother left her in the home for two months and then removed her, finding that she could not support herself without the child's assistance.[11] The Poor Law Inquiry of 1836 acknowledges the role children played in begging and the census returns of 1851, for example, noted, that of persons under fifteen, 254 were described as rag and bone dealers and a further 23,356 were returned as labourers or domestic servants.[12] Two elements, education and protection, were at the core of all philanthropic work with children. It was in the larger towns and cities that child care work predominated but the provision of education for poor children was to be found in all parts of the country.

The earliest formal philanthropic work of women with children before mid-century was marked by the establishment of poor or charity schools. It is difficult to gauge the number of such schools

---

[7] Census of Ireland,1851.
[8] *Report of the select committee on criminal and destitute children* ... 1852–53, HC 1852–3 (674), xxiii, 510–11.
[9] Mary E. Daly, *Dublin, The Deposed Capital* (Cork, 1984), p. 85.
[10] *The Classified List of Child Saving Institutions* (Reformatory and Refuge Union, London, 1915), pp. 92–7.
[11] Annual report of the William Henry Elliott Home for Waifs and Strays, 1889, p. 5.
[12] Census of Ireland, 1851.

which were run by women either free of charge or for a small fee. In Clonmel in 1789 the Quakers established a charitable school which originally catered for boys and girls but from 1804 taught girls only.[13] In the same town in 1826, there were twenty-one schools operating. Of these eight were run by women, including one free school run by the Presentation sisters.[14] For women, particularly 'genteel ladies' who were in a financially precarious position, teaching was the only acceptable form of work which they could undertake without being socially stigmatised. Whether undertaken for humanitarian, or partly financial reasons, such schools proliferated. Amongst the earliest established to provide a free education were those schools founded by Nano Nagle, later to found the Presentation Order, in Cork in 1769.[15] A group of women opened a Charitable Repository and School of Industry in Bandon in 1811. Its purpose was to provide a rudimentary education to poorer children. It appears to have catered only for girls and the curriculum followed was intended to provide 'a moderate proficiency in reading, a knowledge of plain and useful needlework and an acquaintance with religious truth'.[16] The highest expectations for the pupils were that they would become upper servants, shop assistants or teachers in 'inferior schools'. The majority were not expected to go beyond the level of minor servants or of using whatever skills they had acquired in the school, outside the confines of their own homes.[17] The women who ran this school recognised the economic value of children within the family unit and as an encouragement to parents to send them their daughters they promised to provide them with clothing 'as some equivalent of the small services of which the parents might be deprived by thus resigning the disposal of their children's time'.[18] The clothing provided served another purpose in that it acted as a type of uniform which helped to distinguish the poorest children and thus make them more amenable to discipline.[19] The school appears to have catered for about 100

---

13 Clonmel Charitable School, annual report 1858.
14 *Second Report of the Commissioners of Education Inquiry*, 1826–7, HC 1826 (12), xii, 1100–57. In Tipperary town there were fourteen schools, eight of which were run by women all of whom charged for their services. See D.G. Marnane, *Land and Violence: A History of West Tipperary from 1660* (Tipperary, 1985), appendix 3, pp. 166–7.
15 Walsh, *Nano Nagle*, pp. 44–5.
16 Annual report of the Charitable Repository and School of Industry, Bandon, 1814, p. 9.
17 Ibid., p. 6.   18 Ibid., p. 9.   19 Ibid.

pupils in 1814 and was supported in part by public subscriptions and also by the knitting and sewing done by the girls.[20]

The Ladies' Hibernian Female School Society, established in London in 1824, also encouraged Irishwomen to open schools within their own localities. Funds were collected by the parent body and distributed to the 'ladies' who organised schools in Ireland though they were not paid for their exertions. The parent body expressed the opinion that 'as the spirit of union, kindness and benevolence becomes more prevalent amongst the higher classes, that of gratitude, the return of kindly feeling and a readiness in receiving instruction will be more widely diffused among the lower orders'.[21] Unfortunately very little information survives regarding this society, although it was still in existence, according to *Thom's Directory*, in the 1890s. By the end of its first year of operation three schools had been set up in Munster and six in each Connaught and Leinster. By 1844 it claimed to have 230 schools under its control.[22] Poor schools were probably established all over the country and it is difficult to gauge their full extent. Many were probably short-lived efforts and there was no overall co-ordinating body or network to look after them. In around 1834 a school for girls was established in Kilkee which 'chiefly owes its existence to the exertions of two benevolent ladies from Dublin during a summer visit'. The success of this enterprise was attributed to the 'superintendence and unwearied exertion of a resident lady'.[23] Such local philanthropy gave the 'lady' involved a worthwhile purpose and these schools were a popular form of philanthropic enterprise. Such operations were of primary importance to the Established church and allowed for a consolidation of their evangelical mission. The exertions of women in this regard were often condemned by the Catholic clergy which saw their involvement as an attempt at proselytism. Elizabeth Smith, the wife of a landowner in County Wicklow, established a school in Baltiboys under the National Board. She took a great interest in its affairs and visited regularly. Her interest was not appreciated by the local

---

20 Ibid., pp. 10–11, the annual income of the school in 1813 was £260; 87 per cent of this was derived from donations and subscriptions while work done in the school accounted for 9 per cent of income.

21 Annual report of the Ladies' Hibernian Female School Society, 1824, p. 13.

22 See *Thom's Directory* for 1845. The society remained listed in this directory until the end of the century and the figure of 230 schools remained unaltered.

23 Mary John Knott, *Two Months at Kilkee* (Dublin, 1836), pp. 108–9.

Catholic priest who tried to stop, without success, the local children attending.[24]

For girls the education provided in these poor schools was limited to reading, writing, needlework and the acquisition of domestic skills. With the spread of convent schools from the 1830s the education of the poor gradually came under the control of nuns, though individual women still continued to earn a living as lay teachers and by providing some form of education through governessing. The education of poor females, whether carried out by religious or lay women, centred on providing them with those skills which were thought essential for their future as wives and mothers. Domestic skills also equipped a girl to become a servant, but this also meant operating within the private sphere, and provided yet further training for her ultimate expected role as wife and mother. Practical skills, such as knitting and sewing, could be used to supplement an income, but like the training provided for poor women, these skills were to be used from the home.

In an analysis of the textbooks used in Irish schools in the last century, Lorcan Walsh has identified the images of women portrayed as reinforcing the 'cult' of motherhood and domesticity.[25] Sections of the readers used were intended for girls only 'for the instruction of females in household and domestic duties'.[26] The stories used presented girls with a model for all those virtues considered necessary to be the 'ideal' woman. To the mother also, was left the spiritual and moral care of the young and religious education was the subject of primary importance. Women, as educators, in the home or in institutions, saw their function as transmitting these values unquestioningly. Since women could not partake fully in public life their one arena of power lay within the institution of the family. In establishing orphanages, poor schools and refuges women extended their power base from the domestic setting to public institutions.

---

[24] Elizabeth Grant, *The Highland Lady in Ireland: Elizabeth Grant of Rothiemurchus*, eds. Patricia Pelly and Andrew Todd (Edinburgh, 1991), p. 47 and passim. A shorter, edited version of this journal appeared as David Thompson and Moyra McGusty (eds.), *The Irish Journals of Elizabeth Smith, 1840–1850* (Oxford, 1980). See also Asenath Nicholson, *Ireland's Welcome to the Stranger* (London, 1847), pp. 40–1, 64–5, for a brief account of schools established by Lady Harburton and Lady Wicklow.

[25] Lorcan Walsh, 'Images of women in nineteenth-century schoolbooks', *Irish Educational Studies*, 4:1(1984), pp. 73–87.

[26] Quoted in ibid., p. 77.

Alongside these schools children were also catered for in 'ragged schools'. These differed from 'poor schools', being designed for a specific clientele, generally the children of the very poor who spent most of their lives on the streets. Mary Carpenter, the great English philanthropist and reformer had played a leading role in the establishment of such schools in England but it is difficult to assess whether the example of these English models was followed by Irish philanthropists in any great detail. Ragged schools appear to have become quite common in Dublin from around the 1850s, although the Mill Street ragged schools were in operation from 1838.[27] In 1852 there were stated to be nine such schools in operation in the city catering for 664 pupils.[28] An Industrial Ragged School also operated in Cork city from the 1850s and was organised by Protestant women.[29] The humanitarian purposes of these schools can be witnessed in an appeal for funds for the establishment of a ragged school in Cork in 1851. The organisers recognised that there were some children whose sole occupation in life was to steal, not for the sake of stealing but in order to survive. It was to be the function of the ragged schools to entice these children away from a life of crime by allowing them physical sustenance and an education and by training them in habits of industry, 'to induce them to seek an honest livelihood, and fit them for the duties of life giving them such sustenance as may, until they can earn some for themselves, supersede the temptation to resort to dishonest practices'.[30] Ragged schools in England were closely identified with evangelical effort and the same appears to be true for Irish schools. In an appeal for funds made by the Cork Industrial Ragged School, in 1859, it was stated: 'surely Christians will uphold an institution thus calculated to meet the wants of those who are emphatically "the dangerous classes", and to rescue from idleness, crime, or degraded superstition, the children of all professing creeds of their poorer brethren'.[31] Mrs Smyly was certainly an innovator in this field but there appear also to have been some Catholic ragged schools in existence.[32] Cullen's pastoral against proselytism delivered

[27] *Report from the Select Committee on Criminal and Destitute Children* . . . 1852–3, HC 1852–3 (674), xxiii. Evidence of J.C. Connellan, Q. 4,260–4,262.
[28] Ibid., Q. 4,263.
[29] Anon., 'Cork industrial ragged school', *The Irish Quarterly Review* 9 (October 1859), appendix, pp. xxxvii–xxxviii.
[30] Quoted in an Appeal for the Cork Central Ragged School Association (Cork, 1851), p. 1.
[31] Anon., 'Cork industrial ragged school', p. xxxvii.
[32] See *Thom's Directory* from the 1850s to the end of the century.

in June of 1856, and which condemned the ragged schools, ensured the opening of Catholic schools in the following months.[33] Some of these were not without their problems. The lay committee of the Catholic ragged schools wrote a long letter to Cullen outlining their problems with the local Catholic clergy. The battle here seems to have been for control over the schools rather than for souls. A tale of insults, dismissals and appointments of teachers, problems over the collection and control of money surfaced, though in this instance the clergy emerged victorious.[34]

Besides poor and ragged schools an extensive network of orphanages was established in the nineteenth century. Thomas Osler, in an 1834 report, noted the existence of twenty-three Catholic establishments in Dublin,[35] and others were established in the cities of Cork and Waterford.[36] The Protestant Orphan Society was established in 1828 and by 1887 it had thirty-five branches around the country.[37] Other religious denominations had their own societies. The Methodist Orphan Society, for example, was founded in 1870 and a Presbyterian Orphan Society opened in Belfast in 1866.[38] These organisations had a national basis and were managed by men. Women also established independent orphanages to look after children of their own persuasion or to evangelise. One of the earliest Protestant orphanages, the Female Orphan House, was opened in Dublin in 1790 by a Mrs Este and a Mrs Tighe. In the original prospectus for the orphanage it was proposed to take in destitute girls between the ages of five and ten years and that they, 'would be clothed, dieted, lodged and taught reading, writing and common accounts; carefully instructed in the Christian Religion, and habituated to cleanliness and industry ... to spin, knit and when able to make their own clothes'.[39] The girls were to be trained in all aspects of household work to enable them to be placed as servants once they reached the age of sixteen. The orphanage, which had the support of many wealthy people in Dublin, received an

[33] Peadar MacSuibhne, *Paul Cullen and His Contemporaries*, 3 vols. (Naas, 1961–5), II, 220, 296, III, 288, 404.

[34] Chairman of the committee of ragged schools (Catholic) to Cullen, February 1856, Cullen Papers, File 339/2/20 (Non-diocesan 1856) (DDA).

[35] Report on Catholic Orphanages and Orphan Schools in Dublin, 1824 by Thomas Oslar (MS 640, NLI).

[36] Robins, *Lost Children*, pp. 118–29.   [37] *Irish Church Directory*, 1899, p. 229.

[38] Barrett, *Guide*, part ii, pp. 18, 21–2.

[39] Anon., *A Brief Record of the Female Orphan House* (Dublin, 1893), p. 6.

annual grant from parliament which, between 1801 and 1823, averaged approximately £650 per annum.[40] The work of the orphans themselves also brought in about £400 per year.[41] Various parliamentary commissions reported favourably on this orphanage and thought of it as an example to be followed by other similar institutions.[42]

Though the Female Orphan House was not seen as a proselytising agency, many Protestant orphanages had that reputation. The need to evangelise, strongly felt, especially in the early nineteenth century, by both Catholics and Protestants, ensured that tensions arose over the care of children. St Bonaventure's Charitable Institution and Orphanage, established in 1820, sought to prevent Protestant agencies receiving Catholic children.[43] Similarly, St Brigid's Orphanage, founded by Margaret Aylward, was begun solely with the purpose of preventing Catholic children being forced, through need, to enter Protestant run establishments. In an appeal for this orphanage, made in 1876, the public were urged to support the charity not alone for its charitable function but because in 'contributing to this charity you save not merely poor orphans but poor orphans whose faith is in danger'. The organisers wanted to 'rescue the children of the Catholic church from the enemies of the Catholic church'.[44] Likewise St Vincent's Female Orphanage in North William Street, Dublin, which was under the supervision of the Sisters of Charity of St Vincent de Paul, hoped to counteract proselytism. Although concerned with the physical destitution forced on children through becoming orphans they feared even more that such children would enter Protestant orphanages where 'many of these innocent victims, unconscious of their sad fate and early doom, are thus lost to the faith of their fathers, which they learn only to abhor'.[45] Many of the Protestant orphanages were indeed self-professed proselytising agencies, particularly those under the control of the Irish Church Missions. One of these, the Bird's Nest, organised by Mrs Ellen Smyly, favoured children of mixed marriages or of Catholic

[40] *Reports of the Inspector of Charitable Institutions, Dublin 1842*, HC 1842 (337), xxxviii, 52.
[41] Anon., *Brief Record*, p. 34.
[42] *Reports of the Inspector of Charitable Institutions, Dublin 1842*, 32.
[43] W.J. Battersby, *Catholic Directory*, 1836, p. 105.
[44] Rev. Mathew Russell, 'St Brigid's orphans', *The Irish Monthly*, 4 (1876), p. 455.
[45] Annual report of St Vincent's Female Orphanage, 1861, p. 5.

parentage as inmates.[46] In 1884 some children were taken from the Protestant run Elliott Home in Townsend Street due to the 'endeavours of the priests to force poor mothers to claim children'.[47] An article published in the *Freeman's Journal* in 1883 was a strong attack on Protestant orphanages and schools. The author, after a visit to one of Mrs Smyly's ragged schools observed 'over a hundred starvelings, as poor and as pitiable as the so-called charity which had fed them that morning'.[48] Concluding, the author urged subscribers to donate to a Save the Child fund which was to be administered by a group of Catholic women.

Within Dublin, at least, women played an important role in the battle for children's souls. Aylward and her helpers, the Ladies' Association of Charity of St Vincent de Paul, regularly visited Protestant schools to ascertain the numbers of Catholic children who attended. One report noted that 'Archbishop [Cullen] has expressed his desire for our co-operation in this most meritorious work',[49] and the women reported regularly to him. They also stood outside the Irish Church Mission Sunday schools speaking to the children and trying to get their names and addresses and those of their parents. The role women played in this battle can best be seen by examining the work of Aylward and Ellen Smyly. Aylward, as we have noted, was instrumental in establishing St Brigid's Orphanage in Dublin in 1856. Among the functions of her organisation, the Ladies of Charity, was the 'instruction of the ignorant, and with the concern of resisting the efforts of Proselytism, carried on through means of anti-Catholic schools'.[50] The concern with which Catholics approached this issue can be seen in the number of written reports sent to Cullen outlining the activities of such Protestant schools.[51] Gauging the numbers of Catholic children within these establishments was a difficult task. A report to Cullen in 1876 enumerat-

---

[46] Barrett, *Guide*, part ii, pp. 11–12. Taylor, describing the Bird's Nest, stated that its 'high walls and locked dormitory denote its true character – a prison for Catholic children', *Irish Homes*, p. 94.

[47] Annual report of the William Henry Elliott Home for Waifs and Strays, 1885, p. 4.

[48] Anon., Save the Child (reprinted as a pamphlet from the *Freeman's Journal* of 1 March 1883), p. 2.

[49] Cullen Papers, 1856, File 339/2/36 and Aylward to Cullen, 8 February 1856, File 339/2/22, 1856 (DDA).

[50] Ladies' Association of Charity of St Vincent de Paul, annual report, 1852, p. 20 (hereafter LAC).

[51] See n 1 above. Protestant schools visited by the Ladies of St Vincent, Murray Papers, File 33/15/4 (Undated); Letter from the Committee of the Ragged (Catholic) Schools to Cullen, February 1856; Cullen Papers, File 339/2/20 (Non-diocesan 1856); lists of Catholic children attending Bird's Nest, Cullen Papers, File 322/7/36 (Laity, 1876) (DDA).

ing the Catholic children in the Bird's Nest in Kingstown (Dun Laoghaire) relied on the testimony of Lizzy Lucas: 'a little girl ten years old [who] was an inmate of this "Home" nearly two years up to the 1st May 1876. She reckons the number of children then in the "nest" as close to 200, and is enabled from memory to name and classify 177 of them as follows – Catholics still faithful 90 names Catholics now indifferent 37 names, Protestants 50 names.'[52]

Aylward was quite determined that such proselytism must be counteracted and the only effective challenge she felt that could be provided demanded 'a large Catholic orphanage'.[53] Through the Ladies of Charity, Aylward's helpers physically removed Catholic children from Protestant institutions. In one case, reported in an annual report of the Ladies' Association, a Catholic woman, whose three children had been sent to a Protestant orphanage in County Wicklow was provided with money by Aylward's committee to 'rescue' the children. This she did without any great difficulty but was followed by the nurse who had charge of the children. A showdown ensued in a Dublin street where the nurse was surrounded by a group of children, and they 'with their baptismal instincts of Catholicity strong in them ... seized the nurse by the arms, and held her fast till our servant reached the lady's house'. The children were rescued by the Lady of Charity and the account ends 'Thus thank God, the mother and her three children were rescued from the Nurse, the Devil, and the Swaddlers.'[54] The reports of the Association are filled with such dramatic accounts of child 'saving'.

Aylward understood that the attraction of the schools organised by the ICM lay in the fact that they provided physical relief for those who attended in the form of food, clothing, training and employment. The ICM were attracting the poorest members of society, their schools and homes were in the poorest parts of the city. Her solution to the problem was to establish an orphanage 'that would not relax [its] efforts until five hundred children should have been rescued'.[55] The clergy were wary and Cullen was not

---

[52] Lists of Catholic children attending Bird's Nest, Cullen Papers, File 322/7/36 (Laity, 1876) (DDA).

[53] Aylward to Cullen, 16 February 1857, Cullen Papers, File 339/6/40 (1857) (DDA). In this emotive letter Aylward describes that 'to see them [Catholic infants] taken from the church – torn from their mother's breast – and dragged in their helplessness into the net of heresy, is what we cannot bear'.

[54] LAC, fifth annual report, pp. 12–13.

[55] Taylor, *Irish Homes*, p. 99.

supportive. It was felt that such an undertaking was too large and the system to be adopted, that of boarding out, open to too much abuse.[56] Aylward continued to exert pressure on the clergy and eventually received their support. In 1857 the first child was received in St Brigid's Orphanage. One way of ensuring the success of this organisation was for Aylward to have complete control. It was she who determined the policies of the orphanage, much to the chagrin of many members of the clergy who continually recommended cases which Aylward refused to admit.[57] The guiding principle was that children should, as far as was possible and practicable, be looked after by their relatives. Like other philanthropists she was concerned that the bond between parent and children be maintained as much as possible. The boarding-out system used by the orphanage was strictly regulated, the foster mothers were well paid, unannounced visits were made to the foster homes and any failure to comply fully with the regulations meant the immediate removal of the children. From 1857 to 1889, 2,717 children were admitted to the orphanage. Shortly after its establishment St Brigid's was seen as the 'chief bulwark in Dublin against the multiplied machinations' of the proselytisers.[58]

Aylward was exceptionally good at publicising the work of the Ladies' Association and St Brigid's. She penned the annual reports which recounted in dramatic detail the 'rescue' of Catholic children from the clutches of Protestant predators. She spoke at annual meetings denouncing their activities. Her trial in 1858 over the Mary Mathews case led to her six month imprisonment on a contempt of court charge. The accusation that Aylward had knowingly allowed the child to be taken from St Brigid's to prevent the child's mother removing her and bringing her up as a Protestant was probably orchestrated by individuals from some of the Protestant homes and the trial in essence was a fight between a 'Roman Catholic institution and a Protestant Institution'.[59] The case was widely reported in the press and a St Brigid's Defence Committee was established to pay Aylward's costs.[60] When Aylward was released her health had

---

[56] St Brigid's Orphanage, fortieth report, p. 10.
[57] For example see Aylward to Fr O'Neill, 29 October 1857, Cullen Papers, File 339/6/24 (1857) (DDA); Gibbons, *Margaret Aylward*, pp. 316–17.
[58] *The Month*, December 1866, pp. 568–9.   [59] *Freeman's Journal*, 18 November 1859.
[60] For accounts of the trial see also *The Times* and the *Irish Times* of the same period. The sentence given Aylward also provoked much comment. See for example, *Morning News*, 3 December 1860, *Irish Times*, 7 November 1861 and *Freeman's Journal*, January 1861. For

suffered a significant decline but she was still determined to continue in her actions against proselytisers. Her next step was to establish schools for the poor and these were sited in the poorest parts of Dublin where the Protestant mission schools were also active. By 1870 six schools had been established. Food and clothing were provided by the schools in an attempt to keep the children from attending Protestant schools which had always provided these necessities.[61] There is no doubt that in the history of anti-proselytism in Dublin Margaret Aylward played a significant and leading role. Through her work she aided the Catholic church in its mission of evangelism and like many other female religious she helped to consolidate the power of the Catholic church in the poorest regions of Dublin city. Her motivation appears to have arisen both from strongly held religious beliefs and also an instinctive desire to physically aid the poor. Like other philanthropists who had 'God on their side' it is difficult to know whether physical or spiritual danger was of utmost concern.

While Aylward was a strong, powerful and influential figure in the Catholic camp she was well matched by women such as Ellen Smyly who played such an important role in expanding the role of the ICM in Irish society. Smyly, in fact, established one of the more extensive networks of schools and homes for orphan and destitute children in nineteenth-century Dublin. Her motivation in founding such homes came again from strongly held religious convictions. She began to seek out such children in the Dublin streets when she was seventeen. On her early visitations to the abodes of the destitute she was always accompanied by another lady as a chaperone as it was considered unseemly for a lady to wander the streets on her own. Married at nineteen, she had a family of nine children but never ceased her work on behalf of destitute children. Her first Bible school was opened near Grand Canal Street in 1850 and other schools soon followed in the Coombe, Townsend Street, Lurgan Street, Grand Canal Street and Luke Street. By the 1880s she had founded nine ragged schools and homes for boys and girls in the city and also operated an orphanage in Spiddal in County Galway. Smyly was a close friend of the Rev. Alexander Dallas, founder of the Irish Church Missions, and her schools and orphanages were closely

---

documents relating to the Defence Fund see Cullen Papers, File 333/8/3 (Nuns 1861) (DDA).
[61] See Gibbons, *Margaret Aylward*, passim.

linked to that organisation,[62] but without impeding Mrs Smyly's control of her homes. The teachers in these schools were supplied by the ICM, but the running of the homes was left to the control of Mrs Smyly, aided in most cases by committees of women. Members of her family were also closely involved in this work. In 1883 the number of children catered for in these various establishments amounted to 1,578, many of whom were infants attending day schools.[63] The committees of these various homes often had to defend their work publicly from Catholic attacks. In an annual report from 1883 the committee of the Bird's Nest noted that 'In the Romish papers, when anything is to be said against Protestantism, it is – THE BIRD'S NEST AGAIN! Sometimes holding it up to ridicule, sometimes describing it as a deadly enemy.'[64] In 1895 the committee of the same establishment refuted the charge of a Catholic priest who had stated that in Glencree reformatory for juvenile delinquents, out of 150 inmates 120 had 'graduated in Mrs Smyly's famous Bird's Nest'.[65] Smyly felt she was doing 'God's work', and the religious and humanitarian aspects of her charity work were as closely bound as they were in Aylward's work.

At least six ragged schools and homes in Dublin were part of the philanthropic empire of Mrs Smyly. The religious and indeed missionary element comes across strongly in the annual reports which have survived. In a report for the Townsend Street Ragged Schools and Home in 1892, it was stated that 'we have had several striking cases of deliverance from Romanism during the year, but of those now in the home we do not wish to speak much, but commit them to Him who has begun the good work in them, and we believe will perfect it unto the day of Jesus Christ'.[66] Indeed the practice of Roman Catholicism, or irreligion, was blamed for much of the destitution experienced by the children. The primary purpose of these schools was to inculcate a degree of discipline in the children

---

62 For a brief, general and uncritical look at Mrs Smyly's work see Vivienne Smyly, *The Early History of Mrs Smyly's Homes and Schools* (privately printed, 1976).

63 Barrett, *Guide*, part ii, pp. 11–15.   64 Annual report of the Bird's Nest, 1883, p. 4.

65 Annual report of the Bird's Nest, 1895, pp. 4–5.

66 Annual report of the Townsend Street Ragged Schools and Girls' Home, Dublin, 1892, p. 6. The Smyly network of homes in Dublin, included the William Henry Elliott Home for Waifs and Strays (est. 1872), the Grand Canal Street School for Little Ragged Children (est. 1852), the Ragged Boys' Home, Grand Canal Street (est. 1857), the Bird's Nest and Mission Ragged School, Dun Laoghaire (est. 1859), the Coombe Ragged Schools and Boys' Home (est. 1853), and the Townsend Street Ragged Schools and Girls' Home (est. 1852).

who would be armed for the future by a knowledge of the Bible. The acquisition of basic reading and writing skills together with domestic skills for girls were the limits of the education provided.

Religious motivation was also behind the establishment of Miss Carr's Homes in Dublin at the end of the century. Lizzie H. Carr established her first home for destitute children in Dublin in 1887. The religious motivation behind her various enterprises comes across clearly in the available annual reports. Elizabeth Carr and her sister Mary, founder of the Kingstown Mission, were both products of an evangelical Protestant upbringing. Their grandfather, the Rev. George W. Carr was reputed to have founded the first temperance society in Ireland and was a close associate of Fr Theobald Mathew, the great temperance advocate. Another sister, Emily, married a missionary and went to China. Though Elizabeth was the main force in establishing Miss Carr's Homes, she received support from both Mary and another sister Anna. In the first report available for the home, and written by Elizabeth, she states that, 'the Lord laid very much upon my heart a few distressing cases of little children who, though utterly destitute, could not, from one cause or another, be received into any of the Protestant homes for poor children which already existed and I felt that He wanted me to care for those neglected little ones'.[67]

All philanthropists, whether Catholic or Protestant, were intent on imparting their own religious views to their charges, and amassing souls for God was seen as part of their duty. Even those charitable institutions run by Protestants which claimed to be non-sectarian, as many were in practice, found it difficult to escape the tag of proselytising. The Belfast Ladies' Industrial National School, which educated poor children, had a policy of providing religious instruction in their school on a non-sectarian basis and had even sought and received the support of the clergy of various denominations in doing so. However, it appears that rumours were spread in Belfast that the school was in fact proselytising and the committee, in 1854, defended itself against this attack by asserting, 'we aim at no proselytising, we believe in no right of ours to interfere between parent and child in this momentous object'.[68] Whether such rumours or accusations had any effect upon attendance cannot

[67] Annual report for Miss Carr's Home for Destitute Children, 1888, p. 5.
[68] Annual report of the Belfast Ladies' Industrial National School, 1855, p. 5.

be ascertained as the records do not give the religious background of its pupils. Clearly, religious intolerance proved to be a divisive force in the development of any close links between workers in the child care field. While many of the Protestant orphanages recommended children to one another, and indeed the same applied to Catholic run orphanages, the religious barrier was never crossed. It is striking also that all of the Catholic run orphanages were operated by religious orders or congregations, those which had been established by the laity being soon handed over to religious control.

Women philanthropists seem to have accepted that poverty was a fact of life and their efforts to help poor children were aimed at making them self-supporting and independent of charity by providing them with the skills deemed necessary for their class. These philanthropists also had a great fear of what life on the streets could do to children. The street paved the way for criminality and prostitution. But for all its dangers it was not until the second half of the century that children were freely taken into homes and refuges. Some of the homes and orphanages in the earlier part of the century were particular about the children they would handle. A House of Refuge, which opened in Baggot Street in 1802, aimed to 'shelter the unprotected'. Young girls who had been brought up in charity schools or who were temporarily without a job could gain entrance to the refuge only by submitting 'unquestionable testimonies of her modesty, honesty and sobriety'.[69] Similarly the Providence Home, established in 1839, took in young girls of 'good character' vouched for by a clergyman. These homeless girls were taught the usual domestic skills and provided with a religious education and the women's committee who ran the home worked on the principle that 'prevention is better than cure'. Homelessness was seen to lead to the practice of the 'grossest immoralities' but within this institution they would be offered some protection and 'put in the way of helping themselves'.[70] Thus situations were secured for them and while in the home they were put to work in the laundry 'to avoid the evils of idleness and to keep up self respect'.[71] For young Catholic girls such protective homes were attached to convents, particularly those of the Mercy congregation which had Houses of Mercy attached to cater for their needs.

[69] Annual report of the House of Refuge, Baggot Street, 1803, p. 1.
[70] Annual report of the Providence Home, 1872, p. 6.
[71] Ibid.

From mid-century philanthropists followed a more open policy of rescuing children from the streets. The ragged schools established in cities throughout the country were intent on rescuing children from the street. The Belfast Ladies' Industrial National School's original motive was to 'preserve a few children from the debasement arising from street begging and waiting for alms at a soup kitchen'.[72] The Helping Hand, a home organised by Mrs Smyly, functioned,

to give a 'Helping Hand' to poor big lads who are homeless and friendless, and who, in their rough, untrained, and often ragged condition, could not possibly obtain employment; and without such timely aid would probably increase the number of idlers who sit around the base of Nelson's Pillar, wander aimlessly, about the streets of our city, and fall into open sin.[73]

Many of these institutions were residential, and although the 'ragged schools' were not, some established refuges for vagrant children. Some of these institutions were called orphanages but did not cater only for orphan children.

For many philanthropists the home was not just a place in which to live. It was felt to be the focus of a moral, spiritual and social life. They insisted that in caring for children in the institutions they established they were rescuing them from moral and spiritual neglect and abuse. They also made explicit judgements about the homes from which children came. Of those who attended the Townsend Street Ragged Schools it was stated that they came 'out of places which it would be mockery to call homes'.[74] In Miss Carr's Home for Children, it was asserted that 'some of the little ones have come from the most wretched homes, where only sin abounds'.[75] Undoubtedly many of the homes these children came from left a lot to be desired but the examples used in the annual reports tend to overemphasise the religious and moral elements in their circumstances. For Mrs Smyly's Bird's Nest orphanage the most immediate danger to children came from having Catholic parents. In a report for 1895 a number of case histories of the children cited this as a reason why children were admitted. For example, the case of,

M— S—, five years old – father Romanist; mother Protestant. Father left mother with her two little girls two years ago; they have since lived with the mother's stepfather, who does not want the children; father's relations

72 Annual report of the Belfast Ladies' Industrial National School, 1855, p. 5.
73 Annual report of the Helping Hand, A Mission Home for Lads, 1892, pp. 3–4.
74 Annual report of the Townsend Street Ragged School, 1885, p. 4.
75 Annual report for Miss Carr's Home for Destitute Children, 1888, p. 6.

strong Romanists, are anxious to get them. Mother seems a sober, industrious woman; she struggled to support her children, but became very poor,
and was most thankful to find a home for one little one in the Nest.[76]

In some homes the children of unmarried parents were not accepted
lest it be construed as an acceptance of immorality.[77]

It is evident from both the annual reports and some of the registers
of these institutions that economic reasons were paramount in the
decision of parents to give up their children. In the Cottage Home
for Little Children, established by Rosa M. Barrett in 1879 in Dun
Laoghaire, the majority of the first 100 admissions resulted from
crises affecting the family. In many cases the death of a father, or his
desertion of the family, had left the mother unable to both hold a job
and look after her children. In some instances a mother had left her
husband because of drunkenness or violence and again, being
obliged to work, could not care for her children.[78] The care of such
children was not taken up lightly by institutions and in the Cottage
Home some financial support for the child accepted had to be
guaranteed. Either the parent or some relative paid a maintenance
fee agreed on with the committee of the home. One reason for this
was to secure some additional financial support but it also reflects
the belief of philanthropists that the poor were ultimately responsible for the welfare of their own children and by requesting a fee for
maintenance they attempted to ensure parental responsibility and
dissuade them from a dependence on charity. In Miss Carr's Homes
the committee stated that they 'seek to relieve the worst cases and
generally refuse all who are able in any way to struggle on without
our help'.[79] In a number of these homes siblings were often separated from each other. This was not a deliberate policy followed by
committees but reflected the fact that many homes only catered for
children of particular age groups. Thus the Cottage Home took in
infants up to six years of age and they were then sent to other homes,
and children of different ages could not be accepted into the same
institution, nor indeed could brothers and sisters as there were
separate homes for boys and girls.

Within some of the homes established by women philanthropists a
policy of emigrating the children was also followed. It is difficult to

---

[76] Annual report for the Bird's Nest, 1895, p. 4.
[77] This was true for the Cottage Home for Little Children and the Bird's Nest.
[78] Admissions register, 1882–1900 (Cottage Home for Little Children, Dun Laoghaire).
[79] Annual report for Miss Carr's Home for Destitute Children, 1891, p. 7.

assess how widespread this policy was as access to the registers of the various homes is limited. From the annual reports available for Mrs Smyly's Homes there is evidence that a number of children were sent to both Canada and America. In 1882 six boys from the Bird's Nest were sent to Canada and 'adopted into farmers' families'.[80] A similar policy of emigration was followed in Rosa M. Barrett's Cottage Home for Little Children. Of the 182 children admitted to this home from 1882 to 1894 at least 10 children were adopted by Canadian couples.[81] From the evidence available the permission of the parents or surviving parent was required before any child could be so adopted. It also appears that Miss Barrett or members of the committee of the Home paid visits to the adoptive homes to ensure that the children were well looked after.[82] It appears also that for the Cottage Home some connection was maintained with Annie Macpherson, a Scots-born Quaker, who began taking groups of children from England to Canada in the 1870s. The children from the Cottage Home may have been sent to England to join Macpherson's emigrant groups.[83] The motivation for such schemes may have been to ensure the children were brought up as Protestants and also that they would have better opportunities economically in another country. It was conducted on a very small scale and does not appear to have been the policy of any Catholic agency. Women philanthropists did not only exert power in organising, managing and controlling the homes, schools and orphanages they established throughout the nineteenth century, they spread their influential net wider by attempting to control the lifestyles of 'neglectful' mothers. A number of women activists in the child-care field sought out the parents, and especially the mothers, of vagrant children, and attempted to teach them the skills of household and child management. The 'ragged schools' operating under the ICM, for example, included sewing and domestic classes for women. In 1885 one report on such classes claimed that not only were poor women able to support their families through the sewing skills acquired, but their attendance at

---

[80] Annual report of the Bird's Nest, 1883, p. 4. Other brief references to emigration are to be found in the reports for 1889, p. 4, 1891, pp. 5–6.

[81] Admissions register, 1882–1900 (Cottage Home for Little Children, Dun Laoghaire).

[82] Brief references to such visits are made in the annual reports of the Home and in a scrapbook of clippings relating to the Home (Cottage Home for Little Children, Dun Laoghaire).

[83] Some reference is made to Miss Macpherson's emigration group in the Admissions register, 1882–1900 (Cottage Home for Little Children, Dun Laoghaire).

meetings, it was believed, had 'altered their characters to a great degree'.[84]

The establishment of such refuges and classes for poor mothers implies a number of pre-conceived ideas about the poor home and poor women as mothers. Women were more responsible for the care of children than men. A poor woman was more likely to be considered a 'bad' mother if her children were found to be begging or working on the streets. Such children were seen to be neglected by their parents and this reflected particularly badly on the mother. Motherhood was the apex of a woman's achievement and for these middle-class philanthropists, most of whom were married with children, it was the prime source of identity. To enforce their own concept of the ideal family life, women philanthropists held classes for these poor women which taught the importance of sobriety, cleanliness and domesticity. It was these factors which formed the basis, not only for virtuous motherhood, but also for a proper home. That poor women were willing to attend these classes reveals a willingness to use the resources made available by these philanthropists. Attendance also ensured consideration when charity was being dispensed. Whether these poor women believed or implemented any of the values propounded by these philanthropists is impossible to ascertain. Throughout the century the relationship of the poor to charitable enterprises shows them willing and able to tell philanthropists what they wish to hear. These philanthropists, for most of the century, seem to have had little understanding of the dynamics of working-class family life, where children worked from an early age for their own support, where mothers themselves were forced to work to feed their families and where a certain degree of independence existed between working-class children and their parents. Through offering advice on household matters to poor women these philanthropists were imposing their own values on working-class family life; mothers in turn were expected to hand such values on to their children. Through the implementation of such values the poor family could become a civilising agency, a more moral form of family life would exist and children would be kept off the streets.

The development of crèches in the last quarter of the century reveals a certain change in attitude amongst middle-class philanth-

---

[84] Annual report of the Schools for Little Ragged Children and Women's Sewing Class, Grand Canal Street, 1885, p. 1.

ropists about poor working women. For the first time there is a recognition of the fact that poor women have to work to support their families. There were at least five crèches organised in Dublin from 1878 onwards. The first of these appears to have been one founded by Rosa M. Barrett in Dun Laoghaire in 1878. Working mothers could not generally afford to pay someone to watch their children and the usual alternative was to leave them unattended or in the care of an older child, resulting sometimes in tragic loss of life. It was to prevent such fatalities that Barrett organised her crèche, based on an earlier one founded, by a Mrs Hilton, in London.[85] Two Catholic crèches were in operation from 1884, one in Holles Street and the other in Gardiner Street, Dublin. The Liberty Crèche, attached to the Sick Poor Institution and Dorset Nourishment Dispensary in Meath street, was in operation in the 1890s and appears to have been run by a group of Quaker women.[86] This latter crèche deemed itself to be 'strictly non-sectarian' and was organised to cater for the children 'of respectable women, dependent on their own exertions away from their homes for means and support'.[87] By providing such a service these women allowed poor mothers out to work, ensured that the children were fed and looked after and also that they stayed off the streets. Some payment had to be made and the usual charge was 1d a day for those who could afford it and a lesser charge was made for those who could not meet this fee. This small fee helped to support the crèche but the imposition of a charge was also to prevent the loosening of the bond between parents and children.[88] In the crèche operating in Holles Street a total of 4,714 children were looked after in 1888.[89] Undoubtedly these philanthro-

---

[85] R.M. Barrett, *The Cottage Home for Little Children. A Retrospect* (Dublin,1905?), pp. 2–3. In this pamphlet Barrett also quotes a case reported in the *Irish Times*, 9 January 1904, to support her move: 'A mother locked her children in the room in the morning (presumably to save them from the dangers of the street) when she went out; later in the day a neighbour, hearing screams, broke into the room and found a tiny child, who subsequently died, in flames.'

[86] See G.D. Williams (ed.), *Dublin Charities: A Handbook* (Dublin, 1902), pp. 92–3, 147; Annual report of the Crèche or Day Nursery, 8 Lower Gardiner Street, 1888–9; Annual report of the Crèche or Day Nursery, 29 Holles Street, 1888.

[87] Liberty crèche, committee minute book, 12 December 1892 (Society of Friends Archive, Dublin).

[88] R.M. Barrett, *Our Kingstown Nursery* (Dublin, 1880), p. 4.

[89] Annual report of the Crèche or Day Nursery, Holles Street, 1888, p. 6. In the crèche at Stephen's Green 2,588 children attended in 1883 and the crèche at Gardiner Street looked after an average of 90 children every week. See Barrett, *Guide*, part ii, p. 4; annual report of the Crèche or Day Nursery, 8 Lower Gardiner Street, 1888–9, p. 6.

pists were catering for a special need and were acknowledging the fact that many mothers had to work but they were also taking the place of the poor mother and reinforcing the ideal of the woman as maternal agent. It was considered unfortunate that these women had to work, and the philanthropists substituted themselves as mothers, abhorring the customary practice of poor women leaving their children, and positing the ideal of women at home looking after their children and keeping them off the streets. Moral judgements were explicitly made regarding the homes of the poor. Crèches were always described as clean and comfortable, in contrast to 'the wretched homes from which these children are brought'.[90]

Working-class homes were thus seen as deficient when it came to rearing children. Discontent and aversion to work were blamed on bad parenting. This aversion could be traced, 'to the slovenly neglect of all the decencies of life, which forms the strange indulgence of the lower orders of this country and indisposes the young, who have been reared in an atmosphere of dirt and idleness, to do other than follow the example of their lazy parent, unless compelled thereto by stern necessity'.[91]

PHILANTHROPISTS AND WORKHOUSE CHILDREN

One individual writing in 1855 stated that 'the natural way of rearing children is as members of a family, with a mother to cherish and a father to control'.[92] Many of the objections women philanthropists made against the workhouse system and large institutions were that they were not created in the family mould. The work carried out by the organisers of St Brigid's Orphanage was praised because it relied on a system of boarding out children to suitable homes in the countryside. Many orphanages, in fact, adopted this policy. Through such boarding out children were placed in a family setting where their characters could be remoulded and desirable behaviour could be taught. Boarding out for girls was seen as particularly important because within a family her work provided her with 'habits of attention and responsibility'. It was in the homes of the respectable cottagers that poor girls could acquire all those

[90] Ibid.   [91] Annual report of the Training School for Female Servants, 1857, p. 5.
[92] W. Neilson Hancock, 'The workhouse as a mode of relief for widows and orphans', *Journal of the Dublin Statistical Society* 1 (April 1855), p. 86.

skills in domesticity 'that men do comfort call'.[93] A number of philanthropic women actively sought to have children, and especially girls, removed from the workhouse as quickly as possible. For Mrs Woodlock, founder of St Joseph's Industrial Institute, children brought up in a workhouse were 'apt to be too fond of the place ... they get accustomed to it, and do not know what a misfortune it is to be there'.[94] Woodlock, as we have seen, was one of the few lay Catholic women to engage in public philanthropy.[95] She had established industrial schools in Cork prior to opening St Joseph's. Crochet, embroidery and laundry work were the occupations of their inmates but the numbers maintained in them appears to have been small with perhaps less than twenty girls receiving training annually.

As we have previously noted women had very little say in the running of the workhouses and where they did act as visitors they were left to deal with other women and children. The policy of boarding out children was one with which women were most concerned and by the end of the century fifteen boards of guardians had instituted women's committees to look after this aspect of their affairs.[96] In the early decades of the twentieth century women were still urging that boards of guardians extend this policy. The novelist and suffragist, Susanne R. Day, writing in 1912, stated that the delay in boarding out children to foster parents or to their own mothers was 'only to foster an evil which it is imperatively necessary to abolish [and] to persist in the manufacture of paupers'.[97] The attitude of these women reformers was to reject institutionalism. Just as they had established their own homes and refuges for destitute children based on family values they wished to remove children from workhouses where they felt corruption abounded. This aim was obviously motivated by a concern with more than the physical welfare of the child and was based on the belief that it was only

[93] Quoted in O'Shaughnessy, 'Some remarks', p. 145. Laura Stephens, writing in 1901, stressed that the pauper child's only chance for survival depended on removal, at an early stage, from the workhouse. She saw boarding out with 'respectable' families as the best solution because it 'restore[d] them to family life, and teaches them that self reliance which can never be acquired in a large institution'. See J.P Smyth (ed.), *Social Service Handbook* (Dublin, 1901), pp. 78–9.

[94] *Report from the select committee on poor relief (Ireland) 1861*, HC 1861 (408), xx, 222.

[95] For the industrial schools see Eblana, 'St Joseph's industrial institute', *Transactions of the National Association for the Promotion of Social Science* (1862), pp. 125–31.

[96] Robins, *Lost Children*, pp. 272–82.

[97] Susanne R. Day, 'The workhouse child', *The Irish Review* (June 1912), p. 179.

through the care provided to children by women, within a family environment, that they could develop into adults who would not be a burden to society and would be independent of charity.

Although we have little information on the influence Irish women had in the workhouses it is clear that they were, at least, effective in having children boarded out in a number of institutions. The fate of children in the nineteenth century gradually improved and a greater awareness of their destitute condition made itself known to the authorities through various investigative committees and the work of individuals, both men and women, who were concerned with these issues. As Robins notes in his study of children, there was a considerable level of legislative protection in place by the end of the century. In 1879 the Children's Dangerous Performances Act was passed which prohibited children under fourteen years from partaking in any public performance or exhibition which was considered dangerous. The Infant Life Protection Act of 1872, and an amendment to that Act in 1897, were intended to safeguard children placed in private fosterage by local authorities. In 1889 the Prevention of Cruelty and Protection of Children Act provided for the punishment of those who neglected or ill-treated children.[98] Women played some role in changing popular attitudes to children and they were influential in ensuring that children benefited from the legislative changes which occurred. The principal organisation which made the greatest voluntary contribution in this area was undoubtedly the Dublin Aid Committee, later known as the National Society for the Prevention of Cruelty to Children.

Many philanthropists welcomed the various Acts introduced to protect children, but they believed that unless some organisation existed to ensure that they were enforced they would be of no use to them. 'The child', it was argued, 'from its very nature, its innocence and inexperience, cannot put the law in force to help itself.'[99] The Dublin Aid Committee was established for the purpose of providing such protection in 1889. The parent organisation had been set up in Liverpool in 1883 and it had been successful in protecting the children with whom it came in contact. The establishment of the Dublin branch of this society was credited to Rosa M. Barrett, founder of the Crèche and the Cottage Home for Little Children in

---

[98] Robins, *Lost Children*, p. 307; John Cooke, 'The state and cruelty to children' in Smyth (ed.), *Handbook*, pp. 111–33.
[99] Ibid., p. 117.

Dun Laoghaire. Apparently Barrett had admitted some children from Tuam to her orphanage. The children were badly undernourished and Barrett went to investigate the home from which they came. There she found 'children sleeping in orange boxes, underfed and sickly'. She then got in touch with the London office of the NSPCC who sent over an inspector, the case was investigated and the person in charge of the home was imprisoned for two years. As a result of this action Barrett called a meeting in Dublin to begin a branch of the society in Ireland.[100]

Barrett herself was very involved in issues relating to children throughout the late nineteenth and early twentieth centuries. She was born in Jamaica but was resident in Dublin from at least the 1860s. She was involved in a number of philanthropic enterprises such as the Philanthropic Reform Association, and Lady Aberdeen's Irish Home Industries Association. In the early years of the twentieth century she helped to establish the Women's National Health Association of Ireland which aimed to heighten public awareness about the prevention of disease, particularly tuberculosis, and she was also an active suffragist. There is little personal information about her life though she remained unmarried and lived in Dun Laoghaire. She travelled extensively in Canada, Sweden and South Africa and was the author of Lock's *Irish Guides* for a number of years. She also wrote a biography of Ellice Hopkins, founder of the White Cross movement, and a number of pamphlets on the status of children.[101]

The Irish founding committee of the NSPCC consisted of thirty-one members, sixteen of whom were women. Besides Barrett there was at least one other woman activist, Mrs Henry Wigham, prominent in the suffrage movement and the Anti-Contagious Diseases Acts campaign.[102] The society was avowedly non-sectarian. In the first annual report it was emphasised that 'religious provision for such children as have to be separated from their parents, it [the society] leaves to be made by the community to which the child

---

[100] A correspondent to *The Times*, 2 September 1936.
[101] R.M. Barrett, her pamphlets on children were *Foreign legislation on behalf of neglected and destitute children* (Dublin, 1896, 2nd edn); *The Rescue of the Young* (n.p., 1899). Some of the facts relating to her life were found in MS 1901 census for the population of Ireland (PRO, Dublin).
[102] Typescript copy of the first meeting of the Society for the Prevention of Cruelty to Children (ISPCC office, Dublin).

belongs'.[103] Although there were Catholics, Protestants and Quakers on the managing committee the organisation failed to secure the public support of the Catholic clergy which remained suspicious of a body which had a number of prominent Protestants in its ranks.[104]

The purpose of this society, which did not see itself as a charity, was to 'prevent the necessity of charity, much of it at least by bringing up the moral nature of parents to do their duty by their children'.[105] It did not desire to split up families but sought to 'furnish aid to those worthless parents who make children wanderers, homeless and destitute and to render other provisions than their own home less necessary'.[106] The committee of this society observed that it was poverty, unemployment and particularly drunkenness which led to children being neglected. It was adamant that parents who neglected their children should be punished and it was the function of the society to keep such parents under surveillance and ensure that the full force of the law would be brought to bear on them. Although claiming not to judge the morality of working-class parents the society made implicit judgements about the poor. It was their habits which led to neglect. 'There can be no doubt', the first report of the society noted, 'that the extremely intemperate habits of the lower classes of the people of Dublin have much to do with the high death rate among children.'[107] One member of the original committee desired public support for an organisation which would 'be of immense benefit to the children of the poor'. The society did laudable work and after two years in existence it dealt with 344 children in Dublin.[108] By 1901 it had nine branches throughout the country. Women seem to have played a prominent role in these local branches; for example, of the twenty members of the Clonmel committee, established in 1899, fourteen were women.[109]

Other agencies were also established to look after deprived chil-

---

[103] Annual report of the National Society for the Prevention of Cruelty to Children, 1889–90, pp. 11–12.

[104] Robins, *Lost Children*, p. 308.   [105] See n 102 above.

[106] Annual report of the National Society for the Prevention of Cruelty to Children, 1889–90, p. 11.

[107] Ibid., p. 20.

[108] Annual report of the National Society for the Prevention of Cruelty to Children, 1890–1, p. 6.

[109] *The Nationalist*, 13 January 1900.

dren. The Philanthropic Reform Association (1897), with a mixed committee, campaigned for changes in the workhouse system with regard to children. It supported the NSPCC and sought further changes in the legal system to 'enforce the responsibility of parents for the maintenance and training of their children'.[110] It was primarily left to the women of the committee to look after the welfare of children and they tried particularly to force children off the streets as traders believing that it ' is one, if not the chief, of the recruiting agents for all classes of the criminal and degraded'.[111] These women also initiated a Police Aided Clothing Scheme which provided clothing to poor children. With police support it was thought that parents would not dare to pawn the clothing provided.[112] Besides these societies which wished to ensure the legislative position of children, women formed other societies to help the children of the poor. One such was the Fresh Air Association, established in 1885, with the purpose of sending sick children to homes in the country where they could recover from illness.[113] The Children's Home, in Delgany, County Wicklow, was organised, sometime in the last decade of the century, for children who 'require permanent care till able to earn for themselves'. The committee also took a special interest in children who were recovering from operations in hospitals and appears to have taken in such patients from the Adelaide Hospital.[114] In 1882 a group of Protestant women formed the Cottage Home for Girls, in Dublin. The committee trained girls for domestic service and payment of £10 per annum per girl had to be made by a guardian.[115]

By the end of the century then, women had become involved publicly in providing for all aspects of child care, from the crèche to the school, through training institutions, and by endeavouring to ensure that children were cared for by their parents. Through this work they strengthened their own position as public workers and carers in society. They also enhanced the position of women as wives and mothers, and strengthened the idea of the family as the cradle of morality and civilisation. If the family could not look after the needs of its children then these middle-class philanthropists were willing to

---

[110] Annual report Philanthropic Reform Association, 1897, p. 5 (hereafter PRA).
[111] A.W. Orr, 'The state and cruelty to children' in Smyth (ed.), *Handbook*, p. 137.
[112] Annual report PRA, 1898, pp. 15, 42–3.
[113] Annual report of the Fresh Air Association, 1909.
[114] Williams (ed.), *Dublin Charities*, p. 331.   [115] Barrett, *Guide*, part ii, p. 3.

institute homes to take their place and to teach poor mothers how to be 'ideal' mothers. If they promulgated the ideal of domesticity it was a domesticity tinged with more than a little sense of reality. By the end of the century women philanthropists were aware of working women's need to leave their children. To prevent accidents these philanthropists took over their care and while they may have 'tut-tutted' over these women's 'lack' of parental responsibility they recognised what would be most beneficial to them. A century of care had also led them to initiate calls for legislative reform which involved them working closely with men and engaging in political lobbying and debate. But behind all women's work with children lay the spectre of proselytism which had not abated by the end of the century. It was the barrier which prevented co-operation and alliances being built to secure mutual interests, the welfare of children.

CHAPTER 4

Prostitution and rescue work

In 1835 Monsignor Kinseley, of Kilkenny, in a conversation with
Alexis de Tocqueville observed in relation to morality that

twenty years in the confessional have made me aware that the misconduct
of girls is very rare, and that of married women almost unknown. Public
opinion, one might almost say, goes too far in this direction. A woman
suspected is lost for life. I am sure that there are not twenty illegitimate
children a year in the whole Catholic population of Kilkenny.[1]

Other travellers of the nineteenth century were to note the chastity
and morality displayed by Irish women.[2] The census figures of 1841
would seem to bear out these impressionistic accounts when it listed
only six individuals engaged in the business of prostitution.[3]
However, behind the cloak of sexual morality lay an abundance of
women who engaged in prostitution and who created a pool of
individuals who had to be 'rescued and reclaimed' by nineteenth-
century philanthropists.

Male and female philanthropists of the last century were concerned with problems relating to sexual morality, the most obvious
and public expression of which was prostitution. But the problems of
unmarried mothers, female intemperance, and the fate of women
ex-prisoners were also grist to the reclamation mill. In this chapter I
will examine the extent of prostitution in nineteenth-century Irish
society and the nature of both official, that is government, and
unofficial, or philanthropic, responses to this problem. Throughout
the century there was little public discussion of prostitution. Prosti-

---

[1] *Alexis de Tocqueville's Journey in Ireland, July August, 1835* (ed.), Emmet Larkin (Dublin,
1990), p. 64.
[2] See for example, *Observations on the Labouring Classes* (Dublin, 1836), p. 12; G. de Beaumont,
Ireland, Social, Political and Religious (London, 1839), II, p. 35; F.B. Head, *A Fortnight in
Ireland* (London, 1852).
[3] *Census, Ireland,* 1841.

tutes were judged as social outcasts and many of the philanthropists who worked in the field of rescuing 'fallen women' seem to have accepted prostitution as an inevitable feature of society. There were no campaigns directed at the social causes of prostitution, and rescue work, carried out mainly by women as a strictly voluntary occupation, was done out of the public eye. It was not until the end of the century, with the campaign to repeal the Contagious Diseases Acts, that double standards in sexual behaviour began to be questioned publicly. Any examination of prostitution reveals a multiplicity of attitudes not alone towards the practice of sexuality in any society but also towards how women are perceived in that society. In Ireland the responses to prostitution were informed primarily by Catholic teachings and beliefs about women's behaviour. Looking at those responses in the light of how women lived their lives as prostitutes reveals a complex interaction of attempted control and rehabilitation, the success or failure of which was determined more by the needs of prostitutes than the hopes or expectations of rescuers.

EXTENT OF PROSTITUTION

One impressionistic account of prostitution in Irish cities, from the earlier part of the century, comes from evidence gathered by William Logan, a mission worker from Leeds who also engaged in rescue work, on a trip he made in 1845.[4] From a 'philanthropic gentleman' he ascertained that Cork contained 85 regular brothels and 356 public prostitutes. Logan noted that in Cork 'a large number of procuresses abound ... Individuals have been known to tender their daughters and other relatives to brothel keepers for money. A man in 1841 voluntarily offered his daughter for £3.' In addition to these women there were thought to be 100 'privateers' who operated from houses not designated as brothels. Logan was

---

[4] William Logan, *The Great Social Evil: Its Causes, Extent, Results and Remedies* (London, 1871). There are numerous earlier references to women operating as prostitutes in the various inquiries made by the government into the condition of the poor. One early reference, found in official records, relates that a flourishing red light district operated in a maze of back alleys and lanes between Aungier Street and St Stephen's Green in Dublin. One of the occupants of this district petitioned the Lord Lieutenant in 1835 to restore order to this 'nursery of human turpitude and hotbed of depravity' where prostitutes 'in a state of nudity openly and wantonly assailed the most respectable persons'. The police, however, claimed that there was little they could do and the area continued as a centre of vice until about 1875. Quoted in Gregory Allen, 'The new police: London and Dublin', *The Police Journal*, 1:4 (October 1977), pp. 307–8.

also told by the Rev. William Robertson, superintendent of the City Mission, that there were 1,700 prostitutes operating in Dublin at the same time. In Belfast he quoted Dr Edgar as saying that 236 prostitutes lived in brothels in that city.[5] Edgar, who became involved in rescue work, was to claim that he knew of a small 'village, where ten sisters in four families are prostitutes, I know four sisters who support their father, mother and younger brother, by the wages of iniquity.'[6] Prostitutes were also to be found in large numbers in all the workhouses in the country. Indeed many guardians feared that some women gained access to the workhouse for the sole purpose of procuring.[7] The concrete evidence of police statistics provides a more accurate picture of the situation. The earliest figures, for Dublin, come from the Dublin Metropolitan Police statistics and cover the years 1838–99. These figures account for arrests and convictions of women accused of soliciting; they do not record the number of rearrests so the number given is obviously higher than it should be. On the other hand it is unlikely that the police arrested every prostitute who operated within the city. The figures are high, with 2,849 arrests in 1838 increasing yearly to a maximum of 4,784 in 1856 and decreasing to 1,672 in 1877, fluctuating around the 1,000 mark from then to the 1890s and reaching a low of 494 in 1899. Not all of those women arrested were actually convicted of prostitution and generally, in the earlier period, an average of 18 per cent were released without being charged. From the 1870s only about 1 per cent were discharged. Under the Dublin Police Act of 1842 all that was necessary for conviction was for a policeman to state that a woman was known to him as a prostitute and he had seen her approach men. It is not clear, from the available evidence, what the circumstances for conviction were or what standards were used to allow a woman go free. In some instances, for those freed, an assurance by some person known to the woman of her future good behaviour was given. It is interesting to note that the greatest number of arrests occurred during the famine years. This may have resulted from an influx of poorer women into the city, who had no other possible source of income. In Belfast the problem of prostitution does not appear to have been as serious as in

[5] Logan, *Social Evil*, pp. 48–52.
[6] Rev. John Edgar, *Female Virtue – Its Enemies and Friends* (London, 1841).
[7] See, for example, *Eighth Annual Report of the Poor Law Commissioners for Ireland*, 1856, appendix, pp. 107–8.

Dublin. In 1865, for example, there were, according to the judicial statistics, 367 prostitutes in the city and in 1901 only 139 women were summarily convicted of prostitution.[8]

The Dublin statistics also provide a breakdown of the ages of those convicted. Throughout the period over 60 per cent of convictions were for women aged between twenty and thirty years. In 1838 twenty of those convicted were between the ages of ten and fifteen years. For the remainder of the period the average annual number of convictions for this age group was ten. For the whole period also the illiteracy level of those convicted averaged 99 per cent. The picture which emerges of the 'common prostitute' reveals her to have been poor and uneducated and ranging in age from twenty to thirty years. Most women appear to have given up the occupation by the time they reached their forties. Indeed many may have contracted illnesses or died by this stage. It is probable also that prostitution was engaged in by most of the women as a temporary occupation, many abandoning it once they married or secured other means to keep themselves. The figures available also detail the number of known brothels which existed within the city. In 1838, for example, there were 402 such establishments. The highest number recorded comes from 1845 with 419; by 1853 the number had declined to 207; in the 1870s it averaged about 96 per year and in the 1890s about 80. It appears also that in the earlier part of the century fewer prostitutes ended up in prison. In 1851, for example, an average of one woman per month was sentenced to Grangegorman female prison on conviction of being a 'common night walker'. The sentence was usually a month in prison or a fine of between 1s and 2s shillings. This had changed quite dramatically by the 1870s, due no doubt to the vigilance of the police, when for example, in the month of February 1871, forty-one women were sentenced and fined for the same offence. The most common sentence at this stage was a fine of 20s, a not insubstantial sum, or fourteen days in prison. It is interesting to note that of these forty-one women only four had not been previously imprisoned.[9]

Table 4.1 provides a more general picture of prostitution throughout Ireland for the years 1870 to 1900. Dublin had the

[8] *Judicial Statistics*, 1868, 1902.
[9] Grangegorman Female Prison, general register, 1 January–31 October 1851, Prisons, 1/9/13, V16–4–2; 24 July 1879–30 September 1880, Prisons, 1/9/13, V16–4–14 (PRO, Dublin).

Table 4.1. *Arrests for prostitution in Ireland, 1870–1900*

	1870	1875	1880	1885	1890	1895	1900
Dublin	3,255	1,462	1,009	1,601	1,077	699	431
Belfast	38	94	225	202	131	84	86
Rest of Ireland	380	283	236	383	159	158	139
Total	3,673	1,839	1,470	2,186	1,367	941	656
Number of alleged prostitutes among other offenders							
Dublin	8,271	4,288	3,419	2,867	4,132	1,692	1,907
Belfast	864	502	294	208	146	147	231
Rest of Ireland	2,729	2,274	1,660	1,292	995	621	832
Total	11,864	7,064	5,373	4,367	5,273	2,460	2,970

Sources: Judicial Statistics (Ireland) and the Dublin Metropolitan Police Statistics, 1871–1901

greatest number in 1870 with 3,255 women arrested, but this had dropped to a low of 431 by 1900. If the figures given for arrests and the number of alleged prostitutes, that is women who were charged with other offences but were known to be prostitutes, are taken together then Dublin had 11,526 arrests in 1870, and even taking account of the fact that rearrests were not recorded, it is a very high figure. For the country in general the combined total for 1870 is 15,537 arrests; this had dropped to 3,626 by 1900. The reasons for this remarkable drop in numbers will be discussed later. Given these figures it is hardly an exaggeration to say that prostitution was a sizeable problem within Dublin during the last century, and that that problem was not confined to the major cities.

Inevitably towns which housed garrisons also provided their quota of prostitutes. Mason, in his parochial survey, noted the immorality which existed in Athlone and the Protestant rector commented that prostitutes,

infest the streets, as well as the hedges and ditches about the town, not only to the destruction of the moral[ity], of the present as well as the rising generation, but even in violation of common decency; to such a pitch is depravity risen, that vice does not hide its deeds in darkness, but boldly stalks abroad in open day.[10]

[10] Quoted in W.S. Mason, *A Statistical Account or Parochial Survey of Ireland*, 3 vols. (Dublin, 1814–19), III, p. 79.

Isaac Weld, writing of Roscommon town in 1832, noted,

that the evil [prostitution] was of far greater magnitude than it appeared at first view. In Castle Street, on the skirts of the town, there was actually a range of brothels, at the doors of which females stood, at noonday, to entice passengers, with gestures too plain to be misunderstood.[11]

In 1847 a Colonel More, writing from Newbridge, which he claimed was 'infested with prostitutes', sought advice on how to punish these women who 'climb over the barracks wall'.[12] The police seem generally to have turned a blind eye to prostitutes unless they created a public nuisance. Often the attempts made to curtail the vice came instead from clergymen. In Tipperary pressure from the local clergy on the town commissioners to clean up the streets resulted in a bounty being paid to night-watchmen at the rate of 5s for every successful conviction of a prostitute.[13]

A Rev. Hegarty of Cork city stated in 1881, after witnessing what he considered to be an act of gross immorality, that if the magistrates did not try to prevent such immorality the only course open to him 'was to employ again some of the Confraternity men'.[14] Similarly, in 1876 the Catholic priests in Cork city, determined to close down the brothels in St Finbarr's parish acted without police aid. The Rev. Henry Reed reported their methods:

There was one street which contained probably 12 or 14 houses of ill fame, and the priests determined to clear out the whole nest; it was in a back lane or alley; we took public action; we called on the people of our confraternities to assist us; and by bringing public opinion to bear upon the question, all these houses were shut up.[15]

The cleric who provided this information declared the success of the action in ridding Cork of brothels; other evidence however, reveals that such activity only drove the problem underground.[16]

In the case histories of prostitutes, often published in the annual

---

[11] Isaac Weld, *Statistical Survey of the County of Roscommon* (Dublin, 1832), p. 407.
[12] MS 1054, Kilmainham Papers, p. 290. NLI.
[13] D. G. Marnane, *Land and Violence: A History of West Tipperary from 1660* (Tipperary, 1985), pp. 72–3, 112, 117.
[14] *Cork Constitution*, 24 March 1881.
[15] Evidence of the Rev. Henry Reed, *Report of the House of Commons Select Committee on the Administration, Operation, and Effects of the Contagious Diseases Acts of 1866–69*, HC 1881 (351), viii, Q. 6,206. Public opinion, he stated, was roused by priests and men from the confraternities walking around the neighbourhood which brought pressure to bear on the landlords to get rid of their tenants, Q. 6,389.
[16] See the evidence of Dr James Curtis in *House of Commons Select Committee ... on CDAs*, 1882 (340), ix.

reports of rescue agencies, they were portrayed as women whose lives were destroyed by sexual experience. Rescuers never accepted that women could choose prostitution as a viable means of earning or supplementing an income, in a country which offered few employment opportunities for women. For rescuers, the passage to prostitution was forced upon the woman. A 'virtuous' woman was first seduced, and thus shamed, after this, due to abandonment by her seducer, she continued as a 'privateer' and finally became so degraded that she took to the streets.[17] Logan, in his study, states that prostitutes came usually from the lower classes 'low dress-makers, and servants; manure collectors, who are sent very young to the streets for that purpose, have also furnished their quota'.[18] Prostitutes, he noted, were not accepted into brothels unless they were well recommended, usually by another prostitute, and paid 8s per week to their mistresses for board; any other money they made was for their own use.[19]

For the poorer prostitutes conditions could be miserable. The 'Bush' was a wooded place near Cobh where '20 to 25 to 30 women ... lived ... all the year round under the furze ... like animals.'[20] Many prostitutes also followed soldiers around from one depot to another. Dr Curtis, who gave evidence to a select committee on the operation of the Contagious Diseases Acts, stated, 'they [the prosti-tutes] are always moving about from Fermoy to Kinsale, and the garrison towns ... and sleeping under forts, and behind the bar-racks'.[21] The 'Wrens of the Curragh' were another notorious band of prostitutes who lived primitively in makeshift huts on the perimeters of the Curragh camp. The numbers of women living in these conditions varied but up to sixty women were stated to live at the Curragh. Many of these were undoubtedly prostitutes but it is probable that some, at least, were also involved in longstanding common law relationships with some of the soldiers, since it was the practice of the army authorities at this time not to recognise soldiers' marriages unless they were living in married quarters in the camp. Even living in such conditions there was a certain bond of solidarity amongst the fifty or sixty women who occupied the nests. The women pooled their meagre financial resources and lived off them. The 'colony' was also 'open to any poor wretch who imagines that

<hr>

[17] Logan, *Social Evil*, pp. 49–50.   [18] Ibid.   [19] Ibid.
[20] Evidence of Dr Curtis, *Select Committee, 1882*, Q. 11,256, 11,257.
[21] Ibid., Q. 11,278.

there she can find comfort'. The poor women who followed soldiers
to the camp were 'made as welcome amongst the wrens as if they did
not bring with them certain trouble and an inevitable increase to the
common poverty'.[22] These women appear to have been badly
treated by the local population and one observer writing of a visit he
had made to the area in the 1840s, stated that it was 'quite common
for the priest, when he met one of them ['wrens'] to seize her and cut
her hair off close'. Similarly local shopkeepers would not serve them
in their shops.[23] Evidence relating to the 'wrens' also suggests that
prostitution was a seasonal occupation. Harvesters sometimes joined
the band of women when they were not working and the numbers of
women at the Curragh declined during the winter when many of
them returned to the city.[24]

   There were also prostitutes who made a good living and who
catered for a better class of client than the ordinary soldier. The area
around St Stephen's Green in Dublin was noted as a place where the
'upper class' prostitute operated.[25] Evidence from the commissions
on the effects of the Contagious Diseases Acts notes the existence of
prostitutes who would not deal with soldiers and who considered
themselves to be of a 'better class' than women who did. It is
impossible to assess how the women themselves felt about their
occupation. For some it may have been freely chosen; for others a
necessity. Despite the dangers of disease, pregnancy and social
ostracism involved, a large number of women took it up.

   One document, dating from the 1820s, purports to be an account
of the life of a Belfast prostitute written by herself on her deathbed,
but is much more a tract written as a warning to young women who
might engage in prostitution and is similar in style to the tales of
regret and repentance found in the case histories published in
annual reports of rescue societies. In the pamphlet the woman
mourns for a life spent in dissipation and warns her 'former wicked
companions' that 'were you here, you would learn the lesson, that

22 The account first appeared in the *Pall Mall Gazette*, 15, 16, 17 and 19 October 1867. It was
    later published by J. Greenwood as *The Wren of the Curragh* (London, 1867), and he also
    included a piece on the 'wrens' in his *The Seven Curses of London* (London, 1869),
    pp. 292–303. See also Padraic O'Farrell, 'Camp followers of the Curragh', *Irish Times*, 31
    January 1988 and Maria Luddy, 'An outcast community: the "wrens" of the Curragh',
    Women's History Review, 1: 3 (1992), pp. 341–55.
23 'Stoning the desolate', *All the Year Round* (November 1865), p. 370.
24 MS 1069, Kilmainham Papers, p. 313 (NLI).
25 Evidence of Dr R. McNamara, *House of Commons Select Committee . . . on CDAs, 1881* (351)
    viii, Q. 6,472.

one hour of a deathbed reflection will completely condemn a whole life spent in the mire and abominable practices of which you and I have been guilty'. In conclusion she implores other women 'either to forsake your former ways, and gain eternal happiness, or persevere in your mad career, and reap eternal misery'.[26] It is a sentiment which is to be found in many of the reports of asylums, which were much more concerned with the spiritual than the temporal welfare of the women who sought their aid.

LOCK HOSPITALS: THE OFFICIAL RESPONSE

The only government institution which catered for prostitutes in the last century was the Lock hospital. There were a number of these operating throughout the country, including one in Limerick, for example, but the largest was the Westmoreland Lock hospital, which opened originally in 1755, in Ransford Lane, Dublin.[27] It was not until the introduction of the Contagious Diseases Acts that such hospitals were opened in Cork and the Curragh.[28] By 1792 the Westmoreland Lock Hospital had been relocated in Townsend Street and initially catered for both male and female patients who suffered from venereal diseases. From 1819 the hospital dealt only with female patients. A certain stigma was attached to patients who suffered from v.d. and there was a great reluctance on the part of voluntary hospitals to admit such patients.[29] A large number, though not all, of the women admitted to the Westmoreland hospital were prostitutes and it was claimed that once 'cured' (there was no medical cure for venereal diseases in the nineteenth century) many of them remained in the hospital to entice other women into prostitution.[30] Admissions to the hospital were high with 26,500 patients

---

[26] Anon., *The Life and Transactions of a Female Prostitute* (Belfast, c.1826).

[27] *The Irish Builder*, 1 May 1897, pp. 89–90. The word Lock derives from 'Loke', a house of lepers. Apparently, in medieval times it was difficult to distinguish some forms of venereal disease from leprosy. See Olive Checkland, *Philanthropy in Victorian Scotland* (Edinburgh, 1980), p. 199.

[28] John Fleetwood, *A History of Medicine in Ireland* (Dublin, 1951). The Lock hospital in Cork was opened in Infirmary Road in 1869 and contained forty-six beds. See *Irish Medical Directory* (Dublin, 1879).

[29] Evidence of Dr McNamara, *Select Committee, 1882*, Q. 6,509–6,512. Dr McNamara stated that the Meath, St Vincent's, the Mater and Jervis Street hospitals had strict rules against admitting v.d. patients. Usually patients with v.d. who entered these hospitals did so without declaring the nature of their illness.

[30] *Report from the Select Committee on Dublin Hospitals*, HC 1854 (338), xii, Q. 1,062.

Table 4.2. *Admissions to the Westmoreland Lock Hospital, Dublin,*
1847–1854

Year	Admissions	Natives of Dublin	Rest of Ireland	Britain and the Colonies	Deaths	Women reformed	Number of beds
1847	667	305	342	20	5	178	130
1848	729	294	400	35	11	213	130
1849	992	430	520	42	9	182	130
1850	1,128	364	730	34	9	236	100
1851	985	267	700	18	1	82	80
1852	1,027	245	754	28	5	61	60
1853	861	253	571	37	3	19	50
1854	575	130	405	40	1	5	50
Total	6,964	2,288	4,422	254	44	976	

Source: Report from the Select Committee on Dublin Hospitals, HC 1854 (338), xii, appendix, p. 20

being treated from 1821 to 1853.[31] The number of beds declined from 150 to 50 by 1854 and the governing committee blamed this on the decline of government funding. The hospital was supported entirely by the government with a grant which averaged £2,500 per annum. The all male committee of the hospital never sought public support or subscriptions for their institution because it was thought that the function of the hospital was too delicate to bring to public attention.[32] The establishment of a Lock penitentiary in 1821 or 1822, where reclaimed prostitutes cured in the hospital could work, seems to have been motivated by financial considerations. The washing for the hospital cost £200 per annum, and a saving of £25 was expected to be made by employing these women to do that work. Although this amount may appear small, for the board of governors, constantly trying to save money, it was a not inconsiderable sum. The women were employed for four hours per day in the laundry but they were not paid for the work they did. Instead, they were allowed to do some sewing, in their own time, which the matron sold for them.[33] Originally eleven women worked in the laundry but by

[31] Between 1792 and June 1808, 22,811 patients were admitted to the hospital. See J. Warburton et al., *History of the City of Dublin*, 2 vols. (London, 1818), II, p. 696.
[32] *Report . . . Dublin Hospitals*, 1854, Q. 114.   [33] Ibid. Q. 121–124.

1854 that number had been reduced to six and the penitentiary, though not the laundry, had been abandoned by the 1880s.[34]

The hospital committee claimed that attempts were made to 'rescue' the women who entered the hospital. However, these attempts subjected the women to a repressive moral regime while making money from their labour. The patients wore a uniform and were placed in separate wards; 'fallen women' were segregated from married women, who had to prove their marital status by producing their marriage certificate, and Protestant was separated from Catholic. Many of the cured patients were kept on as wardsmaids and to do the kitchen work of the hospital. The inmates had all their correspondence opened and read by the matron.[35] The reason given for this was that many brothel owners offered employment to women once they were cured. The women who worked in the laundry were not allowed to have visitors without the permission of a governor of the hospital and it appears that, in general, visitors were not encouraged. The porter kept a record of all visitors and the doors of the hospital were locked at five each evening. Nurses, in case they might go on messages for inmates, were strictly timed regarding their absence and were fined and reprimanded if it was thought they had remained outside the hospital for an excessive length of time.[36] The quality of the nursing staff of the hospital, particularly in the first three-quarters of the century, was of a highly dubious character and there are numerous references, in the records of the institution, to their being often drunk on duty and insubordinate to both doctors and matrons. A Nurse Shack, for example, 'in consequence of the impropriety of [her] conduct ... and her unfitfulness to superintend wards ... from her occasional habit of drinking', was removed to another ward in the hospital where her pay was reduced and her work considered less important.[37]

The claims made by the committee in terms of rescuing women

---

[34] Ibid., also *Dublin Hospitals Commission: Report of the Committee of Inquiry of 1887* ... [C.5042], HC 1887, xxxv, Q. 2,182.

[35] Ibid. Q. 2,199; 4,576. There was much discussion among the board of governors of the hospital regarding this matter. After requesting the opinions of both chaplains and doctors it was decided to continue the system as it was. The Catholic chaplain was in favour of retaining the system while the Protestant chaplain thought it 'an unnecessary humiliation of the patients'. See Minutes of the Board, Westmoreland Lock Hospital, vol. 5, 6/3/1886; 13/3/1886; 3/4/1886 (RCPI).

[36] See MS Visitor's Book, Westmoreland Lock Hospital, 1825–89 (RCPI).

[37] Ibid., 14/6/1828. Other examples of the nurses' conduct can be found in MS Registrar's report book for the period 1870, and in all the Board minute books (RCPI).

were exaggerated, and appear to have been made in order to get the government to increase the hospital's grant. For the ten years, 1875 to 1885, out of a total of 7,456 admissions, 910 women were said to have been reformed. The majority of these 'reclaimed' women were actually sent to rescue homes.[38] Since patients spent, on average, thirty-one days in the hospital it is unlikely that the hospital authorities can accept responsibility for any reform made in the characters or situation of the women. Protestant or Catholic clergymen were the only visitors allowed and they may have made some conversions. Women visitors, allowed into other hospitals, were not granted entrance to the Lock hospital until 1889, when Protestant visitors were only allowed visit their few co-religionists who were patients.[39] The majority of the board of governors, when pressed at a hospital commissions inquiry in 1887, declared they had no major objection to the suggestion that the Mercy nuns should nurse there. However, this seemed to be an attempt to appease the commission rather than showing any great willingness to allow entry, as the nuns were never asked to work there. Mr Edward Fottrell, a governor of the hospital in 1887, stated that the nuns could not improve the hospital any more than was being done by the lay staff.[40]

Even in preventing the spread of venereal diseases the hospital was quite inefficient. For example, in 1867 the seventy patients who entered the hospital had, on average, already been inmates on three previous occasions. In fact, one of these women, a Bridget Tutnell, aged twenty-six, had received treatment on fourteen previous occasions.[41] Women entered the hospital voluntarily and could not be detained against their will. They were often in the full throes of the disease by the time they entered and had ample opportunity to infect others before receiving treatment. Of the seventy women mentioned above the majority had become aware

---

[38] *Dublin Hospitals Commission ... 1887*, xxxv, Q. 4,359. Of the 914 rescued patients, 417 were sent to other asylums or penitentiaries; 155 were returned to friends; 82 went to the workhouse; 250 were employed in the hospital as staff, while 10 got situations outside the hospital. Of the 232 patients treated in 1877, 41 were sent to asylums or penitentiaries, 12 returned home, 19 went to the workhouse, 18 were given employment in the hospital, 2 were sent to other hospitals, the remaining 140 remained unaccounted for. See *Twenty-First Report of the Board of Superintendence of the Dublin Hospitals for 1880* [C.2565], HC 1881, xxiii, 22.

[39] See chapter 6 for the work these women did within the hospital.

[40] *Dublin Hospitals Commission ... 1887*, Q. 2,312.

[41] General register of patients, Westmoreland Lock Hospital, vol. 4, 1857–68 (RCPI).

that they were infected at least three weeks before admission.[42] The treatment of syphilis and gonorrhoea was still in a primitive state and many women were released in the mistaken belief that they were cured. During the secondary stage of syphilis victims appear to have recovered as the disease is quiescent but the tertiary stage was always fatal. Because of the double standards relating to sexual behaviour which existed, there was no serious attempt to treat male patients.[43] Soldiers were not treated in confinement as women were and they obviously infected a large number of women. Of the 6,550 unmarried women admitted in 1850 half were believed to have been infected by soldiers.[44] It was also believed that the establishment of Lock hospitals for women, in garrison towns, was the best means of preventing the spread of v.d. among the soldiery.[45] The Lock hospital was an institutional device, sanctioned by government, which sought short-term solutions to the diseases associated with prostitution. Although they were primarily medical institutions, they also sought, in some degree, to influence the morality of their patients. No serious effort at reclamation was made, however, comparable to the work done by female religious and lay women in the numerous penitent asylums which they established.

RESCUE WORK: THE PHILANTHROPIC RESPONSE

In the nineteenth century at least twenty-three asylums or refuges were established to rescue and reclaim 'fallen women'. Of these at least fourteen operated in Dublin,[46] three in Belfast and most others

---

[42] Ibid. One woman named Eliza Smith, aged nineteen, had been infected for three months before seeking treatment.

[43] *Report Select Committee ... CDAs, 1881*, Q. 6,523, 6,546, 6,567, 6,569. Dr McNamara states that men were able to look after themselves but the women needed protection.

[44] *Report ... Dublin Hospitals, 1854*, Q.39

[45] Ibid., Preface, p. iv. M.C. Hime, *The Moral Utility of a Lock Hospital* (Dublin, 1872).

[46] The figures given here are not absolute as some homes opened for short periods of time under different management and different names. Many refuges, which were not primarily for prostitutes, like the Olive Mount Institution of the Good Samaritan, took in 'fallen women'. There is some confusion also regarding refuges which existed in northern Ireland. There is a reference to an Ulster Female Penitentiary existing c.1816. However, the sixth annual report of the Ulster Female Penitentiary dates its foundation from 1822. There is another reference to an Ulster Female Penitentiary which dates its foundation in 1835 and the Ulster Magdalene Asylum was certainly founded in 1838. The Ulster Female Penitentiary of 1816, 1822 and 1835 may have been the same establishment reformed under new committees. The Rosevale Home, which opened in 1862 near Lisburn, may also have been a Magdalen home. One annual report of its activities is available but the description of its work is so circumspect that it is difficult to be sure of its function. For reference to all of

were attached to convents, especially those of the Good Shepherd Sisters, the Sisters of Charity and the Mercy nuns, in towns and cities around the country. Six of the Dublin asylums were run by religious congregations or Catholic clergymen, the rest had Protestant clergymen as trustees, governors or committee members. In these latter institutions the laity played a greater role in their organisation and management. Throughout the century there was a direct link between institutional religion and the asylums, strongest in those refuges run by female religious. While there were certain similarities between the organisation of lay and religious asylums the differences were important and they will be treated separately here.

LAY ASYLUMS

The earliest refuge established was the Magdalen Asylum in Leeson Street which opened in 1766. Lady Arbella Denny, who founded this home, had become interested in rescue work while involved in the reform of the Dublin Foundling Hospital. There she came across unmarried mothers who were forced to give up their children. The plight of these women, abandoned by their families, moved her to action. She opened a fund and received many contributions from her wealthy friends and on 17 August 1767 the first inmate was received.[47] The patroness, vice-patroness and governesses of this asylum were 'fully invested with the internal government of the house, without control of the president, vice president, guardians or any of them'.[48] A committee of fifteen ladies was chosen annually to act as visitors and in 1796 a governess or guardian paid £1 a year for the privilege of being associated with the institution.[49] In the

these institutions see Letter from Rev. Mark Cassidy D.1088/22, c.1816, PRONI; sixth Annual Report of the Ulster Female Penitentiary . . . for the years ending 1825, 1826, 1827 (Belfast, 1828); *Third Report of the Commissioners for Inquiring into the Condition of the Poorer Classes in Ireland*, HC 1836 [43], xxx, appendix C, part 1, 15–16; Mr and Mrs S.C. Hall, *Ireland: its Scenery and Character*, 3 vols. (London, 1841–43), III, pp. 59–62; annual report of the Ulster Magdalene Asylum for the year ending February 1905; Twelfth Report of the Rosevale Home . . . for the year ending 1873 (Lisburn, 1874). For a complete list of these refuges see Luddy, 'Women and Philanthropy'.

[47] For the work of Lady Denny in the Foundling Hospital see Robins, *Lost Children*, ch. 2. For the life of Lady Denny see Beatrice Bayley Butler, 'Lady Arbella Denny, 1707–1792', *Dublin Historical Record*, 9:1 (December 1946–February 1947), pp. 1–20.

[48] *Rules and regulations for the asylum of penitent females with an account of receipts and disbursements . . .* (Dublin, 1796), p. 2.

[49] MS board of guardian minute book, November 1841–January 1853 (Denny House, Dublin).

eighteenth century it was decided that the 'penitents' as the inmates were called, should spend between eighteen months and two years in the asylum and that they were to leave only if their future could be guaranteed in some way, either through acquiring a position or returning home. It appears that these policies were also in force in the nineteenth century. Within this asylum women would be sheltered from 'Shame, from Reproach, from Disease, from Want, from the base Society that has either drawn you into vice, or prevailed upon you to continue in it, to the utmost hazard of your eternal happiness'.[50] This refuge was based on a similar asylum which had been established in London a number of years previously. The organisation and ethos of the Magdalen asylum was taken up by other refuges which appeared in Ireland later on in the eighteenth and nineteenth centuries. The title 'Magdalen asylum', used by many refuges, reveals the influence of religious symbolism using Mary Magdalen as the model of repentance and also of spiritual regeneration.

In order to gain entry to an asylum, particularly to the earlier ones, women had to be recommended by a subscriber. For the Dublin Female Penitentiary a petition had to be signed, which read: 'that your petitioner is an unfortunate female sensible of the offence which has plunged her into guilt and misery, and deprived her of every means of getting an honest livelihood; and being desirous of quitting her vicious courses ... prays admittance'.[51] The use of petitions was soon abandoned and may initially have been a means of gaining subscribers to the charity with a personal interest in the homes, thus ensuring sympathy and funds for its purpose. Penitents most often gained entry by making their own way to the refuge. One reason given for rejecting penitents was the lack of room available in the institution, and many of the homes certainly catered for small numbers and had limited funds. However, judging from some of the reports, it appears that a number of asylums also operated on a discriminatory basis. In those institutions under lay control penitents were more acceptable if they were 'young, unskilled ... and not hardened in the ways of vice'.[52] The Magdalen asylum in Leeson Street took in Protestant women who were most often under twenty years of age, or were expectant mothers, and the stated aim

[50] Quoted in J.D.H. Widdess, *The Magdalen Asylum, Dublin 1766–1966* (Dublin, c.1966), p. 5.
[51] Annual report, Dublin Female Penitentiary (hereafter DFP), 1815, p. 19.
[52] Annual report, DFP, 1814, p. 12.

of the home was to afford protection to young women after a 'first fall'.[53] The Ulster Magdalene Asylum in Belfast also wished only to take in women under twenty.[54] The attitude of the committee of the Dublin Midnight Mission and Home towards prostitutes was quite different. Its members, who appear to have been male, went onto the streets to gather in prostitutes, usually after midnight. They accepted all 'penitents' and if there was not enough room in their own establishment they found other places of refuge or lodgings for the women immediately.[55] The majority of asylums did not discriminate on a religious basis and accepted penitents of all religious persuasions; in practice, however, Catholic women tended to go to the religious run asylums and Protestants to the lay homes.

The policies of the lay Magdalen philanthropists seem to have excluded the admission of hardened prostitutes. From the case histories provided in some of the annual reports, many of the women appear not to have been prostitutes at all. Many were 'seduced' women who on abandonment by their seducers and families turned to the asylums for protection. It was also probably easier to reclaim young and 'seduced' women than hardened prostitutes and the greater the success rate claimed by the asylums in the reform of penitents the more justification they had for their existence and the greater their claim on public support, on which the lay asylums depended, particularly in their earlier years. The reports of these asylums included case histories of young, vulnerable females as an attempt to engage public sympathy and to open purses. The only requirement common to all these institutions in allowing entry was the expressed desire on the part of the 'penitent' to reform. After that, asylums selected penitents to suit their own facilities. Almost no public opposition to the establishment of these refuges is evident, though some objections were raised in 1813 regarding the opening of the Dublin Female Penitentiary, on the basis that a public asylum could only encourage prostitution by providing the vice with publicity and that there were sufficient refuges within Dublin already to cater for reform.[56]

---

[53] Barrett, *Guide*, part iii, p. 4. The Rescue Mission Home, established in the North Circular Road in 1875, stated that it was for the 'reformation of a better class, socially, of young women than those in other homes' (p. 6).
[54] Report of the Ulster Magdalene Asylum, 1887.   [55] Barrett, *Guide*, p. 3.
[56] Anon., *An Address to the Ladies Forming the Committee of the Intended New Dublin Female Penitentiary in Consequence of their Appeal to the Public* (Dublin, 1813). The objections raised in this pamphlet were answered in Anon., *Four Letters in Answer to an Address to the Committee of*

What was life like for the women who entered these institutions? Once within the walls of a refuge the penitents were generally issued with a uniform, one outfit for Sundays and another for everyday wear. In some institutions the women were separated into different classes. In the Dublin Female Penitentiary the classification was carried out with reference 'to their [the inmates] former education and habits of life',[57] suggesting a social rather than moral classification. The institutions were 'designed to comfort and relieve the distressed soul who has happily perceived the error of her ways and loathes her former vileness'.[58] The women were 'wretched outcasts desirous of forsaking the evil of their ways'.[59] There was a seemingly contradictory attitude towards the women accepted. In many of the reports the belief that the women, in themselves, were not evil is expressed. Rather it was the keeping of bad company or other harmful influences which led them astray. The Female Penitent Refuge, in Summerhill, wished to remove the young female 'from the contagious influence of her former associates'.[60] In the Ulster Female Penitentiary inmates were removed from 'the common jails, and the low dens of infamy and crime'.[61] In the reports available for the Dublin Female Penitentiary the blame for the fall into vice was laid at abuse by seducers.[62] In a pamphlet published in 1805 the male reader was castigated, 'let them [men] not disdain to look for a moment into the awful distress which many of them have contributed to produce and encrease [sic] ... they shall know that those who act the part of fiends in thus marring the good creation of God, shall, without repentance, share the fate of fiends for ever'.[63] It was

---

the *Dublin Female Penitentiary* (Dublin, 1813). The Rev. Mark Cassidy, in a private letter to the committee of the Ulster Female Penitentiary in 1816, objected to the composition of the committee. According to him the management of the asylum was entrusted to Protestant evangelicals and the interests of the home, being confined to one sect, could only be damaged because other religious bodies would be prevented from co-operating with the managers of the home. See Ulster Female Penitentiary, Letter from Rev. Mark Cassidy, D 1088/22 (PRONI).

57 Annual report, DFP, 1814, p. 6.

58 Quoted in Bayley Butler, 'Arbella Denny', p. 10. The Magdalen Asylum in Leeson Street was 'a shelter that will afford you time to reflect how gravely you have offended that gracious Author of all good'. *Rules and Regulations for the Asylum for Penitent Females* (Dublin, 1785), p. 10.

59 Hall, *Ireland*, III, p. 62.   60 Murray Papers, File 31/1/4 undated (DDA).

61 See n 59 above.

62 See the case histories in the annual reports of the DFP, 1814–16.

63 Anon., *New Edition of the Tract which gave Rise to the Institution of the Lock Penitentiary* (Dublin, 1805), p. 10.

one of the few acknowledgements publicly made of men's role in 'ruining' women.

Within the institutions, however, responsibility for their actions was laid firmly on the shoulders of the penitents themselves. A strict regime was followed in the asylums which stripped the women of their former identity and moulded a new one for them. Penitents were forbidden to use their own names or to speak of their past. In the Magdalen asylum in Leeson Street the penitents were given a number and known as Mrs One, Mrs Two etc. In religious run asylums they were given the name of a saint.[64] But even in rejecting their past the penitents were never allowed to forget that they had sinned. Their daily life was made up of prayer, labour, recreation and silence. This programme of reform and discipline made no allowance either for maternal feeling. The children of penitents were usually sent for adoption. An attempt by the trustees of the Asylum for Penitent Females to allow infants to remain with their mothers was unanimously rejected by the committee in 1858.[65] Within all the asylums there was an exaggerated rejection of the penitent's past. 'Until the penitents forget the past', as one report stated, 'nothing solid can be done towards their permanent conversion.'[66] All contacts with her past life were broken, they could not write or receive letters without the matron first reading them, they were rarely allowed visitors and if they were they had to meet them with the matron present. The control these institutions attempted to exert over the women even extended to selecting topics of conversation among the inmates: 'all occasions which might give rise to improper mental associations are ... carefully guarded against ... all light and trifling conversation is strictly inhibited'.[67]

Within the asylums the inmates had to do a certain amount of work. A policy of religious instruction coupled with vocational training was normally followed. To effect reform and rehabilitation the homes inculcated a sense of guilt in the penitents and united this with lessons in sobriety and industry. The conversion of the inmates depended on them being constantly employed; an idle life was considered to be prejudicial to their good. The inmates it was

---

[64] See Bayley Butler, 'Arbella Denny', and also the registers of the various asylums.
[65] Minutes of the Penitent Relief Society, July 1858. M1133 (PRO, Dublin).
[66] *Abstract Report and Statistical Sketch of the Magdalen Asylum, High Park, Drumcondra June 1881* (Dublin, 1881), p. 17.
[67] Annual report, Asylum for Penitent Females, 1831, p. 11.

stressed were changed by work, industry allowed 'the mind to be tranquillised and made the penitents more amenable to religious instruction'.[68] The aim of the work was not only to keep the inmates busy but also to train them for new occupations once they had left the asylum. In the Female Penitent Asylum the women were taught, 'to weep incessantly over their sins, and pray without intermission for their pious benefactors, their time being usefully filled up in washing and working for the public, and no opportunity was lost to refit them, to fill, at some future date, their proper station in society'.[69]

All the asylums engaged in needle and laundry work. Although the main reason given for engaging in such work was the desire to discipline the penitents and to give them a trade, such work was also a vital source of financial support for the institutions. Generally these charitable efforts were well supported by the public initially but public interest usually waned after the first years of an institution's existence. The Ulster Female Penitentiary established on a non-denominational basis in Belfast in 1820 owed much of its original success to the work of the Presbyterian minister John Edgar. In 1839 he saved the penitentiary from financial difficulty by raising over £2,000 in funding from the public in the space of a few weeks.[70] The Dublin Female Penitentiary earned 11 per cent of its annual income from needle and laundry work in 1815, compared to 27 per cent from subscriptions and donations. By 1824 the income derived from subscriptions and donations had dropped to 9 per cent whilst that from laundry work had increased to 55 per cent.[71] The pattern of becoming almost self-supporting through laundry work occurred in all of the asylums. Generally, subscriptions dropped after the first few years of an institution's existence and they had to rely on the laundry for financial support. Penitents did receive some money for their work, usually when they left the refuge. In the Magdalen

---

[68] Annual report, DFP, 1816.   [69] Murray Papers, File 31/7–9, 1840 (DDA).
[70] W.D. Killen, *Memoir of Dr Edgar* (Belfast, 1867), p. 134.
[71] Annual reports, DFP, 1812–25. The Dublin by Lamplight Institution accounts show a similar pattern. In 1856 subscriptions and donations accounted for 98 per cent of income, and laundry work 2 per cent. By 1867 subscriptions and donations had dropped to 39 per cent of income while laundry receipts had climbed to 56 per cent. See annual reports, Dublin by Lamplight Institution 1857, 1858, 1868. This institution also took over a 'concern known as Duffy's factory in Ballsbridge' in 1856, probably to use as a laundry and make the institution more self-supporting. See *Irish Ecclesiastical Gazette* (September, 1856). Another source of income for an asylum was provided by the charity sermon which usually accounted for about 5 per cent of an institution's annual income.

Asylum in Leeson Street this was determined by the length of time and conduct of the woman while she resided in the refuge and ranged from a few shillings to seven or eight pounds.

In these lay run establishments women stayed, generally, for a period of up to three years. When leaving after this time they were usually placed in domestic service if they did not return to their families. By the middle of the century the Dublin by Lamplight Institution also provided some women with the funds to emigrate. However, if a penitent left of her own accord, as many of them did, or was dismissed for any reason, she was not helped by the committee.

Only one register for an asylum that remained in lay hands appears to have survived from the nineteenth century. This, the register of the Magdalen Asylum in Leeson Street Dublin, gives us some indication of how lay asylums dealt with their inmates. As we can see from table 4.3 the total number of entrants from 1809 to 1828 numbered 384. Unlike many of the religious run asylums the re-entrance of individuals was not a common phenomenon within this asylum. One individual, Mrs 689, had resided in the refuge for two years before returning home to her mother 'against the wish and remonstrance of the vice patroness'. Less than two months later the woman sought readmittance and it was granted only after she brought a 'certificate from her mother of her not having left her roof and behaving well and also of her quiet and good behaviour to that day'.[72] It may be an indication of the refuge's success in placing their inmates that so few sought readmittance. There was also a much higher rate of entry through recommendations from employers or guardians and governesses than is found in the religious run homes. The age range of these entrants also tends to be much lower than that which existed for religious run homes. The youngest individual to enter in Leeson Street was aged nine and the governesses do not seem to have taken in anyone older than twenty-five. It appears that the 'success' rate of this institution was quite high. A much higher proportion of the inmates ended up in situations than is evident for the religious run homes. Mrs 677, for example, was taken out by a resident of Grafton Street as 'children's maid to her family'.[73] A number of women were also returned to their families once they were considered to be 'rehabilitated'. Quite

[72] MS Magdalen Asylum Register, 1809–28 (Denny House).   [73] Ibid.

Table 4.3. *Inmates of the Magdalen Asylum, Leeson Street, Dublin, 1809–1828*

Sources of entry

Voluntary	Religious referrals	Family	Police/Prison	Other	Unaccounted
34	39	90		203	12
8.85%	10.15%	23.44%		52.86%	3.13%

Reasons for leaving

Left voluntarily	Expelled	Situation	Emigrated	Magdalen Class	Hospital	Deaths	Escaped
15	45	59	5		36	7	47
3.9%	11.71%	15.36%	1.3%		9.38%	1.82%	12.24%

Home/Friends	Other convents	House of industry	Lunatic asylum	Unaccounted	To marry	To work
149		5	1	15		
38.8%		1.3%	0.26%	3.9%		

Total number of entrants   384 (includes re-entrants)
Total number of re-entrants   6 (1.56%)

Source: MS Magdalen Asylum Register, 1809–28, vol. 3 (Denny House, Dublin)

a few of the women also 'eloped' or escaped from the refuge. Some of these women had spent some time in the refuge while others escaped after a few days; they usually took their asylum clothes with them. Time spent in the refuge varied from a single day to just over seven years for one inmate. The average length of stay was about two years, again in contrast to the religious run refuges where individuals could spend up to forty years in the home. The governesses also expelled almost 12 per cent of the inmates in this period. Mrs 753, for example, 'behaved very ill, after repeated remonstrances has obliged to be put out and sent to the House of Industry'. Mrs 770, had been sent to hospital 'where she did not behave well, [and] on that account [is] not to be readmitted'. Many of the individuals who returned home were sent there because the governesses could not deal with them in the refuge.[74]

It is difficult to assess how successful these institutions were in reforming or rescuing their inmates. Clearly claims made regarding the rehabilitation of the penitents, in such annual reports as have

[74] Ibid.

survived, should be treated with caution. In the Magdalen Asylum, Leeson Street, the total number of inmates from 1767 to 1784 was 251. The committee claimed a reform rate of 52 per cent or 130 of the women and a failure rate of 36 per cent or 90 inmates.[75] The remaining 12 per cent were resident in the home when these figures were compiled. The Magdalen Asylum in Limerick was run by a Miss Reddan until the Good Shepherd Sisters took it over in 1848. It is one of the few lay run refuges for which a complete list of penitents can be found. From May 1828 to June 1843 the total number of penitents admitted was 218 (see table 4.4). Of these, 47 were placed in situations and 34 were restored to friends or returned home. All of these penitents would have been seen as reclaimed and if we include the five deaths which occurred in the home, the ultimate redemption, 39 per cent of the women were rescued. Some homes claimed a high success rate. The Rescue Mission Home in Dublin, for example, pronounced a success rate of 65 per cent in 1899.[76] This home was very selective in choosing its inmates and the figure may indeed be accurate. Other institutions seem to have admitted high rates of failure. The Dublin by Lamplight Institution appears to have had, in 1899, a failure rate of about 70 per cent and a success rate of 13 per cent, the remaining 17 per cent being resident in the home when the figures were compiled.[77] Although these samples are too small to make any generalisation about the successes of the asylums, a recent study of prostitution in York suggests that many penitents placed in situations usually slipped back into their old lifestyles.[78] Many women also left or ran away from the refuges before their allotted release date, about 2 per cent of the inmates of the Limerick Magdalen Asylum did so. It seems likely that many of the women used these homes as a temporary refuge and had no intention of reforming, an aspect which will be looked at later.

Lay women played an important role in running these establishments. All of the lay homes had male governors, patrons or

[75] Asylum for Penitent Females, Rules and Regulations, appendix, p. 3.
[76] Williams (ed.), *Dublin Charities*, p. 60. The refuge admitted 19 during the year 1899–1900. Of these, 4 returned home, 1 married and 8 were placed in situations.
[77] Ibid. p. 153. For the year 1899, 254 penitents were admitted to the home; 178 left before the allotted probation period of 18 months, 31 were sent to situations and 2 to friends. The remaining women were resident in the home when these figures were compiled. See Table 4.5 for the fate of women in the lay Magdalen Asylum in Townsend St. Dublin.
[78] See Frances Finnegan, *Poverty and Prostitution, A Study of Victorian Prostitutes in York* (Cambridge, 1979).

Table 4.4. *Inmates of the Magdalen Asylum, Limerick, May 1828–June 1843*

Sources of entry

Voluntary	Religious referrals	Family	Police/Prison	Other	Unaccounted
	170			48	
	77.98%			22.02%	

Reasons for leaving

Left voluntarily	Expelled	Situation	Emigrated	Magdalen Class	Hospital	Deaths
42	39	47			15	5
19.27%	17.89%	21.56%			6.88%	2.9%

Home/Friends	Other convents	Workhouse	Lunatic asylum	Unaccounted	To marry	To work
34				36		
15.59%				16.59%		

Total number of entrants   218
Total number of re-entrants   unknown

Source: MS Registers of the Asylum of the Good Shepherd, Limerick, 1828–1900 (4 vols.)

committee members and they all had ladies' committees or lady visitors. The ladies' committees effectively took charge of the running of the institutions. Even when men made policy decisions they were influenced by the women who did the routine work of ensuring that the homes ran smoothly. All the employees of the homes were female, usually with the exception of a male porter or carter who brought in the washing. In the institution founded by Lady Arbella Denny the women's committee ran the home completely and rarely sought advice from the male governors. The work these women did for the refuges covered three areas; firstly, the administration of the day to day running of the home; secondly, the instruction of the inmates in religion, reading and needlework and thirdly, the raising of funds. Groups of women generally visited the home a number of times during the week and recommended policy changes to the male governors. In the raising of funds the women mainly sought financial aid from other women. The committee of the Dublin Female Penitentiary sought money 'from all ... but chiefly [looked] to their own sex, whose bosoms must beat with corresponding sentiments of anxiety to become instrumental in rescuing an unhappy fellow creature, a sister, from temporal and possibly, from spiritual destruction'.[79] Although, as we have noted, subscriptions generally decreased after an initial period of enthusiasm, over the first ten years of its operation women averaged 52 per cent of subscribers to that home.[80] In the Dublin by Lamplight Institution they generally made up 40 per cent of subscribers.[81] Most of the lay asylums also ran repositories which were run by women where needlework or articles donated to the home were sold. Women also organised bazaars where substantial amounts of money were often raised. The asylums also depended on a regular supply of laundry to ensure financial viability and it was women in charge of households who kept them supplied with such work. Without the voluntary and financial support of women it is certain that many of these refuges could not have functioned.

Managing committees were separate and each asylum appears to have had both a male and female committee. In a number of the lay asylums husbands and wives were members of the managing committees. In the Dublin Female Penitentiary, for example, at least 50 per cent of the women on the ladies' committee were related by marriage to male committee members. In the Asylum for Penitent Females all the women involved were married to members of the trustees committee. This latter asylum, in fact, was established by men, and it was not until 1836, at least six years after the establishment of the home, that the trustees committee appointed eleven women to act on a ladies' committee. According to the Trust Deed of the institution the function of the ladies' committee was 'to inspect and superintend the concerns of the asylum and to report their observations to the trustees ... and to perform such duties as the trustees shall from time to time appoint'.[82] In effect the women ran the institution but they had no control over its financial arrangements which remained firmly in male hands. It is obvious also from the minutes of this institution that the male trustees took very little interest in the practical running of the home and were more involved in its financial affairs and the appointment of chaplains to

---

[79] *An Appeal to the Public from the Committee of the Intended New Dublin Female Penitentiary* (Dublin, 1812), p. 20.
[80] Annual reports, DFP, 1813–25, subscription lists.
[81] See annual report of the Dublin by Lamplight Institution, 1868.
[82] Quoted in the minutes of the Penitent Relief Society, M1133 (PRO, Dublin).

the chapel which had been erected in 1833. The male guardians of the Magdalen Asylum in Leeson Street were similarly more concerned with church affairs and building repairs than with the actual day to day running of the asylum.[83] The motivation of the women who ran these refuges was apparently Christian charity. Although life within these asylums was difficult, those who ran them did so with a genuine measure of humanitarianism and it was obvious to these philanthropists that prostitutes were certainly better off in the homes than on the streets. The purpose of this type of charity work was to provide a home which was a 'shelter from the scorn, derision and temptations of the world'.[84]

All the asylums were extremely conservative in their approach to the problem of prostitution. They concentrated all their energies on saving the penitent. In the earlier part of the century prostitution was an evil because it was 'injurious in its effects on society'.[85] If left unreclaimed a prostitute could not 'fill with credit the character of child, wife, mother, friend'.[86] The principal aim of the homes was to give back to society a virtuous being. Through discipline and work the prostitute learned self-control. A prostitute could be a corrupter of female innocence and if left unreclaimed could corrupt others. Not only was her temporal life a misery but if she continued on her way she would also lose eternal life. These philanthropists believed that the causes of prostitution lay with the individual; if the woman could be reclaimed then the vice would be eliminated. Religious salvation was even more important to them than temporal salvation. These refuges were established in response to social demands. The alarming number of prostitutes who operated openly in the city was generally given as the reason for their existence. Women were not expected to be sexual beings, hence the pretence in these homes that prostitutes had no past life.[87] The prostitute, by her 'unwomanly' behaviour in displaying her availability for sexual acts, was seen as an affront to 'respectable' women who were supposedly sexually ignorant. The function of such homes was not to question the existence of a sexual double standard, nor did the women who ran these homes express any degree of solidarity with their fallen sisters.

---

[83] MS Board of guardian minute book, November 1841–January 1853 (Denny House, Dublin).

[84] Murray Papers, File 33/1/20, undated (DDA).   [85] Ibid.

[86] Annual report, DFP, 1816.

[87] See annual reports and asylum registers.

They wished to elevate the 'fallen woman' to an acceptable level of womanhood, to carry out her dutiful role in society without acknowledging her sexuality.

CONVENT REFUGES

The refuges run by nuns are of especial interest in regard to the idealised picture of women common in Ireland in the last century. In these refuges the 'purest' women looked after the most 'impure'. As in other charitable endeavours in which they became involved, female religious provided an extensive, organised network of refuges which operated throughout the country. The Good Shepherd nuns ran homes in Belfast, Cork, Limerick, New Ross and Waterford. The Sisters of Mercy ran a refuge in Galway and Tralee and another in Dun Laoghaire. The Sisters of Our Lady of Charity of Refuge operated the largest asylum in the country in Drumcondra and a branch of that congregation ran a home from Gloucester Street in Dublin. The Sisters of Charity also operated a home in Cork and one in Dublin. After 1830 no lay Catholic asylum was established to look after prostitutes and those begun earlier in the century were all taken over by religious congregations.[88] The Good Shepherd asylum in Cork appears to have been the only religious run asylum established to meet the demand for a refuge resulting from the implementation of the Contagious Diseases Acts in the 1860s.[89] For example, the Order of Our Lady of Charity of Refuge was invited in from France to run a home established by the Rev. John Smith in 1833. When this home was begun it had only seven penitents and the laundry brought in £7 per week.[90] The nuns generally took over institutions which were already in existence but which through both managerial and financial considerations had run into difficulties. It

---

[88] For details see Luddy, 'Philanthropy', appendix, 2.

[89] See *Select Committee ... CDAs 1881* (351), viii, Q. 6,231. The Good Shepherd nuns approached Cullen in 1870 with a proposal to establish a branch of their convent in Dublin, specifically to take over the care of the penitents in an asylum in Mecklenburgh Street. Nothing came of this proposal. See letter to Cullen from the superioress of the Good Shepherd convent, Limerick, 13 February 1872, Cullen Papers, File 335/1/6 (Nuns, 1872 DDA).

[90] MS Annals of the Convent of Our Lady of Charity of Refuge. These annals are very detailed and provide a lot of information about the coming of the order to Ireland and the difficulties the nuns had in wresting control of the asylum from the Rev. John Smith; Anon., *The Order of Our Lady of Charity of Refuge, 1853–1953, A Centenary Record* (n.p., n.d.) provides a synopsis of the information contained in the annals.

was a very practical move to bring the nuns in because they had the personnel, commitment, organisation and financial support which many of the Catholic lay asylums lacked. It is clear that the Catholic hierarchy felt that the only worthwhile impact to be made on Magdalens could come from nuns.[91]

The Sisters of Charity took over a Magdalen asylum in Cork in 1846 which had been established in 1809. A letter from the Rev. Mother to Mary Aikenhead records that there was 'not a sound bit of timber in the place . . . rusty locks . . . no cutlery . . . very dirty . . . nothing in the house . . . the wash[room] is low and dark, when the water is taken from the troughs they [the penitents] are up to the ankles in it . . . the women are there without shoes'.[92] The nuns had to build a new washroom and with thirteen penitents in the home refused to take in any more until they could be adequately looked after. A Miss Lynch established a refuge in Galway in 1834, which appears to have been run by herself until infirmity and old age forced her to seek assistance. She invited the Sisters of Mercy to take over the refuge, which they did in 1847.[93] All the religious congregations insisted on having complete control over the asylums and once they had gained this control ran efficient homes.[94] Though the nuns had immediate day to day control over their refuges they were still ultimately answerable to the clergy. The Magdalen asylum operated by the Sisters of Charity in Donnybrook in Dublin, for example, sent regular reports of their work, along with detailed financial accounts, to their bishop.[95] The power which could be exerted by clerics is shown clearly in a number of letters emanating from St Mary's Penitent retreat, the asylum which was operated by

---

[91] See chapter 2.

[92] Letter from M. Chantal, Cork to Mother M. Aikenhead dated 14 June 1846, File 1/13/97 (RSCG, Milltown). The Magdalen asylum in Townsend Street was run by a Mrs Ryan, a niece of Archbishop Troy, from 1798. By the 1830s Mrs Ryan, through illness, was unable to control the penitents under her care. As a penance the penitents were not allowed to change the straw on their beds and to ensure that this rule would be kept Mrs Ryan had the ticken, which held the straw, nailed to the bed posts. When the Sisters of Charity entered the asylum they discovered that as a result of Mrs Ryan's action the beds were crawling with maggots. See Typescript Annals of the Sisters of Charity, Donnybrook, vol 1, 1833, pp. 277–9 (RSC, Donnybrook).

[93] Personal correspondence with the Sisters of Mercy, Galway.

[94] The Sisters of Charity in Cork would not take over the asylum until they were guaranteed full control by the previous lay committee. See annals and letters of that convent kept at Milltown. Our Lady of Charity of Refuge sisters had enormous difficulties in trying to take control of the refuge in Drumcondra.

[95] See Annals of St Mary's Magdalen Asylum (RSCG, Milltown) for copies of the accounts sent to the bishop.

the Sisters of Mercy. Sr Gertrude Howell had the temerity to ask the secretary of Charitable Donations and Bequests when a legacy of £500 which had been left to Archbishop Cullen for the refuge would be paid to them. Cullen was obviously informed of the letter and within two days the same nun was writing to him, with the most abject apologies, for daring to presume to interfere in this matter.[96] Overall, convent asylums were larger and catered for more individuals than the lay run establishments. Most of the lay asylums put between 30 and 50 women through their homes annually with room for 40 penitents at the most. Some of those refuges run by religious could house 150 to 200 inmates at a time. None of the religious run asylums published annual reports but the majority did keep registers of their inmates.[97] These documents provide fascinating details about the women who entered these refuges and it is worth looking at them in some depth.

The general impression gained from reading any of the contemporary literature published about the asylums is that they were virtual prisons and that the women who entered them were unlikely ever to leave. The evidence of the registers disproves this. Tables 4.6 to 4.12 provide a detailed breakdown of the inmates of seven asylums run by religious congregations during the last century. Overall, these asylums, for the period covered, catered for a total of 10,674 women. Of this number approximately 2,219 entered an asylum more than once. This is an underestimate as not all the registers account for repeats. The majority of women who entered these refuges did so voluntarily, approximately 7,110, or just over 66 per cent, and a number of women entered up to ten times. Thus entering a refuge was, for the majority of women, a matter of choice. While it is true that many such women had only the workhouse or the Magdalen asylum to turn to in times of utter distress, it would appear that the

---

96 Sr M. Gertrude Howell to the secretary, Charitable Donations and Bequests, 27 January 1875; Sr M. Gertrude Howell to Cardinal Cullen, 29 January 1875, Cullen Papers, File 322/1/4 (Nuns 1875 DDA).
97 There are five published accounts dealing with the refuge in Drumcondra. The most detailed of these, *Abstract Report, June 1881* gives an insight into the running of the home. In rhetoric and style it is similar to the reports published by the lay asylums and appears to have been published in an attempt to raise funds for the home. See also the *Report Showing the Foundation and Progress of the Monastery of the Order of Our Lady of Charity of Refuge* (Dublin, 1857); 'Second report of the Order of Our Lady of Charity of Refuge', *Irish Quarterly Review*, 9 (January 1860), appendix: 'The Magdalens of High Park, *The Irish Rosary* 1 (April 1897); *Souvenir of the Golden Jubilee of Our Lady of the Charity of Refuge, High Park, Drumcondra* (Dublin, 1903). All of these works were written anonymously.

Table 4.5. *Inmates of the Magdalen Asylum, Townsend Street, Dublin, December 1796–December 1832*

Sources of entry

Voluntary	Religious	Family	Police/Prison	Other	Unaccounted
	35			82	13
	26.92%			63.07%	10%

Reasons for leaving [a]

Left voluntarily	Expelled	Situation	Emigrated	Magdalen Class	Hospital	Deaths	Escaped
10	9	27	2		4	2	11
10.42%	9.37%	28.12%	2.08%		4.16%	2.08%	11.46%

Home/Friends	Other convents	House of industry	Lunatic asylum	Unaccounted	To marry	To work
19	4		6			2
19.79%	4.16%		6.25%			2.08%

Total number of entrants   130
Total number of re-entrants   unknown.

Note: [a] These figures exclude 34 women who were still in the refuge when it was taken over by the Sisters of Charity and are included in table 4.10
Source: MS Register of the Asylum, 1796–1899, Convent of the Sisters of Charity, Donnybrook, Dublin

Table 4.6. *Inmates of the Good Shepherd Magdalen Asylum, Belfast, April 1851–December 1899*

Sources of entry

Voluntary	Religious referrals	Family	Police/Prison	Other	Unaccounted
294	130	37		27	406
32.89%	14.54%	4.13%		3.02%	45.41%

Reasons for leaving

Left voluntarily	Expelled	Situation	Emigrated	Magdalen Class	Hospital	Deaths	Escaped
412	69	31	17	14	40	49	11
46.09%	7.72%	3.47%	1.9%	1.57%	4.47%	5.48%	1.23%

Home/Friends	Other convents	Workhouse	Lunatic asylum	Unaccounted	To marry	To work
95	14 [a]	4	3	116		19
10.63%	1.56%	0.45%	0.34%	12.96%		2.13%

Total number of entrants   894
Total number of re-entrants   266 (29.75%)

Note: [a] Five of these women went to lay asylums
Source: MS Register of the Entrants to the Magdalen Asylum, Good Shepherd Convent, Belfast, 1851–1900

Women and philanthropy

Table 4.7. *Inmates of the Good Shepherd Magdalen Asylum, Cork, July 1872–December 1899*

Sources of entry

Voluntary	Religious referrals	Family	Police/Prison	Other	Unaccounted
902	569	74	103	93	8
51.57%	32.53%	4.23%	5.89%	5.32%	0.46%

Reasons for leaving

Left	Expelled	Situation	Emigrated	Magdalen	Hospital	Deaths	Escaped
808	206	76	112	23	178	44	23
46.2%	11.78%	4.35%	6.4%	1.32%	10.18%	2.52%	1.32%

Home/Friends	Other convents	Workhouse	Lunatic asylum	Unaccounted	To marry	To work
136	27	3	15	91	7	
7.78%	1.54%	0.17%	0.86%	5.2%	0.4%	

Total number of entrants   1,749
Total number of re-entrants   592 (33.84%)

Source: MS Register of the Magdalen Asylum, Good Shepherd Convent, Cork, 1872–1900

Table 4.8. *Inmates of the Sisters of Charity Magdalen Asylum, Cork, June 1846–December 1899*

Sources of entry
Unknown

Reasons for leaving

Left voluntarily	Expelled	Situation	Emigrated	Magdalen Class	Hospital	Deaths	Escaped
1,005	23	5	6		24	119	1
79.32%	1.81%	0.39%	0.47%		1.89%	9.39%	0.08%

Home/Friends	Other convents	Workhouse	Lunatic asylum	Unaccounted	To marry	To work
27	10		6	41		
2.13%	0.78%		0.47%	3.23%		

Total number of entrants   1,267
Total number of re-entrants   unknown

Source: MS Register of St Mary's Magdalen, 1846–99, Good Shepherd Convent, Cork

Table 4.9. *Inmates of the Magdalen Asylum, High Park, Drumcondra, Dublin,*[a] *May 1839–December 1899*

Sources of entry

Voluntary		Family	Police/Prison	Other	Unaccounted
	Religious referrals				
	211	22	37	117	2,246
	8.01%	0.84%	1.41%	4.44%	85.3%

Reasons for leaving

Left voluntarily	Expelled	Situation	Emigrated	Magdalen Class	Hospital	Deaths	Escaped
1,403	232	16	21		211	147	1
53.29%	8.8%	0.61%	0.8%		8.0%	5.58%	0.04%

Home/Friends	Other convents	Workhouse	Lunatic asylum	Unaccounted	To marry	To work
103	3	3	4	489		
3.9%	0.1%	0.1%	0.15%	18.57%		

Total number of entrants   2,633
Total number of re-entrants   434 (16.48%)

Note: [a] Operated by the Sisters of Our Lady of Charity of Refuge
Source: MS Register of the Magdalen Asylum, 1839–1904, Convent of Our Lady of Charity of Refuge, Dublin

second was the favoured option of many. The length of stay in the asylums varied from one day for some women to an entire lifetime, of thirty or forty years, for others. It was generally women who entered in their teens, or who were in their thirties or older, who remained in the homes. One woman, in the Donnybrook asylum, died in 1881 after spending nearly fifty-one years in the home. The decision to stay was made by the women themselves and although the nuns certainly did not encourage women to leave, they had little choice in the matter if the woman was determined to go. It would seem, from the number of re-entries that some women may have used the asylums as a temporary shelter and once they thought it possible to return to the outside world they did so. It is obvious also that the diet within the homes was of a higher standard than that to be obtained elsewhere, and this may have encouraged some women to stay (see table 4.13). The stability of life within a refuge, the order and discipline imposed may have given a sense of security to others and made it an attractive option to remain.

Women and philanthropy

Table 4.10. *Inmates of the Sisters of Charity Magdalen Asylum, Donny-brook, Dublin, January 1833–December 1899*

Sources of entry

Voluntary	Religious referrals	Family	Police/Prison	Other	Unaccounted
568	520	16	35	186	62
40.95%	37.49%	1.15%	2.52%	13.41%	4.47%

Reasons for leaving[a]

Left voluntarily	Expelled	Situation	Emigrated	Magdalen Class	Hospital	Deaths	Escaped
633	345	26	9		106	128	4
44.48%	24.24%	1.83%	0.63%		7.45%	8.99%	0.28%

Home/Friends	Other convents	Workhouse	Lunatic asylum	Unaccounted	To marry	To work
115	34	10		11		
8.08%	2.38%	0.70%		0.77%		

Total number of entrants   1,387[b]
Total number of re-entrants   unknown

Notes: [a] This figure includes the 34 women resident in the asylum in 1833
[b] This figure excludes 34 women who were resident in the asylum when the Sisters of Charity took over
Source: MS Register of the Magdalen Asylum, 1796–1899, Convent of the Sisters of Charity, Donnybrook, Dublin

The second largest source of referral, after voluntary entries, came from religious, either priests and in some cases bishops, or nuns in other convents. Lay referrals concern either parents sending their daughters to a refuge, or matrons from hospitals or employers sending women to a home. It appears likely that those women who were unaccounted for entered the homes of their own choice. The homes in Dublin appear to have catered almost exclusively for women from the Dublin area. In the Good Shepherd asylum in Cork the majority of women, or 91 per cent, came from the city, 4 per cent came from the county and the remaining 5 per cent from places as far away as Dublin, Liverpool and even Scotland.[98] The asylum in Limerick received women from the Limerick, Clare and Tipperary area generally but took in women from other parts of the country as

[98] The registers usually give details about where the women were born. However, recommendations were generally made by the inhabitants of a particular town. In Cork, for example, most penitents were obviously operating in the city and were recommended by individuals from the city.

Table 4.11. *Inmates of the Good Shepherd Magdalen Asylum, Limerick,*
1848–December 1899

Sources of entry

Voluntary	Religious referrals	Family	Police/Prison	Other	Unaccounted
675	902	29	27	81	325
33.10%	44.24%	1.42%	1.32%	3.97%	15.94%

Reasons for leaving

Left voluntarily	Expelled	Situation	Emigrated	Magdalen Class	Hospital	Deaths	Escaped
907	384	81	37	9	199	88	47
44.48%	18.83%	3.97%	1.81%	0.44%	9.76%	4.32%	2.31%

Home/Friends	Other convents	Workhouse	Lunatic asylum	Unaccounted	To marry	To work
142	13	12	7	113		
6.96%	0.64%	0.59%	0.34%	5.54%		

Total number of entrants 2,039[a]
Total number of re-entrants 873 (42.82%)

Note: [a] This figure includes 30 women who were resident in the asylum when the nuns took it over in 1848
Source: MS Register of the Asylum of the Good Shepherd, Limerick, 1828–1900 (4 vols.)

Table 4.12. *Inmates of the Good Shepherd Magdalen Asylum, Waterford,*
July 1842–December 1899

Sources of entry

Voluntary	Religious referrals	Family	Police/Prison	Other	Unaccounted
350	250	34	11	53	7
49.65%	35.5%	4.82%	1.56%	7.52%	0.99%

Reasons for leaving

Left voluntarily	Expelled	Situation	Emigrated	Magdalen Class	Hospital	Deaths	Escaped
359	50	5	4	16	27	48	3
50.92%	7.09%	0.71%	0.57%	2.27%	3.83%	6.81%	0.43%

Home/Friends	Other convents	Workhouse	Lunatic asylum	Unaccounted	To marry	To work
45	5	2	5	136		
6.38%	0.71%	0.28%	0.71%	19.29%		

Total number of entrants 705
Total number of re-entrants 54 (7.66%)

Source: MS Register of St Mary's Magdalen Asylum, 1842–1900, Good Shepherd Convent, Waterford

Table 4.13. *The maintenance of penitents in the Magdalen asylum,*
Donnybrook, 1840

The expenses of each penitent's support in detail

Each penitent for 1840	£9–16–1
Each penitent for one week	0–3–9¼
Each penitent for one day	0–0–6½

£323–11–7 for 33 penitents:
allowing them bread, butter, tea, sugar for breakfast. Sunday, Monday, Tuesday, Thursday beef soup and potatoes. Wednesday and Friday potatoes, butter and milk. Saturday rice, butter, eggs, tea, sugar for dinner and also an extra allowance of mutton, bacon, flour, tea, sugar on all the holy days of the Church and on all the usual festival days of the Blessed Virgin or the different seasons of the year. The expenses of the invalids and all other casual sickness is included in this item.

Description of penitent diet
The best black tea, second best sugar, second best bread, second best potatoes, apples, second best butter, rounds and laps of prime beef on holy and festival days. A hind quarter of mutton and twenty four bacon and 1½ stone of flour with ½lb. of tea, – ¼lb. stone of sugar.

Description of penitent clothing
One stiff gown for Sunday and Holy days with suitable caps and handkerchiefs to compound. Two blue working wrappers. Two blue serge petticoats. Two linen chemise. Two neck handkerchiefs. One pocket handkerchief. One large shawl. One pair woollen and pair cotton stocking. Two pair shoes. Two fine linen caps.

Bedding
Each subject has: One iron bedstead, one hair mattress, one straw ticken, one feather bolster, two plain sheets, one plain blanket, two quilts.

Source: This document is an exact copy of a MS in the Murray Papers, File 31/9/30, 1841–2 (DDA)

well. The majority of women who left the asylums did so of their own wish. Over the period 5,527 or approximately 52 per cent of the women did this. It appears that some form of permission to leave had to be granted by the nuns and a small number of women, about 1 per cent, ran away or escaped from the homes. One woman, who left the asylum in Donnybrook, at her own request after spending four years there, was intriguingly noted in the information column of the register as 'having Protestant tendencies' coupled with a bad temper.[99] Another woman in the same refuge asked and was granted

---

[99] Penitent no. 427, MS Register of the Asylum (RSC, Donnybrook).

permission to leave after a few weeks stating she could not survive a life in the home without smoking![100]

About 14 per cent, or 1,309, were expelled from the refuges. Insubordination, violence, madness or a refusal to attend to religious duties or ceremonies were the reasons usually given for dismissal. One penitent in Donnybrook was dismissed after ten years residence. She was described as 'extremely slothful, irreligious and [having] a shocking tongue'.[101] Another woman in Limerick was expelled in 1891 after a month in the home. It was her sixth time in the refuge and the record of her dismissal states 'not to be admitted again ... a very bad spirit'.[102] Many penitents were also dismissed for engaging in lesbian relationships, or 'particular friendships' as such were termed, with other women in the home. Whether this involved actual sexual activity or not remains unrecorded. Nuns themselves were warned against forming 'particular' attachments to other nuns because they had to devote all their energies to serving God. They may have seen intense friendships between the women under their care as dangerous because it could distract them from the purpose of their stay in the home, total self-abnegation, the suppression of their own desires and repentance. It was undoubtedly difficult for the nuns to control many of the penitents and they were probably glad to see the back of many of them. Expulsion did not mean that a penitent would not be taken back into the refuge again at a later stage. Indeed the nuns did not operate on any discriminatory basis and seem to have taken in any women who came to their doors. It is interesting to note that the small number of Protestants who entered the Good Shepherd asylum in Belfast were converted to Catholicism before they departed again.

Using the information provided in these registers and uniting it with the information available from the Lock hospital and police records it is possible to produce a general profile of the life of a prostitute. It can be taken for granted that these women were poor. Although no occupational category is listed in the asylum registers, such a column was used in prison registers; the majority of women imprisoned for prostitution were accorded no occupational status. In the census registers for 1901,[103] asylum inmates were generally

---

[100] Penitent no. 346, MS Register of the Asylum (RSC, Donnybrook).
[101] Penitent no. 721, MS Register of the Asylum (RSC, Donnybrook).
[102] MS Register of the Asylum (GSC, Limerick).
[103] MS census records, 1901 (PRO, Dublin).

listed as penitents or laundresses. This latter status would have reflected their position in the refuge rather than refer to a position previously held outside the asylum. What is obvious also from these sources of information is that most of the women had migrated to large centres of population from country areas. For example, of the seventy women admitted to the Westmoreland Lock Hospital in January, 1867, only twenty-eight were natives of Dublin city or county, although the remainder had Dublin addresses.[104] Likewise a large percentage of the inmates of the Magdalen asylums had been born outside large towns or cities. These women had therefore migrated to large towns and cities seeking occupations or indeed with the intention of going on the street. Since these women have left us no record of their own, we can only assume what their intentions were. Being, as we have seen, almost totally illiterate there were very few options open to them. Manufacturing industry offered few opportunities in Ireland and where women found work in factories it normally proved to be a tedious, harsh and badly paid means of earning a livelihood. The largest opening for women would, of course, have been domestic service. This was not a very attractive choice for many women since the lives of domestic servants were extremely confining and they too were badly paid.[105] Prostitution, then, may have been seen as a legitimate means of earning a relatively large amount of money without excess toil. It also allowed the women a certain degree of independence. There is no reference, in the existing records, regarding the presence of pimps in these women's lives and they may have had a greater control over their own fate than many other working women.

Another interesting feature of the Lock hospital and prison records is the recurrence of residence in the same areas of Dublin city. Moore Street, Mary's Lane and Purdon Street appear as addresses frequently given for arrested or hospitalised women. Like the 'wrens of the Curragh' they may have had their own community support networks. It appears that it was police policy to restrict the area of prostitution to certain streets and alleys and that women who removed themselves to such areas suffered less harassment from the authorities.

As we have already seen many women had given up the trade by

---

[104] General register of patients, Westmoreland Lock Hospital, vol. 4, 1857–68 (RCPI).
[105] See Mona Hearn, *Below Stairs: Domestic Service Remembered in Dublin and Beyond, 1880–1922* (Dublin, 1993).

the time they had reached forty and were most active in their twenties and thirties. Of the women who entered, and remained, in the refuges the majority had either entered very young, at sixteen, or were in their late thirties. It would seem then that the latter group had given up their life on the streets and purposely entered the refuges with the intention of 'retiring'. Unless they had saved enough money to establish a business, or had married there was very little choice for them other than the workhouse. Many of the women who entered and left the refuges on a regular basis were in their twenties and thirties and were obviously using the homes as a temporary refuge from their occupation. One other fact which emerges from the evidence of the registers is that the majority of women involved were without an immediate family. Most often both parents were dead and in some few instances parents had emigrated without taking their children with them. The home was often disrupted also by the death of one parent with the surviving parent remarrying and in a number of cases it seems that the children of the first marriage were not welcome in the new home. The disruption of the family and migration to large centres of population would have removed the woman from the constraints of family life and expectations. The need to support herself and perhaps the desire to be independent may have made prostitution a viable option in a world where there was little else a woman could do to maintain an existence. Even if prostitution was a chosen career, it was, as we have seen, also a hazardous one.

In terms of rehabilitation it is easier to judge the success rate of the religious run asylums than their lay counterparts. If we take the women who were provided with situations, emigrated, entered a Magdalen class, returned home or entered another Magdalen asylum and those who died (the deaths recorded in the tables refer to those women who died while in the home) 1,926, or 18 per cent, of the women would be deemed reclaimed by the nuns. This percentage is probably much more accurate than that claimed by the lay asylums. Contact with the penitents was not maintained once they had left the asylums and neither lay nor religious refuges provided any after-care services for the women.

Life in the religious run homes was similar to that in the lay run establishments. Like their counterparts in the lay asylums the penitents were well looked after physically. Their diet especially was better than anything they could have managed outside the refuges.

The penitents' days were made up of work, prayer, silence and recreation. In the refuge run by the Sisters of Our Lady of Charity of Refuge the penitents addressed the nuns as mother and were referred to privately as children. In public and when being instructed the title penitent was always used in order to make the inmates realise its true meaning.[106] The penitent was not treated as an adult and had no control over her life in the refuge. The nuns organised her day and took away all the responsibility of decision making. Also within this refuge the women were never allowed to be left alone for a moment. In some of the religious run homes the penitents could also join a Magdalen class.[107] Within these homes the penitents were classed in three groups, the ordinary penitents, Children of Mary and the 'consecrated', which was also called the 'class of perseverance'. The women could move from one class to another by displaying piety and discipline. The highest class was that of the 'consecrated' or class of perseverance. The women who entered this class took a form of religious vow similar to that taken by the nuns themselves. If consecrated the penitents were expected to remain in the home for life and were given special privileges within the community. They also wore a habit similar to that worn by the lay sisters.[108] The nuns' own ideal of austerity and holiness was offered as the ideal for the rescued penitents, but they could never become 'real' nuns nor be totally integrated into the community. Those 'consecrated' remained part of the penitent community and were, by their example of piety, thought to influence other penitents for good. Although treated as children these women could never be full members of a religious family; the nuns kept their distance from their charges. 'The sisters must inspire the children (penitents) who are generally headstrong and obstinate, with confidence, without familiarising themselves with them in the slightest degree.'[109]

The nuns reached out to more penitents, numerically speaking, than did the lay women who ran the other asylums. In the annals of those convents to which asylums were attached there are many stories related of women who led a holy and penitent life within the refuges and great satisfaction was expressed by the nuns in the saving of these souls. These annals are full of anecdotes about the

---

[106] *Abstract Report*, p. 25.
[107] This system did not operate in those refuges run by the Sisters of Charity or the Sisters of Mercy.
[108] *Abstract Report*, pp. 26–7.   [109] Ibid., p. 25.

relationship between the nuns and the penitents. They generally refer to requests by penitents to leave and it is only the superior wit of the nun in charge which tricks them into remaining.

The social world of these refuges reproduced the patriarchal and class order of society in general. Women in the nineteenth century had a carefully defined sphere of action and this can be seen clearly in the operation of the Magdalen asylums. The women who ran these refuges played out their maternal role creating homes for the penitent 'child'. They sought to inculcate in the penitent the correct attitudes and behaviour expected of women in that age. Penitents were trained in deference and subordination in isolated refuges which shielded them from the world, the source of possible temptation. They stressed the importance of personal guilt and that only personal discipline could lead to salvation. Any individual expression of personality or sexuality was denied to the women in these refuges and this was in keeping with what was considered correct behaviour for all women at this time. Judging from the large numbers of women who left these refuges voluntarily, it is obvious that these standards were unacceptable for many.

The Catholic discourse on prostitution was informed by the virginal and spiritual natures attributed to female religious. For society both groups epitomised the extremes of womanhood. The sexual identity of nuns and of prostitutes rested on their opposition and their difference. A contemporary description of the arrival of a penitent at the gates of a religious run Magdalen asylum shows clearly this opposition:

with the tears of a penitent upon her young and sinful face, she turns to the portals of the church and there ... she finds the very ideal of purity – the highest, the grandest, the noblest of the Church's children. The woman who has never known the pollution of a single wicked thought – the woman whose virgin bosom has never been crossed by the shadow of a thought of sin! The woman breathing purity, innocence and grace receives the woman whose breath is the pestilence of hell![110]

Another description, written more than twenty-five years later reiterates this oppositional comparison: 'Innocence and guilt face to face ... the bright cheerfulness of unsullied virtue so near to the most abject wretchedness of multiplied sinfulness! The spotless lily side by

[110] Burke, *Vindication*, p. 21.

side with the foul smelling weed! The consecrated nun speaking to the polluted outcast.'[111]

There is a dramatic confrontation between purity and impurity within these asylums and the battle raged, often to be lost by the forces of respectability. Nuns and prostitutes would appear to be worlds apart but as women they were connected in a number of ways. One was through the definition of women in Irish society according to their sexual activity. There were four stereotypes: the nun, the mother, the spinster and the 'fallen' woman. Although the nun was the ideal, held out as a beacon by the Catholic hierarchy, there are unexpected parallels between the lives of nuns and prostitutes. Both were removed from 'normal' society. Nuns voluntarily removed themselves and were also physically isolated by the limits placed upon public access to their convents. Similarly 'fallen women' were often voluntary, and sometimes involuntary, outcasts in society and removed from the wider community. For example, prostitutes used to congregate in particular areas of towns and cities where they created their own community networks. Likewise there was almost no public access to prostitutes in the Magdalen asylums. The behaviour of both nuns and prostitutes was governed by men. Ultimate authority in convent life, and hence in Magdalen asylums, rested with priests and bishops. For prostitutes on the streets, authority in the shape of police officers governed their lives. There is a further similarity in the position of nuns and prostitutes within the Magdalen asylums. Both were denied individual expression of personality and sexuality, particularly in each other's company: nuns because of their strict vows of obedience and celibacy, prostitutes as a condition of their penitence.

Within both lay and religious run asylums and refuges no serious consideration was given as to the causes of prostitution, or at least there is no evidence to suggest that any such discussion took place, and the only cure seemed to be to attempt to rescue the fallen. None of the women who ran these refuges appears to have played any role in the Contagious Diseases Acts agitation, a campaign which attempted to alter, to some extent, women's perception of their role in society and which suggested that illicit sexual behaviour on the part of men was a threat to society and to women's place in it.

[111] Anon., *Magdalens of High Park*, p. 179. See also Clear, *Nuns*, pp. 153–5.

THE CONTAGIOUS DISEASES ACTS: EFFECT AND RESPONSE

In 1864 parliament passed the first of three statutes which permitted the compulsory inspection of prostitutes for venereal disease in certain military camps in both England and Ireland.[112] The three Acts of 1864, 1866 and 1869 were introduced to control the spread of venereal disease among the soldiery. In Ireland the areas designated 'subjected districts' were Cork, Cobh and the Curragh camp. In effect the acts subjected women who were on the street to arbitrary and compulsory medical examination. If the woman inspected was infected she was forcibly detained in a Lock hospital for a period of up to nine months and registered as a prostitute. There was no similar check on men. As a result of the introduction of the Acts Lock hospitals were established in both Cork and the Curragh in 1869.

Evidence of the effects of the CDAs in Ireland is contradictory. Numerous commissions, to judge the effects and effectiveness of the Acts, were conducted from 1869 to 1884. Depending on the stance taken by the person giving the evidence the Acts were reported to have reduced the numbers of prostitutes operating in the designated areas and led to the reclamation of many women who were forced into the Lock hospitals, or, they encouraged women to remain in the trade and merely drove the vice more underground, without reducing the number of people suffering from venereal diseases. Evidence to the commissions in this country came solely from men, mainly clerics, medical doctors or those who claimed to have an interest in the subject. No Irish woman was invited to give evidence. It is impossible to gauge the accuracy of the information relating to either the decline or increase in prostitution put forward by the witnesses. In Cobh, in 1874, there were, according to census returns, only 6 prostitutes operating in the town, which seems to be a highly

[112] For the operation and resistance to the CDAs in England see J.R. Walkowitz, *Prostitution and Victorian Society: Women, Class and the State* (Cambridge, 1980). Walkowitz, 'The making of an outcast group: prostitution and working women in nineteenth-century Plymouth and Southampton' in Martha Vicinus (ed.), *A Widening Sphere: Changing Roles of Victorian Women* (London, 1977); Walkowitz, 'Male vice and female virtue; feminism and the politics of prostitution in nineteenth-century Britain' in A. Sninton, Christine Stansell and Sharon Thompson (eds.), *Desire: the Politics of Sexuality* (London, 1984); J.R. Walkowitz with D.J. Walkowitz, "We are not beasts of the field"; prostitution and the poor in Plymouth and Southampton under the Contagious Diseases Acts' in M.S. Hartman and Lois Banner (eds.), *Clio's Consciousness Raised: New Perspectives on the History of Women* (New York, 1974).

unlikely figure. In Cork the number of prostitutes known to the police was reported to be 116, and in the Curragh to be 57. The *Medical Enquirer* noted in 1876 that the number of prostitutes in Cork had increased from 90 in 1866 to 114 in 1875. It also stated that the incidence of venereal disease had risen in the city since the introduction of the Acts.[113] Dr Curtis, who was a visiting surgeon to Cork Lock hospital asserted that when the Acts came into force in Cork,

nearly 400 phrynes of the lowest type nightly paraded the chief thoroughfares, so sunk in vice that one could hardly fancy them human beings. Of the large number of prostitutes [400] there now remain in the district but 181 of which latter there are usually in hospital, prison and workhouses 104, leaving the actual number at present in Cork, Queens town and district 10 miles but 77 at large.[114]

It seems unlikely that the number of prostitutes diminished significantly with the introduction of the Acts; since prostitution resulted above all from poverty and was a means of earning a livelihood, and the conditions for the gainful employment of women had not improved in any dramatic way in the 1870s. What the Acts probably did was to force the women to be more secretive about their occupation without diminishing their activity.

Opposition to the Acts arose for a number of reasons. Their implementation was seen, by some groups, as an interference with civil liberties and by others as the recognition and support of vice by the state. The National Association for the Repeal of the Contagious Diseases Acts had a large and active membership of women and one of the chief reasons they opposed the Acts was because they applied solely to women, leaving men untouched.[115] For them the implementation of the Acts marked the legitimation of the double standard of sexual morality which existed in society. In England a number of associations were established to enforce the repeal of the CDAs. Amongst these were the National Association for the Repeal of the Contagious Diseases Acts, formed in 1869, and the Ladies National Association, formed also in 1869; both of these organisations had branches in Ireland. By 1871 three branches of the LNA had been established, in Belfast, Dublin and Cork. Both Isabella Tod and Anna Haslam were involved in the campaign from the beginning and Tod also served on the executive committee of the

---

113 *The Medical Enquirer* (October 1877), pp. 133–6. 114 *The Shield*, 15 April 1871.
115 Walkowitz, *Prostitution*.

London based LNA until 1889 when Haslam took her place.[116]
They both served on the general council of the NARCDA, although
this society was run by men,[117] and women council members had
little impact on policy.

The LNA, in Ireland, was a very localised and small affair.
Throughout its active period, from 1871 to 1885, it never had more
than forty-nine subscribers, the majority of whom were residents of
Dublin, Cork and Waterford.[118] Although the association was small
its very existence marked a new departure for Irishwomen. For the
first time they were willing to discuss openly matters pertaining to
sexual morality and to initiate a public campaign to question and
alter the sexual double standard which existed. In England there
was a certain degree of hostility towards women's activism in this
area[119] and although there is no direct evidence of such hostility
towards women activists in Ireland, the size of the association
indicates how few were willing to be associated with such a campaign. One witness, before the select committee on the effects of the
Contagious Diseases Acts, in 1871, a Catholic priest, when asked if
women were involved in any way against the Acts stated, 'there are
a great many ladies who exert themselves very much and we Catholic clergy do not approve of their putting placards before young
females inviting them to read these acts of which women never heard
before'.[120] That the matter was a delicate one even for the women
involved is revealed in a number of instances. Mrs Henry Wigham
who spoke at a drawing room meeting in Dublin in 1880, sympa-
thised 'with the natural repugnance felt by women in approaching
so loathsome a subject', but she urged that women 'must lay aside
our tastes and inclinations, and the veil of blissful ignorance in
which we indolently shroud ourselves, and come face to face with
the evil in its most repellent forms'.[121] Those women who played an
active role in the association clearly were very courageous. That
some women were either embarrassed or wary of working with men
in this area can be seen in the fact that whereas the original
committee of the NARCDA in Dublin was a mixed one, in 1878 a

---

[116] Annual reports, Ladies' National Association (hereafter LNA), 1871, 1889.
[117] Annual report of the National Association for the Repeal of the Contagious Diseases Acts, 1880–1.
[118] Annual reports, LNA, 1871–86.   [119] Walkowitz, *Prostitution*, pp. 137–9.
[120] *Report Select Committee ... CDAs 1871*, HC 1871 (C.408–1), xix, Q. 18,798.
[121] *The Shield*, 21 February 1880.

sub-committee, for women only, was established as 'some ladies', it was stated, 'are not yet prepared to join a mixed committee'.[122]

The function of the LNA in Ireland was to support the aims of the parent body in London. In practice this meant raising funds, organising petitions to parliament against the Acts, attempting to alter public opinion by distributing pamphlets and papers on the subject and by holding meetings. The majority of meetings were held in the drawing rooms of activists and were attended by women only. These meetings always began and ended with prayers.[123] A number of petitions, favouring repeal, were forwarded to London and between 1870 and 1881 these mustered 85,759 signatures. Of the 88 petitions forwarded, repeal associations sent 16 with 85 signatures, and groups of unidentified Irishwomen sent in 9 petitions with 8,770 signatures. It is likely that these were organised by the LNA. Four petitions, with 188 signatures, were sent in favour of the Acts.[124] In 1877 the Belfast branch of the LNA claimed that the enlargement of the Lock hospital in that city, which patients entered voluntarily since the city was not one of the 'subjected districts', resulted from the committee's attempts to improve the treatment of women afflicted with venereal diseases. They were thus proving that individual action could prevent the spread of such diseases and that the CDAs were essentially unnecessary.[125] The Belfast branch of the LNA was active in trying to ensure that the Acts would not be extended to that city. They claimed that their efforts in bringing the operation of the Acts to the attention of the public had averted 'the terrible danger and degradation of being subjected to the direct operation of the Acts'.[126] They saw the implementation of the Acts as an affront 'to the decency and purity of society – the dignity and independence of every woman in the land'.[127]

The parent body in London was quite anxious to extend its range of activities in Ireland and sent a number of its agents and members to give public talks on the subject there.[128] In 1878 the annual

---

122 *The Shield*, December 1878.
123 See annual reports of the LNA, 1871–88, for numerous references to these drawing room meetings.
124 *Report Select Committee . . . CDAs 1882*, HC 1882 (340), ix, appendix, 596.
125 Annual report, LNA, 1877, p. 16.
126 *To the Members of the Belfast Committee for the Repeal of the Contagious Diseases Acts* (Belfast, 1878), p. 1.
127 Ibid., p. 2.
128 In 1874 Mr Burgess, an organising agent employed by the English LNA, visited Ireland and arranged meetings in Cork. Another agent, a Mr Bligh, organised a meeting in

general meeting of the association was held in Dublin, and was attended by Josephine Butler. The women held their own meeting in the Antient Concert Rooms and a public conference was organised, for a mixed audience, in the Rotunda. Amongst the speakers at the latter was Sir James Stansfeld, MP, one of the leading advocates for repeal, and Butler herself also spoke. When Stansfeld rose to speak there were cries that the women in the audience should be put out and a number of young men began to disrupt the meeting; the police had to be called to clear the hall and the meeting had to be abandoned. A further meeting was held on the following day, again with a mixed audience.[129] The committee blamed the disruption on a group of disorderly students but it is clear that the campaign was unpopular in some quarters.

The women who were active in the movement in Ireland were predominantly Quakers. Anna Haslam, Mrs Henry Wigham, Mary Edmundson, Mrs Henry Allen and all the women in the Webb family were subscribers.[130] Isabella Tod was a Presbyterian, and it appears that very few, if any, of the women were Catholics. One of the characteristics of repeal activists was the involvement of members of the same family in the campaign. Thus, for example, Henry Wigham, Henry Allen, Alfred Webb and Thomas Haslam, all active in the NARCDA, amongst others, were married, or related to, members of the LNA.[131] The degree of such family support probably encouraged activists to continue in their campaign. In fact Anna Haslam's husband Thomas published a pamphlet on the Contagious Diseases Acts in Ireland. In it he analyses the causes of prostitution as lying in some degree in the lack of occupations open to women and the poor pay of some men which does not allow them to marry; drink is also a factor and society's attitudes to women who are 'the victims of seduction' further complicate the problem. But he maintains that 'it is men's unchastity and men's injustice which are mainly responsible for this crying wrong'. The CDAs were, he wrote, 'a dangerous piece of legislative bungling' and he called for their immediate repeal or radical amendment.[132]

    Dublin and later travelled to Carlow, Wicklow, Wexford, Waterford and Limerick, where he put up posters against the Acts. Annual report, LNA, 1874, p. 13.

129 For details of the meetings see *The Shield* (16 November 1878), pp. 273–80.

130 See annual reports, LNA 1871–86; NARCDA 1880–1.

131 Ibid.

132 T.J. Haslam, *A Few Words on Prostitution and the Contagious Diseases Acts* (Dublin, 1870).

Some of the women involved in the Contagious Diseases Acts campaign had philanthropic interests, though it is impossible because of lack of information to discern the philanthropic interests, if any, of the majority of those women who supported the LNA in Ireland. Both Anna Haslam and Isabella Tod were to the forefront in campaigning for women's rights in Ireland. Haslam established a suffrage society in Dublin in 1876. Indeed, in an interview she gave to the *Irish Citizen*, in 1914, she stated that the fight for the repeal of the CDAs 'threw the suffrage movement back for ten years, we were all so absorbed in it'.[133] Tod was a temperance activist, suffragist and campaigner for the extension of educational opportunities for women and was later involved in the Prison Gate Mission in Belfast. Mary Edmundson had been active in the anti-slavery movement and later helped to found the Prison Gate Mission in Dublin.[134] A number of the other LNA activists were to become active in the suffrage movement. A belief in the equality of women was one of the common bonds uniting the members of the LNA, and their interests extended to improving the social and political status of women generally.

The LNA in Britain worked on the premise that one standard of sexual morality, for both men and women, should exist. This campaign against the CDAs itself was a moral rather than a social crusade. Like the philosophy espoused by rescue workers, self-discipline and a higher moral standard were advocated by the repeal associations. The recognition and articulation of the sexual double standard which operated was fully expressed in this campaign. A higher moral standard for men particularly was demanded. Women, it was believed, naturally possessed this high standard and it was the ideal which they expected of men. Isabella Tod, in a speech to the Christian Women's Union, articulated the problem and proposed the solution;

the greatest and most consistent force at work, both in lowering the moral tone throughout all classes, and in bringing about not only individual acts of vice, but in degrading a number of women into a class where occupation is vice, is that unspeakably wicked idea that most men may be expected so to sin, and that in them it is a venial offence ... We must utterly refuse ... to acknowledge the existence of any such class of men, in any rank, as inevitable; or any class of women to meet their horrible demands ... We owe a duty to men ... to awaken their consciences to pull down the selfish

[133] *Irish Citizen*, 21 March 1914.　　[134] *EWR*, 1880.

screen which society has set up ... We have the power of the newly awakened conscience of women, as to their duty to protect their poorer and weaker sisters, and to withstand and enlighten those who would seek to assail them.[135]

The work of the women in the LNA was also used by Tod to support women's claim for the vote. The success of the repeal movement had, according to Tod, shown how effective women's activism could be. 'It was not only for the help which women must give to women, but even more, for the discharge of their special duty to the whole state – a duty which God has entrusted to them, and which no man can do – women are bound to demand their immediate admission within the electorate.'[136]

One important aspect introduced by the LNA was an attempt to analyse why women became prostitutes. They accepted that prostitution was the result of poverty and the Irish activists in the LNA, with their involvement in societies to improve the educational, work and political prospects of women, were hoping to improve conditions for all women. It is interesting to note that although the English branch of the LNA advocated that its members become involved in rescue work none of the Irish activists was so involved.[137] Tod's and Edmundson's activism in this area was confined to the fate of female ex-prisoners, who were not necessarily prostitutes and none of these activists are listed in any of the committees of the rescue homes which existed. The impact of the repeal campaign on Irishwomen, in general, is impossible to gauge. The Acts were repealed in 1886 and in Ireland the membership of the LNA had declined steadily in the latter years of the campaign with only ten subscribers from 1884.[138] Because of their religious affiliations and indeed their political and social activism, the women of the Irish branch of the LNA were unrepresentative of Irishwomen in general. They were part of a reform tradition rather than the more common benevolent tradition which the majority of women philanthropists subscribed to in the last century.

The LNA in England argued it had set the pace for the social purity movement established by Ellice Hopkins, the White Cross Army, founded in England in 1883, in an attempt to improve the

[135] *EWR*, 15 October 1883, pp. 438–40.
[136] Isabella M.S. Tod, 'The new crusade and women's suffrage', reprinted from the *Pall Mall Gazette*, c.1885.
[137] Walkowitz, *Prostitution*, p. 132. [138] Annual report, LNA 1885.

sexual behaviour of men.[139] Only men were recruited and they pledged, among other things, to ' treat all women with respect . . . to endeavour to put down all indecent language and jests . . . to maintain the laws of purity as equally binding on men and women'.[140] This society quickly became associated with the Church of England and it made its first appearance in Dublin in 1885. Hopkins herself visited Dublin in 1885 and her rousing speech was claimed to have initiated the formation of the Dublin White Cross Vigilance Association.[141] Besides attending lectures, members of the association engaged in 'patrol work'. In effect this meant keeping watch outside known 'evil houses' and through such harassment forcing them to close. In 1888 one brothel owner, it was reported, offered a bribe of £1,000 to the members of a patrol if they would desist in watching his premises.[142] Also in 1888 the committee of the association succeeded in successfully prosecuting one hotel owner for keeping a brothel in the city.[143] In 1891 the association claimed to have fourteen branches in Dublin with 530 members.[144] In another visit, in 1893, Hopkins revitalised the WCVA and a group of about twenty-four members accosted customers leaving the city's brothels.[145] Through the activities of this movement thirty-five brothels were claimed to have been closed down and Mecklenburgh Street cleared of prostitutes in the 1890s.[146] These societies were run and organised by men, and women had nothing at all to do with them. These societies, like the refuges, were treating the symptoms rather than the causes of prostitution.

Attempts to inculcate purity among men were also carried out by Catholic agencies, particularly through confraternities. For example, the case previously cited of the priests' campaign to close brothels in Cork city, was carried through with the aid of men from

139 R.M. Barrett, *Ellice Hopkins: A Memoir* (London,1908), passim.
140 Annual report, Dublin White Cross Association, 1898.
141 Barrett, *Hopkins*, p. 166.   142 *The Vigilance Record*, April 1888, p. 35.   143 Ibid.
144 Ibid., April 1891.
145 Edward J. Bristow, *Vice and Vigilance: Purity Movements in Britain Since 1700* (Dublin, 1977), p. 104.
146 Ibid., p. 163. These claims are probably exaggerated. The Mecklenburgh Street area was a notorious red light district in the city. The police rarely interfered in the business conducted in this area and it was only with the campaign organised by Frank Duff and the Legion of Mary in 1921 that prostitution declined in this district. For further accounts of the work of the WCVA in Ireland see, *The Vigilance Record*, March 1888, p. 21; February 1888, p. 12; 15 April 1887, pp. 19, 51; August 1889, p. 77; April 1890, p. 29; April 1892, p. 23; May 1893, pp. 28–9; *The Sentinel*, June 1892, p. 75; June 1894, p. 79.

a confraternity.[147] The energies of Irishwomen generally in the control of sexual immorality centred almost completely on rescue work. This was, in general, a defensive activity which made little social impact save for the few women who were supposedly 'reclaimed'. Refuges in a sense bolstered the sexual double standard by concentrating all their energies on the victim rather than the seducer. The introduction of the Criminal Law Amendment Act of 1885, which gave the police power to summarily convict brothel keepers and allowed imprisonment for repeated offences in this area, went some way to reduce the vice in Dublin. The WCVA, whose members worked closely with the police, took credit for the improvement in the streets of the capital.[148] The decline in prostitution noticeable in the police statistics may reflect some influence of the purity movements. It is much more likely that raising educational standards, increased work opportunities and declining population were more influential. There were also a myriad of other societies which may have helped reduce the number of prostitutes operating in the country. A number of institutions were established which took in poor girls and trained them for employment in an effort to prevent them from falling into vice. An analysis of their role completes the picture of moral guardianship pioneered by women in the last century.

A number of what could be termed clubs were established in Dublin from the 1870s to provide recreational facilities for working girls. The principal objective was to provide a room where such girls could meet for 'instruction or recreation' where they could pass their free time and be 'saved from the temptation of passing these hours in places and in a society which would be for them the high road to ruin and shame'.[149] The scheme was initiated by an unknown Protestant English woman and later Catholics were urged to introduce a similar scheme. The Catholic plan was to go further than providing recreational facilities and the best proposal was thought to be to establish a residential home where such girls could reside.[150] In 1880 St Martha's Home was founded. This not only provided accommodation but also acted as a registry where young women could seek employment.[151] This type of institute was, of course,

---

[147] See n 14 above.   [148] *The Vigilance Record*, 15 April 1887, p. 19.

[149] Mrs Charles Martin, 'Our young work girls', *The Irish Monthly* (1879), p. 469.

[150] Anon. 'St Martha's Home', *The Irish Monthly*, 10 (1882), pp. 157–60.

[151] Ibid., p. 158.

similar to those operated by the Girls' Friendly Society and the Young Women's Christian Association.[152]

One other aspect of women's work in the moral sphere can be seen in the establishment of societies to protect unmarried mothers. Again the philosophy behind such homes was to prevent the women from pursuing a life on the streets. The Dublin Hospital Girls' Aid Association was founded in 1880 by a group of Protestant women.[153] The association was managed by women but they also organised a 'consulting committee of gentlemen' whose functions were not outlined. The association appears to have developed from the practice of hospital visitation. The function of the ladies' visiting committee was to enquire into all cases of unmarried girls, under the age of twenty-one, who were about to become mothers. If the young woman agreed to be assisted the ladies firstly tried to return her to her family, and if that failed, to secure some form of shelter and secure employment for her. Without such assistance, it was believed, such women had little option but to turn to a life of prostitution. The women of the association felt it would be better 'if they were rescued before entering upon such a career'.[154] This, of course, implies that by having an illegitimate child the woman had, in some way, already 'fallen'. The Rotunda Girls' Aid Society was founded in 1880 and may have taken the lead set by the DHGAA.[155] It is interesting to note that the reports of this society were published for private circulation only. Its work was similar to that of the DHGAA. The society organised nurses for the children of these women, for which the women paid a small fee, and which allowed them the freedom to earn a living.

As with many charitable institutions, not every unmarried mother was allowed to use the facilities of this society, it was, as the report stated, 'only those who fell for the first time, only to those who gave promise of future blameless lives, only those who were prepared to do their part in supporting their unhappy offspring, has the society extended its helpful hand'.[156] Whether these rules were always enforced remains unknown. In the year from March 1887 to March 1888, fifty-six women and their children were catered for. Of this number thirty-five women were placed in service, four were helped by the society to emigrate to America and one to England; six

---

[152] See chapter 4.   [153] *EWR*, 15 September 1881, pp. 414–16.   [154] Ibid., p. 415.
[155] Annual reports of the Rotunda Girls' Aid Society (hereafter RGAS), 1887–8, 1892.
[156] Annual report, RGAS, 1892.

women returned to their homes, two married and three were receiving hospital treatment. Two women refused to make regular payments for the keep of their children and two other women abandoned their offspring with the society. These latter two children were placed immediately in the workhouse where one of them later died.[157] Indeed the care provided for the children was hardly the best and the mortality rate was very high. In 1892 out of eighty-three children put out to nurse by the society at least twenty-three died.[158] It is not clear, from the available information, what the denominational affiliations of the women who ran this society were. Like the work carried out by the women in the asylums and refuges, that which concerned unmarried mothers was also conducted out of the public gaze.

In general, and especially in the latter half of the century, women were playing a major role in providing for the needs of 'outcast' women in society. The work and philosophy of the societies and institutions was profoundly conservative. Despite this conservatism there was some attempt made to meet the practical needs of women who were, by their habits of life, ostracised from society at large. The help provided, whether in Magdalen asylums or societies for unmarried mothers, was geared towards moral betterment. The work was rarely publicised and the intention was to reform the women who had, by their actions, moved beyond the pale of acceptable behaviour. The women who engaged in this campaign of moral reform felt it to be their duty to rescue these unfortunate women and to mould them into characters who would practise the virtues of the ideal woman. The practical implications of their work should not be undervalued. Although they may not have questioned the roles assigned to women, they did, in some ways, make life more comfortable and secure for those women who lived on the edge of society.

It is clear that the range and extent of rescue agencies and refuges expanded quite dramatically during the nineteenth century. It is also obvious that much more control was exerted over the lives of 'outcast' women at the end of the nineteenth century than was apparently exerted at the beginning of the century. Attempts to separate and classify women in moral terms developed from attitudes expressed towards the correct expression of sexuality. Women who found their way to Magdalen asylums were immediately label-

---

[157] Annual report, RGAS, 1888–9.   [158] Annual report, RGAS, 1892.

led. Within workhouses also attempts to classify and label women are evident.[159] Prostitutes mixing freely with other women came to be seen a source of 'contamination' in all workhouses. The poor law commissioners commented on this subject on a number of occasions and definite steps were taken by guardians to ensure that no mixing would take place. Married women were also separated from single women in the Lock hospital at Westmoreland Street. The work of women philanthropists and female religious in the area of rescue and reform played an important role in constructing an ideology of proper behaviour for women in public. By the end of the century there were homes and institutions which catered for all groups of 'outcast' women; whether prostitutes, unmarried mothers, female ex-prisoners or drunks, few could escape the 'rescue' net.

[159] See, for example, the discussions which took place at the board of guardian meetings for the Clonmel workhouse. Minute book, Clonmel Union, January 1857–July 1857, County Museum, Clonmel, County Tipperary. The poor law inspector who covered the Carlow/ Kilkenny area noted 'As far as can be done, females who live a life of open profligacy are separated, when in the infirmary, from females of good character . . . In Kilkenny Union, a separate apartment and yard are appropriated for prostitutes.' For further examples see *Eighth annual report, Poor Law Commissioners for Ireland, 1855*.

CHAPTER 5

Prison work

'No one', argued Mary Carpenter, the great prison reformer, 'can calculate the amount of crime which may be saved to the country by the rescue of a single woman from a vicious life.'[1] Her words did not go unheeded in Ireland either by prison reformers or philanthropists who sought to rescue ex-prisoners from returning to their 'vicious lives'. Women prisoners benefited from the reforms implemented in the Irish prison system throughout the nineteenth century. Much of this reform was brought about by men. Female philanthropists had little impact on prison policy but they did play an important role as prison visitors and also set up independent refuges to cater for the needs of ex-prisoners. Several areas are of interest in relation to Irish women prisoners: their conditions within the general prison system and the attempts made to rehabilitate them within that system; the origins and implementation of a separate prison system for women; the development of an intermediary prison for women convicts and finally the establishment of refuges, by philanthropists, for women who had left the prison system. Like so many other areas of the social history of the nineteenth century the incarceration of women in prisons deserves to be looked at in greater detail. The following gives only a general impression of the situation as a background for the initiatives taken by women philanthropists in this area. Before looking at the formal prison system some evidence regarding the level of female criminality in nineteenth-century Ireland will place the subject in context.

WOMEN AND IMPRISONMENT IN NINETEENTH-CENTURY IRELAND

Women, on average, made up approximately 40 per cent of those apprehended for criminal offences in the Dublin Metropolitan

[1] Mary Carpenter, *Our Convicts*, 2 vols. (London, 1864), II, p. 205.

Police District from 1840 to 1890. For example, in 1840, the total number of persons arrested was 36,758 and of this number, 17,282 were women. In 1850 the total number of apprehensions was 64,244, of which 25,371 were women. This was the general pattern, in this district, throughout the century. Although officially there were five categories used to distinguish offences they can be divided into three main groups: crimes against the person, which included murder, attempted murder, manslaughter and assault; crimes against property, which included larceny and forgery; and a third category which covered crimes such as being drunk and disorderly, prostitution and vagrancy.[2] This last category will be referred to as crimes against behaviour. The major types of crime committed by women fell into this last category and women's criminal activity, judging from the available statistics, seems rarely to have involved serious crimes against the person. Using the three categories of crime outlined above throughout the period 1840–90 it is clear that for both men and women, it is the third category, relating to behavioural offences, which accounts for the highest number of arrests. In 1840, 75 per cent of arrests for women were in this category, with the figure for men being 73 per cent. In 1890, this category accounts for 87 per cent of female arrests and 84 per cent of male arrests. Of the 438 offences committed against the person, by women, in 1840, 83.3 per cent were for assaults and the remaining 16.7 per cent offences ranged from obstructing the police to concealing the birth of infants. Similarly in 1890, of the 674 women arrested in the same category, over 95 per cent were arrested for assault and the remainder for other offences.[3]

If these figures are accurate (and we must consider the possibility that crimes were underreported), then women were not imprisoned for committing violent crimes against the person to any great extent. Offences against property in 1840 accounted for 22 per cent of female arrests and in 1890 it was just 6 per cent. Women who committed crimes against the person and offences against property made up, on average, over the period covered, approximately 19 per cent of the total number of women arrested. The bulk of these offences for

---

[2] The official categories were as follows; offences against the person, offences against property with violence, offences against property without violence, forgery and crimes against currency, and lastly, other crimes, which covered all offences committed in the preceding categories.

[3] Dublin Metropolitan Police Statistics, 1838–90.

Table 5.1. *Total committals to prison in Ireland, 1870–1890*

Year	Male	Female	Total
1870	29,935	16,154	46,089
1880	24,615	13,892	38,507
1890	29,173	17,236	46,409

Source: Judicial Statistics (Ireland), 1871 [C. 443], lxiv; 1881 [C. 3028], xcv; 1890–91 [C. 6511], xciii

which women were arrested come under the third category, behavioural offences. In 1840, of the 12,984 women arrested, just over 90 per cent were taken up for either prostitution, vagrancy or being drunk and disorderly. The same percentage held for women apprehended in 1890.[4] Women, who deviated in their personal behaviour from acceptable moral standards, therefore, swelled the ranks of arrested women. Women, more so than men, were likely to be arrested on morality offences than on any other charges. Table 5.1 shows the number of men and women committed to prisons in Ireland for the period 1870 to 1890. These figures represent all those imprisoned in large prisons, bridewells, what were termed lock ups, minor local prisons, lunatic asylums, industrial and reformatory schools. It is clear from table 5.1 that women were incarcerated on a wide scale throughout the century. In deciphering the mass of official statistics available on criminals the pattern for the apprehension of women in the country as a whole is similar to that which we saw for the Dublin area: the majority were arrested and imprisoned for behavioural offences.

From the evidence available in official sources about the occupations of imprisoned women it is clear that the majority of female criminals lived economically marginal lives. In 1870, for example, of the total of 14,698 women imprisoned in the larger prisons, 10 per cent had no occupations, 54 per cent gave their occupation as prostitute, 15 per cent as domestic servants or charwomen, 4 per cent stated they kept shops or were dealers, which probably means they were street traders, and only 17 per cent were skilled workers, factory workers or clerks.[5] The primary occupational status of women imprisoned was prostitution. Criminal activity by women

[4] Ibid.
[5] *Judicial Statistics (Ireland)*: 1871 [C. 443], lxiv; 1881 [C. 3028], xcv; 1890–1 [C. 6511] xciii.

Women and philanthropy

Table 5.2. *Occupations of women incarcerated in Ireland, 1870–1890*

Year	No occupation	Domestic servant	Charwoman/ needlewoman	Factory worker	Skilled worker	Shop woman/ clerk	Profes- sional worker	Shop- keeper/ dealer	Prostitute
1870	1,498	652	1,518	170	109	5		542	7,970
1880	5,869	625	1,203	367	85	12	4	1,164	4,553
1890	2,774	884	1,182	552	223	34	6	1,830	7,213

Source: Judicial Statistics (Ireland): 1871 [C. 443], lxiv; 1881 [C. 3028], xcv; 1890–91 [C. 6511], xciii

was to a great extent economically motivated. Few of the occupations listed by female criminals, with perhaps the exception of prostitution, would have provided women with a reasonable income. Throughout the century women had limited opportunities to earn money and of course the wages paid to women, whether as domestic servants, needlewomen or even factory workers, placed them in a marginal economic position in society.

Prison reformers, throughout the century, were very concerned about the numbers of women incarcerated and the level of female criminality. Looking at this objectively, and in the light of the above figures, we can discern that this interest, in its most fundamental state, was a concern with the behaviour of women. Any deviation by women from imposed moral and social expectations, was a matter of concern for philanthropists generally. In the traditional ideology women were the stabilising forces in the family and thus contributed to the stability of civilisation itself. Any deviancy on the part of women could therefore have a detrimental effect on society at large. It was considered to be of utmost importance then that women should be rehabilitated and returned to their proper sphere in society, as 'good' wives and mothers.

THE REFORM OF PRISON CONDITIONS

In the early years of the nineteenth century all Irish prisons were mixed institutions in that women, men and children were incarcerated together; the only distinction made being the provision of separate wings for men and women. Conditions could be quite horrific with problems ranging from overcrowding, little or no sanitation, brutality with regard to punishments and the mixing of all criminals, whether for serious or minor offences, together with those who suffered from mental illnesses. Gaolers abused the system by charging fees to inmates for particular services such as the provision of bedding.[6] In 1819, the inspector of prisons, described Kilkenny prison as one of the better run establishments of its kind in the country. Here prisoners were allowed 5d worth of food per day from the prison authorities but they were also allowed to purchase their own food to supplement this meagre ration. The same inspector observed the presence of prisoners, mostly women, in the bridewell in Galway city, who were confined by chains on their legs. On further inquiry he discovered that the women had been committed to the gaol for being idle 'in the streets at night'. One woman had actually been confined in these conditions and for this offence for a year.[7] From the very beginning reformers were adamant that prisoners should be separated according to their sex. In 1839 it was required of all prisons that they operate separate wings for women and men and this appears to have been complied with. Elizabeth Fry, the prison reformer, went further and suggested that women be incarcerated in separate prisons and it was through her work in this field that the first all female prison was opened in Ireland at Mountjoy in 1858.

The British Society of Ladies for Promoting the Reformation of Female Prisoners was established in London in 1821, under Fry's direction. She was a Quaker, born in 1780, and her greatest work of philanthropy began when she visited Newgate prison in London, in 1813, and found that the conditions in which the women inmates lived were horrifying. In 1817, in association with twelve other women, the majority of them also Quakers, she established the Association for the Improvement of the Female Prisoners in Newgate.[8] Her original intention had been to influence the inmates of this prison to reform through religious instruction, but the conditions they lived under caused her, first of all, to attend to their physical circumstances. The association then attempted to bring about the reformation of the prisoners through the implementation of systematic discipline, religious instruction and education. The plan was that these changes would be brought about, under the direction of the ladies of the association, by organising the inmates

[6] *Report from the Select Committee on the State of Gaols 1819*, HC 1819 (579), vii, passim.
[7] Ibid., pp. 201, 203, 211–12.
[8] Prochaska, *Philanthropy*, pp. 145–6.

into an hierarchical system with various duties being delegated to each rank. The changes brought about in the prison, on a physical and behavioural level, were noted by the governors and those interested in prison reform and Fry urged the institution of other such associations throughout the British Isles.[9]

In 1825 Fry published her influential book, *Observations on the Siting, Superintendence and Government of Female Prisons*,[10] which advocated a separate prison system for women. Such a system, she believed, would allow women to be rehabilitated because it would allow them to be classified, according to their offences and ages, rather than simply on a gender basis. She also demanded that these prisons should be staffed and run by women. Fry had had her own difficulties with prison administrators and in this book she cautioned women who proposed to enter prisons as visitors, not to interfere with prison authorities. In this tract she also argued that women prisoners could be reformed and that it was through the work of women that such reformation could be best ensured. Work was stressed as a means of reformation and she also elaborated on a complex system of rewards which could be used to induce rehabilitation. Women convicted of crimes had to pass through four classes. In the first class were those women who had almost finished their sentences. The second and third class women would be given privileges and rewards on a lesser basis than those of the first class. Women in the fourth class were those considered to be 'hardened criminals' and who had undergone imprisonment on a number of previous occasions. It was hoped that these women could be raised to the higher classes.[11] Although Fry's schemes were abandoned in many of the English prisons where they were established, and indeed were never instituted in the majority, her work was to have a profound influence on the development of a women's prison system.[12]

It is difficult to establish when women first began to enter prisons

---

9 See Catherine Frazer, 'The origin and progress of "The British Ladies' Society for Promoting the Reformation of Female Prisoners", established by Mrs Fry in 1821', *Transactions of the National Association for the Promotion of Social Science* (1862), pp. 495–501. These guidelines were probably followed by the women's associations in Ireland.
10 Elizabeth Fry, *Observations on the Siting, Superintendance, and Government of Female Prisoners* (London, 1827).
11 Ibid., pp. 26, 31, 34 and passim.
12 See Estelle B. Freedman, *Their Sisters' Keepers: Women's Prison Reform in America, 1830–1930* (Ann Arbor, 1984), passim, for the impact of Fry's ideas on prison reform in America.

as visitors in Ireland but they were certainly active in this enterprise by the second decade of the nineteenth century. They did so, at this stage, under the auspices of the Association for the Improvement of Prisons and Prison Discipline in Ireland. The parent society operated from London and a branch was formed in Dublin in 1818. The society was managed by an all male committee but from the beginning ladies' committees were inaugurated to visit women prisoners. The purpose of the Association was to provide 'instruction ... [for] any who are willing to learn'.[13] By 1821 another society, the Association for Bettering the Condition of the Female Prisoners in Dublin, had been established and this was organised and managed by women. It seems to have developed from the work carried out by women in the AIPPDI but it is not clear what their connection to this society was, although accounts of the work of the women's association were reported in the annual reports of the AIPPDI.[14] It is clear from the evidence available, that the women's work was inspired by that carried out by Elizabeth Fry and they were well acquainted with the work the London association was doing. In the Richmond bridewell, women visitors instituted the reading of scripture and operated a Sunday school. Their work, it was reported, had brought 'an evident improvement in the appearance and habits of the female prisoners ... several of whom have learned the government of their tempers and are obedient, diligent, orderly and cleanly'.[15] In these early years the women visitors also brought about some small changes in prison policy. For example, the ladies' committee in Kilmainham jail reported, in 1821, that the Grand Jury had complied with some of their requests, namely the removal of the hangman from his residence in the centre of the women's ward and a ban on all male turnkeys from entering the women's section of the prison. By 1831 there were thirty-one women on this visiting committee making monthly visits to the jail.[16]

Visiting associations also existed outside Dublin. In Clonmel, women prisoners, under a matron and a ladies' committee, were employed in spinning, knitting, sewing and plain work. To facilitate

---

[13] Annual report, Association for the Improvement of Prisons and Prison Discipline in Ireland (hereafter AIPPDI), 1821, pp. 35–6. Complaints were made by the committee regarding the classification of prisoners, with young and old being housed together. It is not clear if the prison authorities took any notice of these complaints.
[14] See annual reports of AIPPDI, 1819–25.   [15] Annual report, AIPPDI, 1821, p. 35.
[16] Ibid., p. 32.

communication a number of ladies learned Irish in order to commu-
nicate with the women prisoners in the County Gaol in Waterford,
when it was discovered the prisoners only spoke that language.
Prison visiting could be a hazardous business. Even three years after
initiating a visiting scheme to Cork City Gaol the women often had
to wait outside until the governor could guarantee their safety
within the prison.[17] It is difficult to discover who these women
visitors were but it is certain that some of them were Quakers.
Enthusiasm for prison visiting appears to have declined gradually
from the late 1820s and many women found it an unrewarding task.
The activities of the women in the prisons was severely circum-
scribed. In Kilmainham jail, the women visitors reported that
'instruction is given as far as local circumstances will admit ...
However earnest their wishes the visitors regret they do not feel
themselves authorised to mention any striking instance of improvement.'[18] Similarly in the Richmond Bridewell the lady visitors
reported that in the 'sick wards ... the visitors are discouraged in
their desires to be useful'.[19] Whereas prison inspectors recognised the
usefulness of women visitors, particularly in the area of improving
discipline, prison governors never relinquished any power to them.

Nuns also played a major role in prison visiting. As visitors they
had access to prisons from the second decade of the century. Mother
Mary Aikenhead and Mother Catherine first visited Kilmainham
jail in 1821, at the request of the governor, to comfort two young
women who were sentenced to be executed.[20] The Sisters of Charity
afterwards continued visiting the women in that prison. In Cork, the
Sisters of Mercy visited the men's section of the city gaol from 1839,
access being granted through the intercession of the influential cleric
Dominick Murphy. The Sisters of Charity were engaged in
visitation at the county gaol from the 1830s.[21] The Sisters of Mercy,
in Limerick, visited the city and county gaols from 1842. They
undertook the religious instruction of the Catholic inmates. Even for
nuns, prison visiting was not always a rewarding task and the annals

---

[17] Annual report, Ladies' British Association for the Reformation of Female Prisoners, 1828,
p. 16; annual report, AIPPDI, 1824, p. 35.
[18] Annual report, AIPPDI, 1822, p. 33. The women blamed the lack of classification of the
prisoners for this.
[19] Annual report, AIPPDI, 1823, p. 32.
[20] Member of the Congregation, *Life and Work*, p. 53.
[21] Bolster, *Mercy in Cork*, p. 6. The priest, a Fr Murphy, was a personal friend of Catherine
McAuley, Mathieson, *Journal of a Tour*, p. 23.

of the Limerick convent noted that 'limited access and consequent bad discipline increased the difficulty of reclaiming the unfortunate creatures met therein'.[22] In Tralee, the Sisters of Mercy, who had established a convent in the town in 1854, began visiting the local gaol from 1855. These nuns provided religious instruction to the male inmates on Sundays. They visited the female inmates three times per week 'which proved to be of great benefit to the poor creatures'. These nuns were more concerned with the religious aspects of their visitation and there is no reference to the actual conditions endured by the inmates of the prison or whether any changes were brought about through the influence of the nuns. According to the convent annals, 'many conversions were brought about, not only of bad Catholics but even of Protestants, who though they could not be instructed there [in the prison] after their release they were prepared at the convent for baptism'.[23]

Nuns were not always welcomed in prisons and often prison officials did not aid their work. An enquiry into allegations of religious intolerance at Grangegorman female prison in 1851 dismissed them, but the investigating officer noted that 'grounds did exist for stating that there has not been at all times a desire to meet the views of the Sisters of Charity'. By the end of the century these sisters were also assisting the chaplains in the religious instruction of the Catholic prisoners in Mountjoy female prison.[24] After 1830 there are few details available regarding visitations by lay and religious women, but we can accept that women, both religious and lay, did continue to engage in such visitation on some scale as passing references are made to this work throughout the century, in the Reports of the Inspectors General on Prisons in Ireland.[25] For lay visitors the inability to alter prison conditions directly may have reduced their enthusiasm for visiting.

[22] Typescript of Annals of Mercy Convent, Limerick, 1844–59 (MC, Limerick).
[23] MS Annals of the Convent of Mercy, 1854–1927, one volume (MC, Tralee).
[24] R. Lohan, 'The treatment of women sentenced to transportation and penal servitude, 1790–1898' (M. Litt., TCD 1989), p. 229; *Reports from the Inspectors of Prisons (Ireland)*, 1898, xlvii, 30.
[25] These reports remark on the continued attendance of women visitors but no information regarding their work or influence is given. See, for example, fourteenth report of *Inspectors of Prisons*, 1836, xxxv, pp. 15–16, which records the visits of a ladies' committee to Kilmainham jail; p. 21 reveals that the county gaol at Armagh was occasionally visited by a group of women; pp. 25–7 records visits to Londonderry gaol and the county gaol in Louth. In 1825 the AIPPDI noted that a ladies' committee sometimes visited Kilmainham 'but not as often as formerly', annual report, AIPPDI, 1825, p. 31.

Both Fry and her brother, Joseph John Gurney, visited Ireland in 1827, ostensibly to stay with Quaker friends, but they also made an inspection of numerous gaols and charitable institutions in the country. Fry was much concerned with the formation of Ladies' Visiting Associations. Some associations of this kind had been formed earlier and Fry stated that in those prisons where these existed she had noted that they had produced

an extensive improvement among the female criminals in Ireland. It was most striking to us, in visiting the jails, to observe the contrast between the state of the prisoners visited by ladies, and that of those who enjoyed no such privilege. The order, decency, and civilisation, prevalent among the former class, afford an ample evidence of the salutary influence which it is in the power of well educated women to exercise over those degraded and unhappy females.[26]

During her visit she held a meeting in Dublin to co-ordinate and extend the number of such associations and this led, within two years, to the establishment of the Hibernian Ladies' Prison Association. A number of new visiting associations were established under its auspices but there are few details available on the work of the HLPA.[27] The Irish committee of the association did forward some accounts of their work to the parent body in London but it was not all good news. In 1835, for example, the ladies who visited the county gaol in Cork city reported 'there are many causes of a local nature which prevent the ladies' committee from being as efficient as in other places'.[28] These 'causes' are not explained but one can presume that the prison authorities were not the most welcoming.

No doubt Fry's visit encouraged the extension of such visiting associations but, as we have noted, such visitation, particularly among lay women, fell off after the 1830s. It is not known if any substantial changes were brought about in the conditions or rehabi-

---

[26] Elizabeth Fry and Joseph John Gurney, *Report Addressed to the Marquess Wellesley, Lord Lieutenant of Ireland, by E.F. and J.J.G. Respecting Their Late Visit to that Country* (London, 1827), p. 5.

[27] Rev. Thomas Timpson, *Memoirs of Mrs Elizabeth Fry* (London,1849), p. 89. In the report of the Ladies' British Association for the Reformation of Female Prisoners, 1828, the following list of ladies' visiting associations was appended; Dublin: Kilmainham, Richmond Bridewell, Smithfield prison, Newgate, Armagh, Athy, Belfast, Carlow, Carrickfergus, Cavan, Clonmel, Cork city gaol, Cork county gaol, Cork depot gaol, Downpatrick, Drogheda, Dundalk, Enniskillen, Galway, Limerick county gaol, Limerick city gaol, Longford, Londonderry, Lifford, Mullingar, Maryborough, Monaghan, Naas, Omagh, Philipstown, Roscommon, Sligo, Waterford county gaol, Waterford city gaol, Wexford, Wicklow.

[28] Timpson, *Memoirs*, p. 89.

liation of female prisoners by these associations. Prochaska has observed that Fry's reforms were not implemented to any great degree in English prisons. He also notes the decline of women as visitors to prisons there from the 1830s.[29] It is likely that branches of the Hibernian Ladies' Prison Association had as little success in implementing their policies in Ireland.

From 1839 gender separation was enforced in Irish prisons, as proposed by Fry in 1827. Grangegorman female prison, formerly known as the Richmond General Penitentiary, was assigned for women prisoners and given over to the care of a female matron in 1836. The exclusive use of this prison for women was an innovative and unprecedented step in penal history in the British Isles. Marian Rawlins was created head matron and she had been chosen personally for this task by Fry because of her extensive experience in Cold Bath Fields prison in England.[30] The staff of this prison were female with the exception of the male governor and eight other male employees. Rawlins was in charge of twenty-five 'class matrons' though her position was difficult and there was a great deal of tension between her and the governor. Although the ideal would have been to have Rawlins act as governor, it was in fact illegal to have a woman as keeper of a prison.

It was not until 1858 that a women's prison, managed by women, was set up for those who had prison sentences of five years or more to serve. This prison was Mountjoy, built to accommodate 600 prisoners, and in 1863 38 women were employed in the prison and 14 men.[31] The development of this prison undoubtedly owed something to Fry's calls for a separate prison for women and was also influenced by the debates which abounded around prison and prisoner reform in mid-century. Chief amongst the reformers was Sir Walter Crofton who was tremendously influential in reforming the Irish convict system.[32] The debates centred on a call for the separation of prisoners on a gender basis with discussions on the forms of discipline to be imposed. Some suggested that total solitary confinement was the best possible means of preventing 'contami-

---

[29] Prochaska, *Philanthropy*, pp. 170–1.

[30] Anne Jellicoe, 'A visit to the female convict prison at Mountjoy, Dublin', *Transactions of the National Association for the Promotion of Social Science* (1862), p. 437.

[31] Ibid., p. 438. *Judicial and Criminal Statistics (Ireland) 1863* [3418], HC 1864, lvii, 653.

[32] Richard S.E. Hinde, 'Sir Walter Crofton and the reform of the Irish convict system, 1854–61', *The Irish Jurist* (1977), pp. 115–47, 295–338.

nation' amongst prisoners while others insisted that group activity, with strict limits placed on the contact prisoners had with each other, was the only viable form of prison structure. The 1840s saw an attempt by government to ensure that prisoners were housed separately and with the ending of transportation in the 1850s officials were forced to reexamine the structure of the prison system to allow for the incarceration of those who could no longer be transported.[33] The building of a separate prison system for women resulted from these changes.

Mountjoy was under the care of the government's directors of prisons but was managed totally by women, having a woman superintendent, the post of governor having been dispensed with for this prison, and women as warders. Delia Lidwell who had acted as deputy matron under Rawlins in Grangegorman, was later promoted to the post of superintendent at Mountjoy. Being superintendent was a formidable task with the management of staff, who could be troublesome, and inmates being only part of her duties. Superintendents also had the task of making daily reports to the directors of prisons. Other posts were also filled by women such as that of schoolmistress, laundry matron, class matron and assistant matron. A marriage bar introduced in 1867 ensured that only single women or widows were employed in the prison service.[34] Although women within the prison service were a common feature in Irish prisons by the end of the century we still have no idea how they influenced prison discipline or conditions or what systems and schemes, which distinctly referred to women, they operated to achieve the rehabilitation of prisoners.

The Directors of Prisons endeavoured to provide an education for all prisoners willing to learn. With regard to work they stated 'we have desired that all the convicts, in turn, receive instruction in cooking, laundry, sewing, knitting, cleaning etc., instead of confining a certain number to a particular occupation'.[35] The work provided for, and indeed expected of, women prisoners was based on assumptions about their innate skills. Thus they were trained in those domestic skills thought necessary for women to be good

---

[33] See the *Irish Quarterly Review*, 1850–60, for various articles regarding the prison system in Ireland and England.

[34] Rena Lohan, 'The treatment of women sentenced to transportation and penal servitude, 1790–1898' (M.Litt., TCD, 1989), chapter 13.

[35] Quoted in ibid.

homemakers. The maternal role of women was recognised only to the extent that children, under two years, were to be permitted to remain with their mothers in the prison. As a result of the reforms brought about in the system, it was noted that there was 'a manifest improvement in their [the prisoners'] general demeanour and conduct'.[36]

The system which operated in Mountjoy prison was that which had been long sought by prison reformers. Separate cells were provided for each prisoner. They were divided into three classes. When first admitted to the prison women were placed in the third class and kept in separate confinement for a period of up to four months and longer if their behaviour warranted it. If of good behaviour they were then placed in the second and then the first class, each stage allowing them additional privileges. They were employed in washing, knitting, sewing and domestic work around the prison. They did the washing for other prisons and made uniforms for male prisoners. One hour per day was spent in a classroom and they were allowed one hour's recreation per day in the prison yard. For severe offences against discipline in the prison the prisoner could be confined in a darkened cell, on bread and water, for three days. For lesser infringements a marking system was used which could delay a prisoner's eventual release. Those who were near their allotted release date were sent to a refuge, either Goldenbridge, for Catholics, or to the Protestant refuge, in Heytesbury Street, where they completed their sentences. Their diet was consistent with that found in other prisons. For breakfast and supper they received bread and milk and oatmeal porridge, for dinner they received potatoes and meat or soup. They were kept at work until eight o'clock in the evening.[37]

In 1862 Mary Carpenter visited the prison and thought it was the ideal to which prisons for women should aspire.[38] She wrote at length about the system operating in Mountjoy and advocated that a similar system be introduced in England. What impressed her most was the extent to which the prisoners were brought to an

---

[36] Quoted in Mary Carpenter, *Convicts*, 2 vols. (London, 1864), II, p. 256.

[37] For the system in operation in Mountjoy see Jellicoe, 'A visit', pp. 438–9; Carpenter, *Convicts*, II, pp. 255–60; MS, Notes on Prisons, Reformatories, Gaols through Ireland and Great Britain taken by Charles Coffin (hereafter Coffin Papers), Charles F. Coffin and Rhoda M. Coffin Papers (Earlham College Archives, Indiana, USA).

[38] Carpenter, *Convicts*, II, passim.

awareness of their own wrongdoing by the 'kindly benevolence' of the prison authorities. She also urged the necessity of refuges to which these women could be sent, before their sentences expired, like that of Goldenbridge. The prison was also visited by an American interested in prison reform. Charles F. Coffin made a tour of prisons in the British Isles in 1871 and visited Mountjoy in November of that year.[39] He was also impressed by the management of the prison and stated that the existence of Mountjoy proved two things, 'the ability of women to conduct, govern and manage a prison for their own sex, and the power to reform many, probably most of those admitted'.[40]

Throughout the century women prisoners were seen to be the most difficult to reform. Carpenter believed that criminals had distinct physiological traits.[41] She also believed that women were the major influence in spreading criminality. If a woman committed any criminal acts, she became worse than men who were incarcerated for criminal activities. Women, since they were thought to be morally superior to men must, logically, in the committal of a criminal act, descend to greater depths of depravity than men. Woman fell from a higher pedestal. As Carpenter stated, 'When a woman has thrown aside the virtuous restraints of society, and is enlisted on the side of evil, she is far more dangerous to society than the other sex.'[42] Fanny Taylor observed in 1867 that the reformation of the female prisoner 'has long been acknowledged to be a harder task than that of the male – indeed, many have deemed it impossible. She has sinned more against the instincts of her better nature, the consequences of her crime have a more hardening effect on her, but, above all, the absence of hope has a fatal effect on her character.'[43]

Women were consequently seen to be much more difficult to manage in prison. Special conditions were thus necessary to bring about reform. For Carpenter this involved lengthy periods of solitary confinement and a sparse diet. Such a scheme would bring the criminal to an awareness of her crime and make her more amenable to rehabilitation. Breaking down the resistance of the prisoners would make them more susceptible to the demands of authority.[44]

---

[39] Coffin Papers (Earlham College Archives).   [40] Ibid.
[41] Carpenter, *Convicts*, II, p. 246.
[42] Ibid., p. 269.   [43] Taylor, *Irish Homes*, p. 53.
[44] Carpenter, *Convicts*, II, pp. 250–4.

This was why Mountjoy was seen as the ideal prison for women. It represented the efforts of women to reform women. The regime was one which allowed prisoners to contemplate their actions and through work, religious instruction and discipline placed them on the road to become fit members of society. Prison reformers always advocated longer prison sentences for women. Sister Mary Magdalen Kirwan, who was in charge of the refuge at Goldenbridge, noted that it was not enough that women be imprisoned for short periods. It was only through a lengthy period of imprisonment that any attempts at reform could be made. 'When', she stated, 'a woman is sentenced to seven years penal servitude ... she gets subdued, and begins to "lay down her mind to be good" ... being fully aware that the term of imprisonment ... entirely depends on her conduct.'[45]

Allied to the formal prison system another type of institution was established to rehabilitate women prisoners. This could be termed an intermediate prison, a quasi-state institution, supported in part by the government and encouraged by their officials, but relying heavily on the voluntary work of nuns and laywomen to enforce its regulations. It was thought essential that women convicts not be released directly from prison. Mary Carpenter noted that 'women could not with safety be allowed the same liberty as men'.[46] The general public, it was believed, did not perceive prisoners as rehabilitated on their release from prison. A 'halfway home', which would be totally associated in the minds of the public with reform, would more likely allow women to secure employment on their release.

The first reformatory was opened in Goldenbridge in 1856 and was operated by the Sisters of Mercy. Female convicts, who had conducted themselves well in Mountjoy prison, were allowed to finish their sentences here.[47] The government allowed 5 shillings per week for the maintenance of each prisoner and the period of detention within the refuge was not to exceed one year. The management of the prisoners was to be 'under the Lady Director of the institution, the Director of convict prisons having a right of general inspection and supervision'.[48] The director was also obliged to report quarterly to the director of prisons on the state of the prisoners. Once in operation it is clear that the director of prisons board did not

[45] Quoted in ibid., p. 273.   [46] Ibid., p. 269.   [47] Taylor, *Irish Homes*, pp. 260–1.
[48] Walter Crofton to Mrs Maguire, House of refuge, 18 March 1856, Cullen Papers, File 339/2/6 (1856) (DDA).

interfere with the running of the refuge and it was ably managed and controlled by the formidable Sr Magdalen Kirwan. Indeed Kirwan did not encourage official government visitors and one member of the board was to note 'I have a feeling that if we went there constantly it would be looked upon as an undue interference on our parts.'[49] Kirwan also had the luxury of choosing the prisoners who would come to the refuge, though by the 1880s the prison authorities took over that role. This institution catered only for Catholic prisoners but a Protestant equivalent was also established. The system of control operating within these refuges was similar to that which operated in the Magdalen asylums. Washing and needle-work were the principal occupations of the inmates and a portion of the earnings was retained for them until they left. In Goldenbridge the gratuity payable on release was £7.[50] The reformation of the character of the woman was the principal aim of these refuges. The ideal of the 'good woman' was promoted. 'These refuges', as one writer noted, 'afford the opportunity of doing for these joint-heirs with us of immortality, what has been so abundantly done for ourselves. Here they are striven with as women by women, won by love to the paths of virtue and respectability.'[51] Lack of self-esteem and inability to secure employment on release were the reasons given why women fell back into crime more easily than men:

If a poor woman endure her sentence patiently . . . she goes out at the end of her imprisonment with very little prospect for the future, save that of fresh dishonesty . . . Who will employ a discharged prisoner? . . . For men there are a dozen modes of hard, rough outdoor employment to which they can turn; but take away from the woman domestic service, charring and laundry work, and there is nothing left to her but wretched needlework, at which even respectable women can hardly earn their bread. It must seem almost a mockery to speak to a poor prisoner of the Mercy of God, when the mercy of her fellow creatures is so sternly withheld.[52]

The refuges attempted to remedy this situation by providing the inmates with training and situations once they left. Through incul-cating habits 'of industry, self-denial, and self-respect, without which no woman can be reclaimed', the refuges 'place[d] her in

49 Comments of William O'Brien in *Preliminary report of the Royal Commission appointed to inquire into the administration, discipline and condition of prisons in Ireland* [C. 4233], HC 1884–5, xxxviii, 466.

50 *Report of the Royal Commission on Prisons in Ireland* [C. 4233–1], HC 188 4–5, xxxviii, evidence of Mrs Kirwan, Q. 3,875.

51 Jellicoe, 'A visit', p. 441.   52 Taylor, *Irish Homes*, pp. 53–4.

circumstances to secure herself from a relapse into crime. To so comprehensive an aim is added the elevating influence of religion.'[53] The policies of these reformatories appear more humane than the system which operated in the 'penitent' refuges. Prisoners with children were allowed to bring them to the refuge and this was thought to have 'a humanising and softening effect on the poor creatures'.[54] The success of these institutions was proclaimed by Anne Jellicoe who asserted that only seven women out of every hundred who passed through them had ever been reconvicted of a crime.[55]

The women had to spend at least twelve months within the refuge, and discipline proved easy to maintain. They had already spent a number of years in prison and had been used to the discipline, and the managers of reformatories also had the option of returning to Grangegorman or Mountjoy any prisoner who proved to be unwilling to co-operate with their attempts at reformation.[56] From 1856 to 1889 only five women had escaped from Goldenbridge.[57] In this institution the average number of inmates was fifty and the highest number there, at any one time, was eighty-four. The women, it was claimed, were treated on an individual basis. Truthfulness was encouraged and an inmate's word trusted. The system of training, one visitor noted, was, 'intended to create self respect without conceit. Kindness is extended to them without familiarity or undue indulgence. No tale bearing of any description is allowed – the mother superioress refusing to hear anything from one inmate about the others.'[58] Ex-prisoners, like their penitent counterparts, were not allowed to speak of their past lives while a new identity was being moulded for them.

From 1856 to 1889 the number of women who passed through Goldenbridge was 1,232. Of this number, the superior of the reformatory, Sr Magdalen Kirwan, claimed that three-quarters of the inmates had 'turned out well'.[59] The policy was to emigrate as many of the women as possible, over 600 by 1889.[60] Indeed emigration for

[53] Jellicoe, 'A visit', p. 442.   [54] Taylor, *Irish Homes*, p. 65.
[55] Jellicoe, 'A visit', pp. 440–1.
[56] For the operation of the refuge at Goldenbridge see *Report of the Royal Commission on Prisons in Ireland*, 1884–5, evidence of Mrs Kirwan, Q. 3,824–3,975; Coffin Papers (Earlham College Archives).
[57] *Royal Commission on Prisons ... 1884*, Q. 3,836.
[58] Coffin Papers (Earlham College Archives).
[59] *Royal Commission on Prisons, 1884*, evidence of Mrs Kirwan, Q. 3,853.
[60] Ibid., Q. 3,864.

Irish women at this period was not an unusual occurrence, and thousands emigrated voluntarily each year.[61] Kirwan believed that it was only through emigration that a female criminal could be truly reformed.[62] Emigration allowed the woman to start a new life and more importantly it kept her away from those friends and haunts which it was believed had originally led her to crime. The superior at Goldenbridge did not provide the prison's board with any annual reports of the management of the refuge, in contravention of the original directions provided by Walter Crofton, nor did she ever seek any information about the prisoners who were to be sent to her. The reason she gave was that the inmates were being recreated as women and their past should have no bearing on their future lives.[63] Charles Coffin, in a visit paid to Goldenbridge, noted it had a family atmosphere, with no guards employed and the sister in charge he stated, 'acts as a mother to them [prisoners]'.[64] The existence of Mountjoy and of these two reformatories made the Irish prison system, according to Coffin, far superior to any which existed in the United States and he advocated that similar institutions be introduced in his own country. The control which the nuns had over Goldenbridge was seen by many as the reason why it was so successful. Their success further enhanced the position of female religious in the provision of institutional services to the needy and outcast.

Protestant prisoners were also catered for in Goldenbridge but a refuge for their use was opened in Heytesbury Street in 1860. This refuge was managed by a committee of women who employed a matron to run the home. Again it was partly supported by a government grant and laundry work carried out in the refuge. This refuge catered for fewer women than Goldenbridge, in 1873, for example, it had only five inmates.[65] One prison expert felt that it was managed badly by 'a comfortable committee of ladies on a narrow and bigoted system' and he claimed that contact with the women had been refused by the committee out of a fear that Catholic clerics or nuns would gain entrance. The general prisons board also looked for an improvement in the conduct of this refuge in its report for 1886.[66]

---

[61] See Fitzpatrick, *Irish Emigration*.
[62] *Royal Commission on Prisons, 1884*, evidence of Mrs Kirwan, Q. 3,914.
[63] Ibid., Q. 3,957–3,958.   [64] Coffin Papers (Earlham College Archives).
[65] *Judicial and Criminal Statistics (Ireland)*, 1873 [C. 1055] HC 1874, lxxi.
[66] *Eighth annual report of the general prisons board* [C. 4817] HC 1885–6, xxxv, 299.

SHELTERS FOR EX-PRISONERS

Outside the formal prison system, women also established refuges to offer after care services for female ex-prisoners, perhaps as a response to the lack of success experienced by women, as visitors, in initiating any changes in the formal prison system. The first such shelter was opened in Dublin, in 1821, and was founded by a group of Quaker women. The reason given for its establishment was that two women, on leaving prison, had been so dejected by their prospects that they had drowned themselves.[67] The Shelter for Females Discharged from Prison was the longest running establishment of its kind and operated for at least fifty years when, after a few years of inactivity, its functions were taken over by the Dublin Prison Gate Mission. A similar institution, the Association for Bettering the Condition of the Female Prisoners in the City and County of Dublin, whose title is reminiscent of Fry's original Newgate association, was, as we have seen, formed in 1821. This society opened a refuge in that year which was under the patronage of the Archbishop of Dublin.[68] There appears, also, to have been a refuge in Cork city, established in the 1820s, but no details of its activities are available.[69]

Discharged prisoners entered these homes voluntarily after completing their prison sentences. Both of these institutions received government grants and were maintained also by the work of the inmates and public subscriptions. Before the establishment of the refuges at Goldenbridge and Heytesbury Street they were the only institutions designed to reform women prisoners as generally Magdalen asylums did not take in ex-prisoners. The Shelter for Females Discharged from Prison stated it was 'the house of mercy [for] the convicted daughters of crime, it is a place of refuge and reformation for persons discharged from prison'.[70] The regime of these establishments was similar to that found in the penitent asylums. The imposition of discipline, constant employment and religious instruction were the methods used to inculcate reform. In the shelter established by the ABCFPCCD inmates were expected to remain for

---

[67] See the annual reports of the Shelter for Females Discharged from Prison (hereafter SFDP), 1821–43. *Report on the Inspection of Charitable Institutions, Dublin*, HC 1842 (337), xxxvii, 151.

[68] Ibid., pp. 152–4. There appears to be no other source of information available regarding this institution.

[69] Fry and Gurney, *Report to Marquess Wellesley*, p. 7.

[70] Annual report, SFDP, 1833, p. 4.

three years.[71] The numbers catered for in these establishments were small. For example, from 1821 to 1842 the number of entrants to the shelter operated by the ABCFPCCD was 486, an average of 23 women per year. Of this number, 177 were said to have been reformed, with 125 women returning to their families, 47 found employment, and there were 5 deaths; 205 women had left the refuge of their own accord and 71 had been expelled for misconduct; 33 women were residing in the home when these figures were compiled.[72]

The existence of such refuges, from the earliest years of the century, reflects the general belief in the natural vulnerability of women. Women, much more than men, needed protection. The SFDP was designed for the 'perfect reclamation of guilty and convicted females'.[73] Through a stay in the home these women would be brought into the 'peaceful paths of righteousness and truth'.[74] All the refuges of the last century were based on the family model. This was the model also used in the Goldenbridge refuge. It was the structure with which women philanthropists were most familiar and it was the one in which they themselves had been socialised. It was a natural progression that they should use this structure in their refuge projects when trying to reclaim 'fallen women'.

These two refuges seem to have been the longest running ones of their kind. Before mid-century two other refuges, the Victoria Asylum and the Olive Mount Institution of the Good Samaritan, founded in 1838 and 1843 respectively, were relatively shortlived.[75] The former closed around 1847 and the latter around 1857.[76] The Victoria Asylum was established by a group of women who appear to have had some connection with Grangegorman female prison and they may have been visitors there.[77] This refuge originally catered for ten women but it was hoped to eventually hold fifty. No details of the working of the home are available and for reasons which remain unclear it ceased operations around 1847.

The second refuge, the Olive Mount Institution of the Good Samaritan, was founded by a Rev. Bernard Kirby, who had been

---

[71] *Report on the Inspection of Charitable Institutions*, Dublin, 1842, p. 154.   [72] Ibid., p. 153.
[73] Annual report, SFDP, 1835–6, p. 1.   [74] Annual report, SFDP, 1837–8, p. 6.
[75] See appendix to the *Forty-first Report of the Inspector General of Prisons, Ireland*, 1862, p. 430; *Thom's Directory*, 1839, 1844.
[76] It was in these years that the last references were made in *Thom's Directory*.
[77] The Victoria Asylum for Female Penitents, advertising leaflet, 1839, Murray Papers, Ordinary, File 31/7/30 (DDA).

the chaplain in Grangegorman female prison resigning in 1843 to establish his asylum.[78] Kirby's plan was an ambitious one. He saw his refuge as a national institution taking in women from prisons all over the country. It was not only to house women who had completed their prison sentences but 'to afford protection to voluntary applicants who desire to escape from street infamy and degradation'.[79] It was to cater for 300 women and Kirby had the support of many of the leading political figures of his day for this refuge. To ensure as many subscribers as possible the level of subscription was limited from 1d to a maximum of 2/6d. Through this method he obviously hoped to attract the support of all sections of the population. By 1845 more than 1,500 individuals subscribed to the charity and in the same year total subscriptions amounted to a little over £2,189.[80] This was quite a phenomenal achievement given that similar charities, like the Shelter for Females Discharged from Prison, received £100, at the most, in subscriptions.[81]

In 1843 the institution was opened with 54 inmates and by 1845 it catered for 140 women which made it the largest institution of its kind.[82] It is unclear if the number of inmates ever exceeded this figure. Kirby appears to have retained sole control of the institution. He wrote the annual reports, solicited funds and catered for the religious instruction of the inmates. Though no details are available regarding the actual day to day running of the institution it would seem logical to assume that he employed some women, such as matrons, to run the home. In 1846 one of the inmates of the refuge complained about Kirby to Dr Murray, the archbishop of Dublin, about the running of the refuge. She alleged that Kirby kept a number of the young women in the institution locked up without providing them with any religious 'sustenance'. She also claimed, that on the eve of a visit by Fr Mathew, the temperance advocate, to the asylum, Kirby had gathered all the women together and given them a general absolution so that they could receive communion from Fr Mathew. Such an event, it appears, would have been a grave dereliction of his priestly duty as each penitent was supposed

[78] *Forty-first Report of the Inspector General of Prisons, Ireland*, 1862, p. 430.
[79] Rev. Bernard Kirby, *General House of Protection for Unprotected Females* (Dublin, 1843), p. 4.
[80] Annual report, Olive Mount Institution of the Good Samaritan, 1846, subscription lists.
[81] See Luddy, 'Women and philanthropy', appendix 10 for details regarding subscriptions to charitable societies.
[82] Annual report, Olive Mount Institution of the Good Samaritan, 1843, p. 6; 1846, p. 10.

to receive absolution on an individual basis. Kirby refuted all these allegations and referred to the complainant as a 'wretched woman' who had to be expelled forcibly from the refuge by the police.[83] The incident may indeed have been an attempt at revenge by the complainant and may not have reflected the actual conditions in the refuge. It is not known what the outcome of this incident was.

Like other philanthropists who worked with women Kirby believed that those who strayed from the paths of virtue established for them were 'fallen', and because they were women they needed particular attention. On the headed notepaper of this institution is a detailed drawing of a 'penitent' at the gates of the refuge. She is dressed in dark clothing and her isolation is emphasised by the space around her. Just inside the gate stands another woman, obviously a matron of the refuge, who is dressed in white, signifying no doubt her purity, and she appears to be beckoning the other woman to her. The institution is surrounded by high walls which mark if off from the outside world. The luxuriant growth of trees seems reminiscent of the garden of Eden, presumably before the fall! Such institutions were designed to re-establish a woman's innate goodness and return her to the world a chaste and moral creature. Whether operated by men or women the ends were the same.

The Olive Mount Institution ceased operating around 1857, for reasons which remain unclear. It may, for instance, have ceased to attract subscribers at the same high rate, for subscriptions to such charities generally declined after the first few years of operation. Within the context of Irish philanthropy large Catholic enterprises such as this do not seem to have survived unless they were taken over by female religious and the Olive Mount Institution was never in the care of nuns. Whatever the reasons for its demise it was the last such refuge established for female ex-prisoners until the 1870s when a number of other institutions were established as part of the general increase in the range of the philanthropic interests of women in the later decades of the century. It was during this period also that the first refuges for men were established, run, of course, by men. One refuge, the Dublin Protestant Prisoners' Aid Society, established in 1881, offered shelter to both men and women. Its stated aim was 'to assist men and women on their discharge from prison to lead a

---

[83] Bernard Kirby to the Rev. Archbishop Murray, 26 October 1846, Hamilton Papers, File 36/7 (Priests, Secular, 1846) (DDA).

respectable life, and so prevent them from continuing among the outcasts of society'.[84]

The Dublin Female Prison Gate Mission was established in 1876 and took over the functions of the defunct Shelter for Females Discharged from Prison.[85] It was organised by Protestant and Quaker women and had a mixed managing committee although it was the women on the committee who ran the refuge. It does not appear that these women were involved in prison visiting, and they met the women at the gates on their discharge from prison. The average number of women attending the Mission was 80 per month between the years 1883 and 1889, and 40 to 50 women were accommodated in the dormitory provided.[86] Those who stayed in the home were employed in laundry work and sewing. In 1883 carpet weaving was introduced as an occupation for the inmates and in 1887 the committee employed a woman from Armagh to teach them glovemaking.[87] The regime in operation was not as severe as that found in the penitent asylums and inmates appear to have been relatively free to leave the refuge during the day and in the evenings.[88] In June 1888, 104 of the women who attended the Mission were taken on a day trip to Howth.[89] In 1881 the committee opened a home for young girls in Baggot Street to 'prevent the lapse into crime of young girls associated with the criminal class through birth, poverty, or ignorance'.[90] This home was seen as a preventive institution which trained the girls for occupations in domestic service. There are no details available on how many of these women would have been deemed reclaimed, but, like other prisoners' aid societies, it did provide funds to allow those women, who so desired, to emigrate.

In 1881 the Dublin Discharged Female Roman Catholic Prisoners' Aid Society, inspired by the work of the Prison Gate

---

84 Williams, *Dublin Charities*, pp. 154–5, provides the only information available on this society. No details about the number of women assisted are given. In 1897 the society dealt with 43 people. Of that number 4 were placed in employment, 2 were sent to sea, 19 were sent to friends, mostly in England, 4 were given tools of work, 5 were provided with food and lodgings, 2 were emigrated, 3 went to Belfast and 4 individuals declined any offer of assistance from the society.

85 Barrett, *Guide*, III, pp. 10–11; Williams (ed.), *Dublin Charities*, pp. 162–3; *EWR*, 5 May, 15 November 1882, pp. 230–3, 311–12.

86 Dublin Prison Gate Mission, minute book, 1883–9 (RCB).

87 Ibid., 23 October 1883; 12 May 1887.

88 Ibid., 15 November 1883.   89 Ibid., 29 June 1888.

90 *EWR*, 15 November 1882.

Mission, was established.[91] Its purpose was to help Catholic women and may have attempted to entice them away from the Prison Gate Mission to seek help from a specifically Catholic society. It was managed entirely by women with Archbishop Walsh and a Fr Kennedy acting as trustees for any bequests which might be made to the society. The DDRCFPAS pursued a vigorous policy of emigrating as many of their inmates as possible. For example, from May 1890 to May 1891, fifty-two women entered this refuge. Of this number nine left voluntarily, six were expelled and twenty-eight emigrated.[92] The Prison Gate Mission also pursued a policy of emigration, though on a much smaller scale. In 1905 the committee opened a second home at Synott Place, in Dublin, which they gave over to the charge of the Sisters of Charity of St Vincent De Paul.[93] With the advent of the nuns the policy of emigrating the inmates to America and Canada almost ceased and it appears that the nuns placed them in situations, mostly in convents, in Ireland and England.[94] It was always easier for nuns to find employment for their inmates through the vast network of convents which existed not only in Ireland, but, more importantly in relation to ex-prisoners, in foreign countries. The annual reports of the DDRCFPAS which are available provide no information about the committee's attitude to the women they helped. One other prison refuge for women was established in Belfast in 1876 and it also took its lead from the Prison Gate Mission in Dublin.[95] The work of the committee of the Belfast Prison Gate Mission was much influenced by the involvement of committee members in the Women's Temperance Association. For these philanthropists alcohol abuse was identified as the primary cause for women's criminality.

As with the penitent asylums constant appeals were made in the

91 Annual report, Dublin Discharged Roman Catholic Female Prisoners' Aid Society (hereafter DDRCFPAS), 1886–7.
92 Annual report, DDRCFPAS, 1891, p. 5. From May 1892 to May 1893, 58 women entered the home. Of this number 22 were emigrated, 6 were taken away by friends or relatives, 10 left of their own accord, 3 were expelled, 2 women died and 13 women still resided in the home at the end of the year. Annual report, DDRCFPAS, 1893, p. 5. In this report a list of some of the women who emigrated is given. From 1885 to 1893, 46 women were thus accounted for. Of these 18 ended up in Baltimore and 11 in Boston, 17 went to Montreal, Toronto or Ottowa. An Alice McCormack, who went to Montreal, was described as 'married very well, and very good and steady'; an M. Meehan, who went to Toronto 'excellent, gets good wages'; K. Moore, who arrived in Boston in 1889 'saved a good deal of money, and went to her sister in Pennsylvania', pp. 6–8.
93 Annual report, DDRCFPAS, 1905–6.   94 Ibid.
95 *EWR*, 15 June 1881, pp. 247–52; annual report, Belfast Prison Gate Mission, 1877.

annual reports of these refuges for funds; once again subscriptions generally declined after the first few years of an institution's existence and the homes had to rely on the work of the inmates to continue. Unlike the penitent asylums, however, most of these refuges received some form of government assistance. Like other charities which were organised by women they also received a substantial number of subscriptions from women. Although the women entered the homes voluntarily not every woman was acceptable. These refuges did not accept convict women. The Dublin Prison Gate Mission had an average attendance of about 120 women, 'none of whom belong to the convict class, but are all from the short sentence prisons – their term of imprisonment varying from three days to three months'.[96] The committee of the Belfast Prison Gate Mission declared that 'it is well known that all who find themselves within the walls of a prison are not equally guilty, and that many are far from being past help: and it is the task of finding out and aiding such to return to a better life, that the ladies forming the committee have addressed themselves'.[97] Some convict women, of course, finished their sentences in the Goldenbridge or Heytesbury Street refuges and would hardly have relished the thought of spending further time in one of these homes.

It appears obvious that philanthropists thought that women who spent a short period in prison for minor offences were less odious than women who engaged in prostitution. They expressed a much more benevolent attitude to their life circumstances than to those of prostitutes. They accepted that women committed crimes from economic necessity or were arrested for drunkenness brought about by the dismal conditions of their environment. It was also necessary that some form of intervention be made in the lives of these women to prevent them from falling back into a life of crime. The ultimate purpose of the refuges was to have the inmates go forth as 'wives and mothers, restored to their proper place of affection and direction in the family'.[98] The means to this end was to offer these women 'an

---

[96] *EWR*, 15 May 1882, p. 231.
[97] Annual report, Belfast Prison Gate Mission, 1877, p. 5. The stated aim of the DDRCFPAS was to help 'prisoners ... who are just commencing a life of crime', see Williams (ed.), *Dublin Charities*, p. 155.
[98] *EWR*, 15 June 1881, p. 250. The Prison Gate Mission in Belfast also urged the public to subscribe to its funds by stating that 'every woman drawn from a life of drunkenness and degradation is not only a direct saving to the state, but is transformed into a contributor to the prosperity of the community', annual report, Belfast Prison Gate Mission, 1877, p. 9.

opportunity of again earning their own bread, in peace and under protection, the provision of womanly kindness ... and most important, the constant, earnest effort to lead them to look for that Divine guidance which alone can help them in the right way'.[99] Life in these refuges for ex-prisoners was not as harsh as that experienced by penitents. For the benefit of society at large they sought to alter the inmates' behaviour by retraining rather than punishing them.

Although not directly connected with the work of refuges, the Philanthropic Reform Association tried, at the end of the century, to make some changes in the conditions under which women were held in police stations. The PRA was one of the more progressive charitable organisations operating within the country.[100] In its first year of existence members of the association, both men and women, visited police stations and courts in Dublin. They were not satisfied with the conditions they saw and made recommendations for improvement to the chief commissioner of police. Amongst the proposals made was that women should be supervised by female officers and that proper care should be taken of children who were with their mothers when arrested.[101] By 1897 some of the recommendations regarding the holding of prisoners had been implemented although female warders were not appointed to look after women prisoners.[102]

Conditions for women in prisons had improved greatly by the end of the century. They were housed in separate sections and later placed in a separate convict prison from men. They were put to work rather than allowed to idle away their sentences. Much of this improvement was brought about by prison reformers who worked for the government, but with regard to women prisoners, both Elizabeth Fry and Mary Carpenter must be credited with bringing their plight to the attention of the authorities. Women visitors to prisons in the earlier part of the century also played some role in humanising these institutions. It was in the care of ex-prisoners that women's philanthropic work was most evident. It was work with women by women which would save not only 'deviant' women but also society. However, women's philanthropic work was not limited to the area of moral reform, though it formed a major part of their work. From the beginning of the nineteenth century women

99 *EWR*, 15 June 1881, pp. 249–50.   100 See chapter 6.
101 Annual report, PRA, 1896, pp. 26–32.
102 Annual report, PRA, 1897, p. 10.

organised societies which catered for all the needs of society that they could imagine. The extraordinary range of women's philanthropic involvement reveals that in nineteenth-century Ireland the development of a comprehensive welfare system was to a large extent the work of women.

Varieties of charity

Throughout the nineteenth century there was a bewildering array of philanthropic organisations managed and run by women. Most of these societies were small affairs which did not attempt to operate on a national scale. Those organised by female religious were, obviously, much more extensive. Aid was provided to the poor and destitute and also to the 'genteel poor', who were treated quite differently, and social class often determined the type of aid given. As the century progressed there was a development in the nature of philanthropy with women becoming involved in reform organisations, the temperance movement and also in political campaigns directed towards altering the position of women in society. For a small group of middle-class women philanthropic involvement played an important role in their politicisation. Before examining these aspects of philanthropy, some general comments about the organisation and structure of these charitable societies will reveal the features common to all charitable enterprises.

The majority of voluntary societies originated from a humanitarian concern for the plight of the poor. The numbers of voluntary societies, managed by either men or women, always increased in times of distress. Thus a proliferation of societies were organised, for example, during the famine. Many such voluntary organisations were short lived and ceased to function once a particular crisis had passed.[1] Many of the women's societies operating in the early part of the century were adjuncts to male run organisations; this was especially true of the Bible and church related associations where women were generally requested by men to set up auxiliary and

---

[1] One such society was the British Association for the Relief of Extreme Distress in Ireland and Scotland which sent funds to aid famine victims. Similarly a committee was appointed to distribute relief to the poor of Dublin during the severe winter of 1814 and disbanded once this function had been carried out.

fund raising groups to support a parent society. Women themselves also organised societies which catered for the needs of outcast groups, such as prostitutes and ex-prisoners, and although often supported by men they were essentially autonomous organisations where women made the decisions and carried out the work for which the society had been instituted. Many of the societies established by women to help the adult poor were run solely by women but the majority of charitable organisations even if run by women had men as committee members, patrons or trustees. For example, the Asylum for Aged and Respectable Unmarried Females, initiated by a Miss Meredyth in 1838, had a mixed managing committee from its inception.[2] By inviting men to partake in a society the organisers were in effect legitimating their purposes. Men's experience with financial affairs was also a bonus and in most societies men acted as treasurers. In the earlier part of the century the position of treasurer was rarely taken by women. An explanation for this may be that women, particularly married women, had no legal right to property and unlikely as it might have been in practice, husbands and fathers could claim control over the funds of a society if they were entrusted to women.[3] Many women's societies also organised annual public meetings where an account of the society's operation for the year was read out by men who chaired the meetings and it was not until mid-century that women took control of such meetings.

The role played by men in many of these organisations was similar to the role they carried out in the home. While the women dispensed the charity the men oversaw the financial details of the society and supported the women through their presence on a committee. Besides organising their own societies women were encouraged by men to establish voluntary organisations which were subservient to the male organisation. For example, the Association for the Relief of Distressed Protestants, founded in 1836, invited some women to form a ladies' committee in 1876. The ladies' committee followed guidelines established by a sub-committee of men which clearly delineated the limits of their activities. The women were not allowed to recommend cases for relief and their function was to distribute

---

[2] Annual reports of the Home from 1838 to 1900. Lists of committee members, trustees and patrons are provided in the annual reports of all charitable societies. See also St John's House of Rest, annual reports 1872–7.

[3] Lee Holcombe, *Wives and Property: Reform of the Married Women's Property Law in Nineteenth-Century England* (Oxford, 1983).

clothing to the needy and administer a blanket fund initiated by the male committee.[4] Throughout the century the majority of women's organisations were not segregated by gender as men's organisations were. The limited role allowed women in male run societies was perhaps one of the reasons women organised their own societies but the prime motivation appears to have been to aid those members of their own sex whose needs were not being met by male organisations. Female philanthropists themselves believed that they were more capable of dealing with the needs of children and other women than men. Men were often an integral part of the charitable society even if they played no active role in that society.

All women's charitable societies had basically the same structure. They began by a group of like-minded women coming together for a specific purpose. What is notable in many of the societies established are the links which existed among members. The primary link was adherence to a particular religious denomination. For example, the Shelter for Females Discharged from Prison was established by a group of Quaker women in 1821.[5] Protestant associations had Protestant members, Presbyterian associations were organised by Presbyterians, and so on. Though membership of an organisation was decided by the amount of subscription paid and generally no distinction was made, on a religious basis, regarding the recipients of charity, the religious homogeneity of the committees of many of these organisations was to preclude any co-operation among women of different denominations until the end of the century. For the whole century then women's charitable organisations were divided by religious beliefs and the problem of proselytism was a constant reminder of the sectarian nature of much philanthropy.

Besides the religious links which existed between members of organisations many members also belonged to the same family and indeed in a number of instances a tradition of philanthropy was established within a family. For example, the La Touche family were involved in numerous charitable endeavours in Dublin throughout the century. Likewise, the Smyly family engaged in philanthropy from the 1850s right up to the present century. Mrs Ellen Smyly, for example, established and ran numerous homes in Dublin for orphaned and destitute children. Her five daughters

---

[4] Association for the Relief of Distressed Protestants, annual report, 1877. Members of the ladies' committee were listed in the annual reports of this society until 1889.
[5] Barrett, *Guide*, p. 10.

helped her in this work and at her death in 1901 the running of the homes was continued by two of her daughters, Ellen and Annie.[6] Philanthropic work was particularly strong among Quaker families. The Webb family, for example, contributed to a large number of charities and were involved in their activities. They supported the anti-slavery societies, the National Association for the Repeal of the Contagious Diseases Acts, the Ladies' National Association, and they were also suffragists.[7]

The purpose of an organisation was always clearly stated. Thus, for example, the Seaton Needlework Association, founded in 1856, aimed to provide employment in needlework to the widows and wives of soldiers.[8] Once a group decided to organise they drew up a constitution upon which the members voted, and generally declared their purpose to the public in an effort to raise financial support. Nearly all of the societies had patrons, trustees, a managing committee and often sub-committees to deal with the affairs of the organisation or different aspects of its work. The Dublin Prison Gate Mission, organised by women, had a general mixed management committee, a building fund sub-committee, a sub-committee for stores and another for looking after the house furniture.[9] The general committee was elected annually by those members who subscribed a certain amount of money to the society, the amount varied according to the society, and committee members had to be subscribers of a stated minimum amount in order to be eligible for election. Societies also had a number of officers such as secretaries and treasurers, all of whom worked without payment.

Charitable societies had a variety of methods for raising funds. Subscriptions were solicited from the general public and a number of societies employed a paid collector to gather such funds; many women also organised collections among their friends, family and acquaintances and kept records by using collecting cards. Charitable societies were scrupulous about listing the names of those who subscribed to the organisation and most annual reports are taken up with lists of subscribers and the amount paid. No doubt such

---

[6] For the work of Mrs Smyly and her family see Smyly, *Early History*.
[7] See chapter 4 for the Webb family's involvement in philanthropy.
[8] Barrett, *Guide*, pp. 40–1.
[9] Dublin Prison Gate Mission minute book, April 1883–December 1889 (RCB library, MS 231.1).

publicity pleased the subscribers and provided an incentive for them
to maintain their support. Also popular was the charity sermon
which was given once a year by a priest or clergyman who was
guaranteed to draw a crowd. In 1815, for example, it was claimed
that £16,000 was raised annually in Dublin through charity ser-
mons.[10] Functions, such as bazaars, were also used to raise funds. In
many of the annual reports of societies details were given on how
readers could make bequests. Some of the societies were almost
self-supporting and this was true particularly of those organisations
which used the employment of the recipients of their charity to meet
their costs, notably the Magdalen asylums and prison refuges which
employed the inmates in needle and laundry work. The work done
by the inmates was paid for, normally at a low rate, and the surplus
used to defray the costs of the society. The financial needs of a
society varied. Institutional charities such as the Magdalen asylums
had to pay for food and the clothing of inmates, the services of a
matron and a porter. Societies which paid fees to a collector usually
lost about 10 per cent of what had been collected. In non-
institutional charities expenses included items like payment for
stamps and stationery, and the cost of advertisements and publication of an annual report. From an organisational point of view
instituting a charitable society was not a task to be undertaken
lightly, and the women who founded such societies had a keen sense
of responsibility not alone to the people they wished to help but also
to those who supported their cause.

Having initiated a charitable society the organisers had to
contend with one major difficulty. Who was to benefit from its work?
Philanthropists, and indeed the general public, were concerned
throughout the nineteenth century that charity be dispensed only to
the 'deserving poor'. These 'deserving poor' were considered to be
men and women, who, although willing to work, were unable to do
so either through illness or lack of opportunity. Such people were
thought to be the most necessitous and on being provided with
temporary relief, either work or loans of money, it was hoped that
they would not come to be dependent on charitable organisations or
a burden to society in general. To ensure that their charity would
not be abused most women's organisations only catered for specific
groups of people and certain guidelines had to be followed before

[10] Anon., *An Address to the Public on Behalf of the Poor* (Dublin, 1815).

any charity would be dispensed. The Dorset Institution, established in Dublin in 1815 aimed to 'provide employment at a suitable price and at their own homes for industrious females whose only support was a precarious supply of needlework'. Women who sought work from the society had to have a guarantor who provided a security of £1.[11] The provision of employment as a means of relief was one way of ensuring that only those who were 'deserving' of charity received aid. By providing employment they were in essence granting individuals who sought aid 'deserving' status. The policy of restricting aid was a practical decision taken by lay female philanthropists. The majority of the societies they established were managed by a small group of people who had limited funds at their disposal. Indeed most of these societies rarely went over budget and the budget was decided by the amount earned through subscriptions and work done for the society. For example, the Home for Aged Presbyterian Females, established in 1871, had in 1884 an income of £140 derived from donations. Ten women were looked after in the home and to make up for any shortfall in expenses each inmate had to have an income of 2s 6d per week.[12] These women philanthropists felt morally obliged not to dispense charity indiscriminately nor to waste the limited resources of their organisations.

A number of features recur in almost all the charitable and philanthropic societies established by women throughout the nineteenth century. They generally operated separately from each other and many had more contact with their foreign counterparts than with other similar Irish organisations. They remained small and localised and were aware of the limits of their actions. However limited these societies might have been, the women who ran them felt it a moral imperative to organise. Moral, humanitarian and religious principles were some of the motivating forces behind the establishment of all women's voluntary associations.

Although this study has concentrated on the expansion of urban charitable endeavour, the provision of charity in rural areas should not be ignored. Ireland was, for most of the nineteenth century, an overwhelmingly rural society. In rural areas female benevolence was dispensed by the wives, daughters and sisters of landowners.

---

[11] Dorset Institution for Industrious Females, annual report 1816, p. 5. Unfortunately this appears to be the only surviving report available for this society which, according to *Thom's Directory*, survived until at least 1900. See also, Barrett, *Guide*, p. 34.

[12] Barrett, *Guide*, p. 17.

Much of that benevolence revolved around visitation, the establishment of schools on estates for the children of the landowner's
tenants and of course these 'landed' women dispensed advice on
household matters to cottagers, some of whom at least they knew
personally. Elizabeth Smith of Baltiboys in county Wicklow, the
wife of a landowner, described the poverty she witnessed in
visitation:

My next visit was revolting from a different cause – dirt and filth and
discomfort of every kind in and around the dwelling of Michael Doyle and
Judy Ryan . . . Jane Ryan literally, not figuratively, nearly naked . . . was in
the field amusing an ugly dirty enough but perfectly well dressed baby. She
helped me over a wall to the dung yard in front of the cabin which was
cleaner than the kitchen floor over which I had to grope in the darkness to
the fire, carefully holding up my petticoats and stepping so as to avoid what
the two fat pigs had been depositing on it. Besides these two beasts on four
legs, two others on two, old Mrs Doyle, smoking, and lame James Quinn
seemed to be in charge of a lately born infant and a wretched little
nursechild both seated in the chimney corner.[13]

   This personalised philanthropy also involved looking after the ill
by providing broth, blankets or comforting words. Some of these
landed women also established Dorcas societies which enabled the
poor to put aside some money for cheap clothing. Mrs La Touche
and a Mrs Wakefield were instrumental in setting up such a society
for the poor in Kildare. Providing 'treats' for the poor was also a
long-standing tradition among the landed gentry and these were
usually organised by women. Mrs La Touche recounts how Mrs
Wakefield organised a Christmas tree in Kilcullen but the local
Catholic priest declined to be part of the festivities and would not
allow any Catholic children to attend.[14] Ladies of the landed class
also provided treats to the inmates of workhouses, particularly at
Christmas.[15] Much of this kind of benevolence was traditional and
conducted outside the confines of an organisation. Besides this type
of local charity women of the landed and aristocratic classes did
become involved in organisations at a national and local level, often
acting as patrons for societies but in many instances becoming
activists in the work of particular societies.

[13] *The Highland Lady in Ireland*, p. 195.
[14] Margaret Ferrier Young, *Letters of a Noblewoman* (London, 1908) p. 130.
[15] See for example, the treats given by the Bagwells to the inmates of the Clonmel workhouse,
    The Nationalist, 3 January 1900.

One organisation which garnered the support of the aristocracy, landed and middle classes was the British and Irish Ladies' Society for the Promotion of the Welfare of the Female Peasantry in Ireland. The BILS was unique in being the first society which allowed Irish women to visit the homes of the poor on a systematic basis; it operated on a national scale with branches in almost every county; it allowed women to organise, raise and control funds and to initiate the development of local industry in rural Ireland. It was also one of the few societies which remained removed from clerical influence and in contrast to many other organisations it was non-evangelical in purpose. The society was established in London in 1822 and the function of the parent body was to raise funds and to correspond with women in Ireland and encourage them to establish local branches to carry out the aims of the society. The society expanded at a rapid rate: by early 1823 it had 135 associated branches organised throughout the country; by 1824 the number had risen to 254 and it was active in 29 counties.[16] The most important auxiliary association was formed in Cork city in 1822 and by early 1823 this branch had 62 district associations under its control.[17] The aims of the local associations, as described by the parent body, were:

1) to visit the families of the poor and obtain a knowledge of their situation. 2) to excite a sense of virtue and piety, to habits of industry, cleanliness and attention to domestic duty 3) to endeavour to procure employment for poor women at their own dwellings 4) to visit the sick and provide temporary assistance in the loan of linen etc., also to procure medical advice where necessary 5) to encourage the poor to send their children to schools and to promote the industry and improvement of the poor in any other way which local circumstances appear to require.[18]

The parent body, while it suggested these areas of action, did not dictate what forms of relief were to be provided and the Irish branches of the society were very much autonomous.

The organisers and members of the society in Ireland were representative of the social elite of the country. Members of the aristocracy, like the Countess of Kingstown, Lady Colthurst, the Countess of Cork, Viscountess Adare and Viscountess Powerscourt acted as patrons of the society. Positions of district secretaries and treasurers

---

[16] Annual reports, British and Irish Ladies' Society for Improving the Condition and Promoting the Welfare of the Female Peasantry in Ireland (hereafter the BILS), 1823, pp. 12–13; 1824, pp. 65–7.

[17] Annual report, Cork Branch, BILS, 1824.   [18] Annual report, BILS, 1823, p. 9.

and visitors were taken by members of the business and gentry classes. Thus we find Mrs Beamish, of the Cork brewing family, on the Cork central committee, for example.[19] Through their involvement with the society many of these women were brought to a heightened perception of the causes of poverty and their reports recount many harrowing circumstances.[20] Laziness, which had long been considered the root of poverty, did not appear to these women as sufficient explanation for the state of the peasantry. The willingness of the peasantry to work was obvious; lack of employment, instruments of work and suitable markets for produce were deemed the causes of wretchedness.[21] The members of the society, as a result of these observations, organised the supply of materials such as linen and flax to the poor, provided them with spinning wheels, taught them skills such as spinning and knitting and gave loans of money for a number of projects. In Fermoy, for example, 110 people were employed by the district association in spinning flax. Some women opened small shops to sell the products of the work done. Loans of money also helped individuals maintain themselves and their families. Among the cases cited in the reports was one 'M.F. [who] by keeping an eating house, turned the loan five times, and deposited 15s in the Savings Bank.'[22] By 1824 the Cork branch of the society reported that they had, over the first year of operation, provided employment to more than 1,000 families and the visitation of the ladies to the homes of the poor had revealed another 3,000 families willing to work. It is difficult to assess the exact numbers helped in other centres as the various branch reports cite individual cases rather than the gross number of people aided.[23]

---

[19] See the membership lists which are in all the annual reports of the BILS, also annual report BILS, 1824, pp. 70–2.

[20] See, for example, the annual report, BILS, 1823, pp. 52–7. In 1823 twenty-one central committees had been organised. The Cork central committee had fifty-one district associations under its control. The central committee for Leitrim, which had its headquarters in Carrick-on-Shannon, had four district associations. In Tipperary the central committee was based in Clonmel and had seven district associations which covered Clonmel, Cahir, Tipperary, Carrick-on-Suir, Cashel, Newport and Thurles (pp. 12–13, 46).

[21] Ibid., p. 17. The report continues 'degrading habits usually spring from a state of external misery . . . it leads to a poor man's forgetfulness of himself as an accountable being, whilst it absorbs the mind in a sense of present suffering, or in the pressure to perserve a mere animal existence'.

[22] Annual report, Cork Ladies' Society in Association with the BILS, 1826, pp. 8–9.

[23] All of the available reports relate the type of work done by each association. For the examples cited see annual report, Cork Ladies' Society in Association with the BILS, 1825, pp. 25, 29; 1828, p. 33.

Besides catering for the temporal needs of the poor it was also an aim of the society to improve and influence their moral conduct. Although this had been originally a primary aim of the society the conditions encountered by the members in visitation soon relegated it to second place. It was primarily through influencing the female peasant they believed that higher moral principles could be taught to the poor in general. As one correspondent stated

by the influence of the ladies over the female peasantry . . . they hope that not only ideas of comfort and cleanliness, hitherto little known, may be introduced, and industry excited by the prospect of due remuneration, but that likewise benefits of a higher nature may be conferred by the improvement of moral principle and the repression of mean, degrading and vicious habits.[24]

It was the belief of the members that they alone, as women, understood the needs of peasant women. It was seen as the function of the 'ladies' of the society to personally supervise the provision of relief. If left to those of an inferior social status the provision of relief was still seen to be charitable but 'while it might be attention to the poor . . . it would be devoid of the Christian grace which condescends to persons of low degree, which conciliates, and attaches while it relieves'.[25] Women had a special mission to their less fortunate sisters. Members of the society advised them on domestic cleanliness and took an interest in all aspects of peasant family life, attempting to bring the order and domesticity of their own homes into the homes of the peasant.

Members of this society held an implicit belief in women as moral custodians; this was the role they played in their own families and through their influence on peasant women they believed that similar standards would pass to the general population. Their influence on the female peasant would result in significant benefits for society at large and especially would help to create a more docile peasantry by 'promoting morality and submission to the laws of the country'.[26] It is one of the few organisations which explicitly saw its function as involving a degree of social control. These women were also reinforcing the position of the landed classes over the poor and they maintained distinct social divisions in their work. Like many other philanthropists of the time, they did not question the structure of

[24] Annual report, BILS, 1823, pp. 26, 39–40.   [25] Ibid., 1824, pp. 41–2.
[26] Ibid., 1823, p. 26.

society and the concept of equality, if they ever thought about it, was anathema to them. Their motivation came from a humanitarian belief in employment as a means of improving the temporal condition of the poor, and, once this was seen to, it was logical for them to believe that work, allied to the example of the 'ladies', would result in an improvement in moral standards. The charity they dispensed was given by a social superior to a social inferior.

There is no doubt that the BILS was extremely popular among Irishwomen. As one correspondent to the London committee stated

I know of no circumstance which has ever united the ladies of Clare in labours for their fellow creatures as your society has done. Many are now not merely denying themselves, but even at the risk of health going in all weathers to stand the whole day in an indifferent cottage, to give out work with their own hands: and these persons of delicate habits, totally unaccustomed to such an employment.[27]

The BILS was popular because it allowed members to become intensely personally involved in the work they were doing. The level of personal responsibility granted to the members, the extent of home visitation and the provision of aid demanded a strong commitment on the part of these women, a commitment which was willingly given. In Wicklow one member observed that 'the ladies have in two instances visited their districts on common carts and submitted to great personal inconvenience'.[28] It was also, obviously, fulfilling some need felt by these women to involve themselves in the provision of charity. No doubt also that friendships among women of the same social background was a unifying force behind the organisation and it is likely that enthusiasm for the organisation was generated by allowing such women, from different parts of the county, to meet each other on a social and business basis. The parent society in London disbanded in 1828, due in part to the decline in subscriptions and also to the collapse of the linen industry which provided work for the peasantry.[29] Within two years the Irish associations also ceased to function. Some residue of the work carried out by the society survived as in 1830 the Carlow and Graigue Ladies' Association for the Betterment of the Female Peasantry seems to have been carrying on the work originally done

---

[27] Ibid., 1823, p. 22.   [28] Ibid., 1824.
[29] See final report of the parent body, BILS, 1828.

by the BILS.[30] In its years of operation the BILS had harnessed the enthusiasm of middle and upper-class women to actively engage in benevolence. One of its more interesting aspects was the fact that its work was carried on outside the institutional churches, which were the prime agencies actively supporting female philanthropy.

A number of charitable societies organised by women in the last century either had parent bodies operating from England or had bases within the country administering relief to parts of the country outside their immediate catchment area. The BILS was an example of this. Larger societies like the Girls' Friendly Society and the Young Women's Christian Association were founded in England and later spread to Ireland. Smaller societies like the AFD Society, established in England by a Miss Hinton in 1859, opened a branch in Ireland in 1872. This society, run by women, gave grants to the poor clergy of the Church of Ireland.[31] While the Irish branches of such organisations were autonomous they did report annually to the parent body and many received funds to support their cause.

The Belfast Ladies' Relief Association for Connaught was organised under the direction of the Rev. John Edgar, the noted temperance advocate, in 1847. The ladies of this society attempted to counteract the effects of the famine in the west of Ireland by aiming to 'improve, by industry, the temporal condition of the poor females of Connaught and their spiritual [condition] by the truth of the Bible'.[32] To this end they raised funds which were used to establish schools where skills such as knitting and needlework could be taught. By 1850 the society had employed thirty-two schoolmistresses within the province who worked under the direction of resident ladies. In the same year the society claimed to have offered employment and education to over 2,000 poor girls and women.[33] Like the BILS the members of the BLRAC sought to change the habits and morality of the poor in general by influencing the

---

[30] Annual report, Carlow and Graigue Ladies' Association for Bettering the Condition of the Female Peasantry, 1830. This association operated in connection with the Society for Bettering the Condition of the Poor in Ireland. However it dealt only with poor women and the members of the association appear to have been influenced by the BILS.

[31] Barrett, *Guide*, p. 26. The title AFD came from the first and last letters of the words A Friend.

[32] Rev. Hamilton Magee, *Fifty Years in the 'Irish Mission'* (Belfast, n.d.), p. 42; John Edgar, *The Women of the West: Ireland Helped to Help Herself* (Belfast, 1849), p. 3.

[33] Ibid., p. 5.

behaviour of women. Through the acquisition of skills and, of course, a religious education the society claimed that a 'reformation of habits and character [had] been largely effected'.[34]

The tragedy of the famine spurred many women to benevolent action. A tremendous amount of activity was carried out by women of all denominations during these dark years. Food kitchens were set up, committees organised to distribute relief and collect money. Nuns nursed in fever hospitals and fed the starving at their convents.[35] One aspect of this philanthropic work during the famine was the development of cottage industries. As one writer noted in 1862, in those years 'ladies burst the bonds of conventionalities, and went regularly into business to procure remunerative employment for the destitute of their own sex'.[36] Women philanthropists attempted a pragmatic solution to the problem of poverty by creating opportunities for employment among the female poor. Generally this type of philanthropy was not carried out under the direction of any charitable society and depended on the enthusiasm of individual women willing to undertake such work. Through individual action 'the female children of the poor became, all over the land, subjects of instruction in the making up of various sorts of articles for sale'.[37] The teaching of needlework skills became an integral part of the education provided by nuns for poor children and many lay women also acted as teachers and benefactors of schools where such skills were taught. By 1851 there were stated to be 902 children acquiring these skills within schools.[38] The provision of this type of education appears to have been particularly prevalent in the Cork area. For example, Mrs Meredith opened the Adelaide School in the city, which employed 'young persons of limited means or reduced

---

[34] Ibid.

[35] See, for example, the *Cork Examiner*, January 1847 for the establishment of a women's relief committee. No full study has examined the extent of private relief provided during the great famine. There are some references made in convent annals to the work done by nuns during these years. For some reference to private philanthropy during this period see Cecil Woodham-Smith, *The Great Hunger: Ireland 1845–1849* (London, 1962).

[36] S. Meredith, 'The cultivation of female industry in Ireland', *EWJ*, 1 September 1862, p. 305; Meredith, *The Lacemakers, Sketches of Irish Character with some Account of the Effort to Establish Lacemaking in Ireland* (London, 1865). This is the same Meredith who became involved in prison reform in England.

[37] Meredith, 'Cultivation'. During the famine years she claimed that 300,000 women were employed in sewed muslin work and 20,000 in the production of lace, Meredith, *Lacemakers*, p. 17.

[38] Meredith, 'Cultivation', pp. 305–6.

circumstances'.[39] Similar work was carried out by the Ladies' Industrial Society of Ireland, established in 1847, which united women to 'carry out a system for encouraging and developing the latent capacities of the poor of Ireland'.[40]

Needlework was a skill with which middle and upper-class women were totally familiar. They made a pragmatic use of this skill by teaching it to poor women and children who could use it to maintain an existence. The provision of employment as a means of relief had the advantage of ensuring that the poor would not be bereft of skills with which to earn a livelihood, and would also make them independent of seeking relief from charitable societies or the workhouse. Acquiring such skills was also thought to be a valuable educational process as it 'necessitated cleanliness, patience and accuracy'.[41] Lady Aberdeen instituted the Irish Home Industries Association in 1886 which also organised local branches throughout the country where 'resident ladies' encouraged knitting, sewing and weaving amongst the female peasantry. She also organised a display of work carried out by the society at the Irish Exhibition in London in 1888 and opened at least two shops, one in Dublin and the other in London, where such work could be sold.[42]

Lady Aberdeen was one of the many titled women who played a major role in philanthropic and benevolent organisations in Ireland in the late nineteenth and early twentieth centuries. Born Ishbel Marjoribanks (1857–1939) in Scotland she married John Gordon, Lord Aberdeen, in 1877. He was to serve as lord high commissioner to the General Assembly in Scotland, as governor general of Canada and in 1886 was sent as lord lieutenant to Ireland by Gladstone. That first period in Ireland lasted only seven months. In 1905 he was again appointed viceroy and this time his stay was more substantial and lasted to 1915. During her first residence Lady Aberdeen toured the country and visited convent lace industries, and it was then she decided to establish the Irish Home Industries Association which would help to market the goods made. She visited

[39] Ibid., p. 308. See also Helen Blackburn, *A Handy Book of Reference for Irishwomen* (London, 1888).
[40] Report for 1852 of the Ladies' Industrial Society for Ireland for the Encouragement of Remunerative Labour among the Peasantry, 1853, p. 3.
[41] Meredith, 'Cultivation', p. 309.
[42] *EWR*, 15 November 1887, pp. 492–4; 15 July 1889, pp. 311–15; 15 May 1890, pp. 198–201; *The Lady of the House*, 15 September 1891, pp. 3–4; *Clonmel Chronicle*, 10 July 1895; Blackburn, *Reference*, pp. 53–7.

Ireland on a number of occasions between 1886 and 1905 and when her husband was reappointed as viceroy she initiated the Women's National Health Association which attempted to combat the spread of disease, particularly tuberculosis. A caravan toured the country with two nurses giving lectures on health and hygiene. By 1910 there were 155 branches of the society throughout the country. Aberdeen herself was also an active suffragist and in 1904 had headed a liberal women's suffrage deputation to Sir Henry Campbell-Bannerman. She was also president of the International Council of Women for three periods: 1893–9, 1904–20 and 1922–36. She led a joint deputation of ICW and the Inter-Allied Conference of Women Suffragists to the League of Nations Commission of the Peace Conference at Versailles in April 1919.[43] Although Aberdeen achieved a great deal she was not universally liked in Ireland.[44] She appears to have interfered unduly with public departments, and was keen on extending her own power and patronage. But like many other titled women she was influential in extending the scope of women's philanthropic activity in nineteenth-century Ireland.

Employment as a means of relief was not confined to the female peasantry. Women philanthropists recognised that women who had been brought up as 'ladies' could also fall on hard times. It was generally believed that these 'genteel poor' were loathe to seek aid from existing charitable societies and a number of organisations were established to cater for their needs. The Irish Ladies' Work Society, established around 1881, attempted to provide support and employment to 'ladies with an insufficient income [as] a means of helping themselves'.[45] The organisers of this society advertised for knitting and needlework orders which would be carried out by these 'ladies'. Similarly, the Association for the Relief of Ladies in Distress Through Non-Payment of Rent in Ireland, was established in 1881 with the purpose of providing financial support to 'ladies, unmarried or widowed' whose income, derived from the rental of land, had ceased or been disrupted by the land war. This society had a mixed managing committee but the women of the society visited those who

[43] See Lord and Lady Aberdeen, *We Twa* (London, 1925), and *More Cracks with We Twa* (London, 1929); Lady Aberdeen, 'Helping Ireland to help herself', *Outlook*, 112 (March 1916), and 'Health and happiness in the homes of Ireland'; W. Fitzgerald (ed.), *The Voice of Ireland* (Dublin, 1924), pp. 434–39; Nellie O'Cleirigh, 'Lady Aberdeen and the Irish connection', *Dublin Historical Record*, 39 (December 1985–September 1986), p. 28.

[44] *Bean na hEireann*, 8 (June 1909).   [45] *EWR*, 15 November 1881, p. 518.

sought its aid. The committee also opened a registry where such 'ladies' could seek employment. Interestingly, no moral judgements were made regarding the recipients of this charity and work was provided only 'where such form of assistance would be most acceptable to the applicants'.[46] The recipients of the charity were of the same class and social background as the women who formed the committee of the association and this fact, together with the realisation that such a fate could also befall them spurred them to action. The possibility that such 'ladies' could be forced to enter a workhouse was greeted with horror. Those who had entered a workhouse appear to have been taken out and granted a monthly pension by the association.[47] The case histories of the recipients of the charity, cited in an account of the work of the organisation, were obviously chosen to arouse the utmost sympathy. Like that of the 'three unmarried ladies, all over 60 years of age, whose father was a deputy-lieutenant and magistrate of the county. Their united income is now £12 10s; and one is suffering from acute rheumatism, one from throat disease, and a third lamed from a railway accident.'[48] The committee also extended their plea for funds to London and organised two local committees in that city. Between 1881 and 1883 the association gave 1,076 grants or loans of money, repayable without interest, educated thirty-three children and enabled four families to emigrate.[49]

Gratuitous relief to poor women was also provided particularly by female religious and by a number of organisations run by men. The Night Asylum for the Houseless Poor, which opened in Dublin in 1838, and which was organised by men, provided shelter to destitute people who could not afford to pay for lodgings. The asylum organisers did not provide food, beds or bedding. In 1843 a total of 37,951 individuals used the shelter, women accounted for 15,758 of this number.[50] The Sisters of Mercy ran St Joseph's Night Refuge

---

[46] Barrett, *Guide*, p. 28; *EWR*, 15 November 1881, p. 518; 14 January 1882, p. 28; annual report, Association for the Relief of Ladies in Distress Through Non-Payment of Rent in Ireland, 1882.

[47] *EWR*, 15 October 1887, pp. 464–5.   [48] Ibid., p. 465.

[49] Ibid., p. 466; Barrett, *Guide*, p. 28.

[50] Sixth Annual Report of the Committee of the Night Asylum for Houseless Poor, 1844, p. 1. In 1873, 62,611 people used the shelter and women accounted for 23,579 of these. By 1875 an average of 64 women and girls were using the refuge each week. See thirty-sixth annual report of the committee of the Night Asylum for Houseless Poor, 1874, p. 7; Reports of the Charity Organisation Committee of the Statistical and Social Inquiry Society as to the Houseless Poor (Dublin, 1876), pp. 3–4.

for Women and Children which had room for 200 individuals.[51] The particular concern shown for homeless women and children was due not to their destitution alone but because it was thought that homelessness could lead to the practice of vice. The shelter was seen to be a preventive institution engaged in the moral protection of women and children. An appeal for public support published in 1860 attempts to arouse public sympathy by dwelling at length upon the dangers associated with homelessness and it is primarily the danger of sexual immorality which is stressed.

Other institutions, homes and refuges were organised by women to cater for the destitute poor. One of the main groups which received support was domestic servants, a group familiar to philanthropic women who generally employed them in their homes. Philanthropists were concerned that servants be proficient in carrying out their duties and one society, the Society for the Encouragement and Reward of Good Conduct in Female Servants, established in Belfast in 1836, attempted to encourage servants to remain in their places of employment. The habit of regularly changing places of employment was considered detrimental to the smooth running of a household and was also a source of concern for the moral welfare of the female servant, because 'by wandering continually from place to place, young women encounter temptations of every description; and many a promising character has thus been ruined and ultimately sunk to the lowest state of degradation'.[52] To counteract this mobility the society guaranteed a servant who completed a fixed number of years, either four or seven years of uninterrupted service in one household, and a sum of money to the amount of 4 to 10 guineas.

Homes for aged servants were also established and it was thought that if servants were aware that they would be taken care of in their old age it would be an incentive to them to behave well while employed. The female committee of the Asylum for Aged and Infirm Female Servants stated that its aim was 'not more to discourage the idle and profligate, than to reward the honest and faithful servant'.[53] Again, many of the refuges established by women in the last century

[51] Ibid., p. 4.　　　[52] Quoted in Mr and Mrs S.C. Hall, *Ireland*, II, p. 63.
[53] Annual report, Committee of the Asylum for Aged and Infirm Female Servants, 1818, p. 4. This asylum began in 1817 and ceased operating in 1839. The very existence of the home, the committee suggested, 'must have a strong though silent effect on those, whose irregularities and want of principle, are but too frequently causes of complaint, interrupting the calm current of domestic happiness'.

saw themselves as preventive institutions which protected the female servant, who was without a situation, from falling into vice. Some of these homes catered for young girls who were given training in domestic service and one of the earliest of such homes appears to have been the House of Refuge established in Baggot street in 1802. The young women had to be of 'respectable character' before being received into the refuge and once inside were taught skills to enable them to function capably in households. The committee of this refuge stated that when in the home young girls 'can be provided with suitable services, they are sheltered when poor and defenceless from the dangers to which they may be exposed from liberty, youth and inexperience'.[54] The Protestant Servants' Home, established in 1873 and under a mixed management committee, was one of the longest lasting homes of its kind. The home was intended for Protestant women servants coming to work in Dublin from the country. In return for a small weekly payment these women were provided with lodgings which would prevent them from getting into 'bad company ... both their religious and moral training shall be carefully attended to, so helping to fit them for the more faithful discharge of social and domestic duties'.[55] In common with other charitable societies organised by women these homes for servants reveal the intention of the organisers to promote not only the temporal but also the spiritual welfare of those they aided. No aspect of the life of the poor was neglected by these philanthropists.

One of the major influences in developing a more scientific attitude to philanthropy came about through the influence of the National Association for the Promotion of Social Science. This Association had developed from the British Association for the Advancement of Science in England in October of 1857. The founders of the association believed that it was possible to develop a 'social science' of society and thus change could be brought about in society in a scientific manner. The NAPSS was an important platform for activists, many of whom were women, who wished to change society. The annual meetings of the association in 1861 and 1867 were held in Dublin and Belfast respectively. When Isabella Tod first entered public life she did so under the auspices of the NAPSS at the 1867 meeting. She later wrote that the meeting had

---

[54] Annual report, House of Refuge, Baggot Street, 1803; Warburton et al., *City of Dublin*, I, pp. 792–5.
[55] Protestant Servants' Home, special appeal, 1874, p. 1.

given her her first experience 'of direct political effort for a social purpose'.[56] Issues concerning philanthropy and women's position in society were debated at the meetings of the association. Anne Jellicoe, who engaged in philanthropy and later established Alexandra College in Dublin, delivered a paper on the Irish convict system at the 1862 meeting. Sarah Atkinson and Ellen Woodlock spoke on the position of children in Irish workhouses in 1861.[57] A number of women philanthropists gained the confidence to express their ideas for change through this association; they also discussed their ideas with other members of the association and developed societies to agitate for change.

One of the societies to spring from the NAPSS was the Dublin Ladies' Sanitary Association, established in 1861 and affiliated to the male run Dublin Sanitary Association. It aimed to 'improve the physical condition of the poor, and to dispel the ignorance of the laws of health that exists among all classes'.[58] To this end they organised lectures where 'ladies' could be instructed in health matters and would then bring their knowledge to the homes of the poor in organised visitation.[59] This society had both Catholic and Protestant members and assured the public that Catholic homes were visited by Catholics and Protestant homes by Protestants. Its exact relationship to the male run DSA is not very clear. While the DSA applied itself to putting pressure on Dublin corporation to execute alterations in the city's sanitary provisions and also, incidentally, employed an inspector to investigate causes of complaint, the DLSA confined itself to lecturing and visitation on health matters. The DLSA appears to have become defunct by 1890 but in closing up their affairs asked the DSA to take over its function in regard to lecturing and visitation. The DSA declined this offer, requesting instead that the DLSA be reorganised and continue its visitation work. This does not appear to have happened but it seems that women from the DLSA continued their work on an individual basis without the support of the women's organisation and apparently without associating with the DSA.[60] Another society to

[56] See *Transactions of the National Association for the Promotion of Social Science* (1861). Helen Blackburn, *Women's Suffrage: A Record of the Women's Suffrage Movement in the British Isles, with Biographical Sketches of Miss Becker* (London, 1902), p. 127; see also an obituary for Tod in *EWR*, 1897, pp. 58–62.

[57] *The Times*, 23 August 1861.

[58] Ibid.; Barrett, *Guide*, p. 50; Blackburn, *Women's Suffrage*, p. 106.

[59] Minute book, Dublin Sanitary Association, 1889–90 (RCPI).   [60] Ibid.

develop from the NAPSS was the Dublin Kyrle Society, established in 1883, which aimed to bring 'cheering influences of natural and artistic beauty home to the people' by, among other things, decorating schoolrooms and working men's clubs, encouraging window gardening amongst the poor and laying out gardens in waste ground around the city.[61] This society was a branch of the Kyrle Society in London, established by Miranda and Octavia Hill in 1876.

Women did not confine themselves only to visiting the poor or establishing societies to provide them with relief through employment. By the end of the century the desire to help the sick poor, considered one of the more deserving groups in society, had brought about changes and improvements in nursing care. Such visitation by lay women appears to have been generally informal until the end of the century, although around 1838 the Marchioness Wellesley Female Tontine Society (a tontine was an annuity fund shared by the members of a society) was formed in Dublin which had a mixed management committee but only allowed women to become members. The aim of the society was to ensure that the members would 'support each other in sickness and distress and that we may be able at all times to relieve each other in death and sickness'.[62] Each member had to contribute one shilling per week to the society which was invested in stocks. During illness a member was then entitled to 6s per week for seven weeks if she could not work and a further 35s for six weeks if the illness continued. On the birth of a child a woman was allowed 10s 6d and members organised themselves to visit any of their number who was ill.[63] The members of this society who visited their ill sisters, like most others who engaged in sick visitation, had no formal medical knowledge.

By the 1870s women came to realise that improvements in health

---

[61] The title 'Kyrle' apparently came from Alexander Pope's *Man of Ross* who, although not rich, beautified his surroundings. See Olive Checkland, *Philanthropy in Victorian Scotland* (Edinburgh, 1980), n 8, p. 310.

[62] Rules and Orders to be Observed by the Marchioness Wellesley Female Tontine Society (Dublin, 1838), p. 1.

[63] Ibid. A woman who fell ill through contracting a venereal disease was not entitled to any relief. Only women of 'good character' could become members and the wives of watchmen, constables or labourers were barred from joining. The women who joined had to bring their husbands along also to be interviewed by the committee regarding the couple's financial circumstances. The rules of this society also laid out specific fines for the misbehaviour of members. For example, any woman found drunk at a meeting was fined 6d and if caught using 'improper language' was fined 1s and any 'sister (member) going drunk to a brother or sister's funeral to be fined 2s 6d'.

care could only be carried through by trained nurses. In 1874 the
first lay society, organised by women to train and employ nurses to
look after the needs of the sick poor, was begun in Belfast. The
purpose of the Society for Providing Nurses for the Sick Poor was to
'visit the industrious poor in their own homes and supply such
ministrations as their care may require'.[64] The society was non-
sectarian and cared for the sick poor of any religious denomination.
The nurses employed by the society were supervised by a ladies'
committee, whose members visited her at work and oversaw the
financial aspects of the care to be provided. The nurses themselves
were to be 'an example of neatness, order, cleanliness and sobriety
and to urge upon her patients the importance of cleanliness in
person and dwelling'. If a doctor was engaged to help in a case she
had to show deference to his superior knowledge and her duty was to
'supplement, not to take his place'.[65] Between 1874 and 1876 the
society's nurses attended to 1,335 patients. At this stage they
employed five nurses, at an annual salary of £34, and twenty ladies
were occupied in visitation.[66] Even in nursing the sick poor the
committee were wary of providing aid to the undeserving: 'the
supervisors continue to investigate carefully every case, seeing as
they do, more and more fully, the evils of indiscriminate almsgiving,
which strikes at the very root of self-respect in the recipient and robs
the really deserving poor of the sympathy and help which is
bestowed on unworthy objects'.[67]

Like many previous societies the members of the SPNSP sought to
influence the health and living conditions of the poor family by
influencing the conduct of the mother, believing that 'the improvement of sanitary conditions is more in their power than in that of any
outside reformer'.[68] By 1884, following the example set by the
Belfast society, other women in Dublin, Lisburn, Downpatrick,
Ballymena, Hollywood and Randalstown had begun their own
societies to engage in district nursing. Again, the idea that the lives
of the poor could be transformed by the actions and intervention of
their social betters was expressed

if the poor are to be raised to a better condition they must be dealt with as

---

[64] Annual report, Society for Providing Nurses for the Sick Poor, 1877, p. 5 (hereafter
SPNSP).
[65] Ibid.   [66] Annual reports, SPNSP, 1878, p. 8; 1879, p. 10.
[67] Annual report, SPNSP, 1880, p. 10.
[68] Annual report, SPNSP, 1882, p. 10.

individuals. For this purpose there can be no agency better than the cultivated woman, who, living in her own home, surrounded by her own interests and connections, goes among the toiling and suffering, with the love of God in her heart, bringing her loving thought and sympathy to bear on the individual households for the time being placed under her care.[69]

The success of the SPNSP was attributed by the committee to the vast numbers of women who worked voluntarily. It claimed to embrace all classes in its work, with the nobility and gentry classes directing its operations, the middle-class women doing much of the visitation and nursing and the servant maid doing her bit by engaging in the needlework guild, making clothing for the patients. It was indeed a microcosm of the way society in general was considered to function harmoniously, everyone knew their place and the nature of the work which they had to do. The provision of trained nurses was a significant innovation at a time when public hospitals and workhouse hospitals did not consider them vital in running their institutions. The undoubted benefits which these sick poor societies brought to the poor cannot be measured but in the area of professionalising both nursing, and indeed social work, as valid occupations for women they were important. Such societies were expressions of a growing belief that women had a right to paid work which, not only provided her with a living, but also allowed her to function as a socially active agent in society.

From the 1840s a number of institutions were established in Dublin which offered both training and accommodation to nurses. St Patrick's Nurses' Home, for instance, in Stephen's Green, provided training and free nursing to poor patients in their own homes from the 1880s.[70] A number of convalescent homes were also established. One of these, St John's House of Rest, was established in 1870 by a Miss Jane Trench. Jane Trench, together with her sisters, Frances and Maria, were involved in the provision of nursing care for the poor over a long number of years. Both Jane and Frances ran St John's House of Rest and Maria was involved in the running of the Dublin Nurses Training Institution. These convalescent homes were essentially charitable and patients were usually treated gratuitously. In St John's House of Rest, for example, between 1870 and 1873 204 people, men, women and children, were provided for. Of this number only 56 paid for their own treatment and the rest were

[69] Annual report, SPNSP, 1885, p. 9.   [70] Barrett, *Guide*, pp. 29, 31.

paid for either by their employers or by the committee of the home from donations received.[71]

Hospital visitation was also undertaken by women in the last century. It appears that such visitation by lay women was carried out mainly by Protestants as on the Catholic side female religious had obviated the need for lay Catholic involvement in such an enterprise. Fear of proselytism was to cause tension between visitors of various religious persuasions. In 1873 the establishment of the Association for Visiting Hospitals was set up to counteract the perceived proselytism of Protestant visitors in Dublin hospitals. The initiation of a scheme to raise funds for hospitals in 1874 was received badly by the Catholic hierarchy who refused to lend its support. The scheme involved the preaching of an annual hospital Sunday sermon and the donated funds would then be distributed amongst the hospitals. Cullen would not lend his support probably because the managing committee was made up of a number of leading Protestants.[72] From the evidence available there appears to have been little if any communication between women hospital visitors and religious beliefs once again acted as a barrier to co-operation between philanthropic women.

Though we have little information about women's role as hospital visitors some details regarding the women's visiting committee of the Westmoreland Lock hospital have survived. Although, as previously noted, the hospital was in operation from the 1770s it was only in 1889 that the board of governors considered allowing women as visitors. The initiative came from a group of Protestant women who wrote to the Board in 1889 and offered their services to the hospital. The Board agreed to allow visitation on four days per week from 2.30 to 4 p.m. The women were allowed to converse with Protestant inmates only and that activity, allied to choosing proper reading material for them, was the limit of their function as decided by the Board.[73] By 1891 it was obvious that the visitors were becoming frustrated in their attempts to help the inmates by the limitations set and they suggested that the Board help them financially to institute a home in which the patients who were cured could be sheltered. Although the Board supported the suggestion it had no right to use

[71] MS Register of Inmates, 1870–7 (St John's House of Rest, Merrion, Dublin).
[72] Hospital proposed to be included in the scheme for hospital Sunday, Cullen Papers, File 335/2/47 (Laity 1872) (DDA); see also *Daily Express*, 17 January 1874.
[73] Minute book, board of governors, Westmoreland Lock Hospital, 1889; 1889 (RCPI).

the funds of the hospital for such a purpose and the home was never established.[74]

In April 1895 one of the surgeons of the hospital made a complaint to the Board stating that the 'ladies visiting the Protestant wards asked improper and inquisitional questions of the patients causing them in many cases to leave the hospital before cured'. The ladies refuted this allegation and insisted on an apology from the doctor involved. When this was not forthcoming they threatened to discontinue their visitation. The Board stood firmly behind the doctor while at the same time regretting the decision of the ladies. It was not until early 1896 that the matter was resolved, without any apology from the doctor, and women resumed their visits in January of that year.[75] How important the visiting committee was in the eyes of the Board is open to question as it passed a resolution in May 1895 which 'prohibit[ed] anyone in the hospital or otherwise asking questions of the patients respecting their past or private life'. The hospital authorities stressed that they were primarily interested in the physical cure of their patients, any attempt at moral reform, which was the primary aim of the visiting committee, was of minor importance.[76] The function of the women visitors was severely limited and any attempts made by them to broaden their role were resisted.

WOMEN IN PUBLIC INSTITUTIONS

The establishment of the poor law in Ireland placed many of those who had sought relief from charitable societies in the workhouse. Irish women, at least in Belfast, had some dealings with the inmates of the poorhouse from 1827. They secured situations for the girls of the institution and visited it at three-monthly intervals and also undertook the education of the children.[77]

Similarly in Waterford some benevolent women visited the House of Industry in the first decade of the century and operated a school there for 'the improvement of prostitutes'.[78] With the opening of the

[74] Ibid., 4 April 1891.
[75] Ibid., 6 April 1895; 4 May 1895; 7 October 1895; 10 October 1895; 2 November 1895; 4 January 1896.
[76] Ibid., 4 May 1895.
[77] Mary McNeill, *The Life and Times of Mary Ann McCracken, 1770–1866* (Belfast, 1988), chapter 14, passim.
[78] Report by P.F. Johnston and E. Moylan on charity in Waterford, 1834 (MS 3,288, NLI).

workhouses women began to seek admittance to these institutions as visitors. Lay women, however, appear to have been less successful in gaining entrance than nuns. Details of lay women's work in work-houses is poorly documented and it is not certain how many work-houses allowed them as visitors. There was certainly a ladies' com-mittee attending the Cork workhouse from at least the 1860s and Susan Dowden, a temperance activist, was on the committee for twenty-five years. On her death, in 1898, the board of guardians proposed a vote of sympathy to her family and 'deplore[d] her loss more especially in connection with the management of the Girls' Home and working of the boarding out system of relief where she was secretary of the ladies' committee, exercised control over the education, treatment, clothing and general well-being of 300 chil-dren placed at nurse'.[79] In 1880 the North Dublin Union allowed Catholic and Protestant ladies to visit 'the sick of their own per-suasion in this house for the purpose of affording them consolation and sympathy'.[80] It appears that women visitors had already been allowed to visit in the South Dublin Union. Also in 1883 a Work-house Women's Aid Society was established in Dublin by a group of Protestant women. Its purpose was to secure situations for Prot-estant women inmates of the North Dublin Union but it is unclear if they actually visited the workhouse.[81] This society operated for a number of years and in the 1890s was taken over by the Dublin Women's Work Association, whose members, both men and women, visited the Protestant inmates of the workhouse hospital and also appear to have employed nurses from the Deaconess' Nursing Insti-tution in Tottenham to look after these patients.[82]

Where women were allowed as visitors they dealt primarily with the welfare of children and other women. It was not until 1899 that the Local Government Board requested that all workhouses which boarded out children should form ladies' committees and by 1900

---

[79] In the *Englishwoman's Journal* of 1 May 1863 the following is noted: 'A fresh discussion has arisen in the Cork workhouse about the training of female children ... Mr Mahoney suggested the appointment of a special committee for establishing a training school. He quoted Mrs McSwiney, one of the ladies of the visiting committee who had said to him, on the occasion of the Board voting £930 for sending a number of paupers to Canada that "it would be better economy to expend £100 in training the children to fill situations at home, where they were much more wanted".' Information regarding the work of Susan Dowden can be found in a scrapbook containing letters of condolences on her death (CAI).

[80] Quoted in *EWR*, 15 April 1880, pp. 172–3.   [81] Barrett, *Guide*, pp. 46–7.

[82] Williams, *Dublin Charities*, p. 252.

there were fifteen such committees in existence.[83] How much control or even influence women had over the internal affairs of the workhouse remains unknown. Both the Irish Workhouse Association and the Philanthropic Reform Association, established in Dublin in 1897 and 1896 respectively, sought to bring about changes in the workhouse system. Both societies were managed by men and women. The IWA aimed for, among other things, 'the improvement of the condition of the sick, the aged, children and other helpless classes'.[84] In 1897 the IWA suggested to the government that it employ at least one trained nurse in every union and after much lobbying from the members of the IWA the government agreed with the suggestion and paid half of the salary of every trained nurse they employed.[85] Through the IWA also, Lady Pembroke's Nursing Scheme was initiated. Lady Pembroke agreed to pay the training expenses of a certain number of nurses who, on completing training, undertook to nurse for three years in a workhouse.[86] The PRA also instituted a number of changes within the South Dublin Union and with the help of Lady Meath introduced the Brabazon Employment Scheme. Through this scheme older inmates of the workhouse were provided with employment to keep them occupied. No payment was made for the work done and a number of women from the PRA taught the inmates the skills required. An attempt by the same society to introduce the scheme to the North Dublin Union failed when the board of guardians refused to allow it.[87]

Although no clear picture of lay women's activities within the workhouses emerges from the available evidence there is no doubt that those women who did act as visitors clearly saw that they could strengthen their position by becoming poor law guardians. Such a belief signals some of the changes which were occurring in women's involvement in philanthropy from mid-century. From this period we can observe the development of two different strands of philanthropic involvement, one was a benevolent strand, the other was more reformist. In the benevolent strand the majority of women philanthropists were content to carry out the work for which their societies had been originated and cared more for the temporal and spiritual welfare of the recipients of their charity than for seeking out the

[83] Laura Stephens, 'Irish workhouses' in Smyth (ed.), *Social Service*, p. 79.
[84] Annual report, Irish Workhouse Association, 1907, p. 2.
[85] Stephens, 'Irish workhouses', p. 87.   [86] Ibid., p. 103.
[87] Annual report, Philanthropic Reform Association, 1899, p. 15.

social causes of misfortune. Those women who formed, or joined, reformist organisations were adamant that legislative changes were necessary to bring about improvement in the care of the poor and destitute. The strongest strand in philanthropic circles was that of benevolence but the second strand was significant, particularly in relation to the politicisation of women in nineteenth-century Ireland. But before examining the role of women within these reform organisations one other movement, which involved benevolent and reformist women, needs to be examined. That movement was concerned with the temperance issue. The various temperance organisations which were operated by women in nineteenth-century Ireland played a significant role in broadening women's perception of their role in society and also their part in the political process.

TEMPERANCE WORK

No study has yet been done on the role women played in the temperance movement, in Ireland. In her recent work, '*Ireland Sober, Ireland Free' Drink and Temperance in Nineteenth-Century Ireland*, Elizabeth Malcolm devotes just a few lines to women temperance activists. She asserts that 'Irishwomen did not play an active independent role in the temperance movement, as was to be the case in the United States. Such female temperance organisations as existed in Ireland were usually firmly under male control.'[88] Without doubt, women's temperance activism in Ireland never reached the heights achieved by their American counterparts,[89] but to dismiss women's role as being subordinate to that of men ignores the very deep commitment and level of independent action undertaken by women temperance advocates in this country. Women not only established their own temperance societies but their involvement in this issue spurred them to engage in philanthropic work which they felt was related to the temperance issue. Thus the establishment of inebriate homes and preventative institutions for girls and women who had fallen into crime through alcohol abuse was directly related to their work in the temperance field.

---

[88] Elizabeth Malcolm, '*Ireland Sober, Ireland Free*', *Drink and Temperance in Nineteenth-Century Ireland* (Dublin, 1986), has three references to women's temperance activism, pp. 161, 176, 286.

[89] See, for example, Barbara L. Epstein, *The Politics of Domesticity: Women, Evangelism and Temperance in Nineteenth-Century America* (Connecticut, 1980).

Ann Jane Carlile was one of the first Irishwomen to actively promote temperance. She was born in County Monaghan in 1775 and married at twenty-five to a Presbyterian minister, the Rev. Francis Carlile, who died eleven years later. She was the mother of six living children. Sometime after 1822 she moved to Dublin and was active in prison visiting and is stated to have visited all the prisons in Dublin before Elizabeth Fry came in 1827. It was through her work in the prisons that she became interested in temperance. In 1830 she established a small temperance society in Poolbeg Street in Dublin which catered for sailors, and in 1834 she founded another society in Cootehill, County Cavan, where she was resident for some time. Her work for temperance became widely known and she was a friend and correspondent of Fr Mathew. In 1843, at the invitation of English temperance activists, she made the first of many visits to England. In 1847 she formed the Band of Hope movement, a temperance society for children, and earlier also she had been involved in forming the Victoria Temperance Society, a women's organisation, in Belfast in 1841.[90] In her temperance work she concentrated her activities on women and children, and wrote three tracts which were widely used in temperance circles: 'Little Mary, or a Daughter's Love'; 'John Miller, the Reformed Sailor' and 'The Reformed Family of Ballymena'.[91] The first relates the allegedly true story of a 'genteel' family who had fallen on hard times due to the mother's addiction to alcohol. The shock of knowing his wife was a 'winebibber' killed the husband and left a lone daughter unprotected. The child was taken in by Carlile and saved from the horrors of an alcoholic mother.[92] In the second tract Carlile stresses the importance of women in the temperance cause. 'On them, chiefly', she states, 'the rising generation are depending for the formation of their religious principles and habits.'[93] The last tract describes the influence of temperance principles on a family. Through tectotalism the husband had regained his health, the family fortunes have been restored, and, not least important, 'family worship was regularly observed'.[94] What

---

[90] For a brief synopsis of her life see D.H. Crofton, *The Children of Edmondstown Park* (Portlaw, 1980), chapter 3. For further information see Frederick Sherlock, *Ann Jane Carlile, A Temperance Pioneer* (London, 1897). Carlile was cited as an inspiration by other women temperance activists like Mrs Byers, later president of the WTA, and Isabella Tod. See Sherlock, *Ann Jane Carlile*, pp. 56–70; *EWJ*, 15 Feburary 1883, pp. 62–3; 15 February 1886, p. 83.

[91] Sherlock, *Ann Jane Carlile*, pp. 72–6.   [92] Ibid., pp. 56–8.   [93] Ibid., p. 73.
[94] Ibid., pp. 75–6.

is evident from these tracts is the stress on the detrimental effect alcohol abuse had on family life. This was a theme referred to again and again by women's temperance societies. Efforts to get men to abstain also revolved around keeping the family from poverty. The second theme which is to be found in women's temperance activism is the importance laid on women as advocates of teetotalism. This was again the expression of women's superior moral and spiritual nature; through her example and influence on the family the standards of a civilised life would be maintained. Another important aspect of women's temperance work was the link between it and religious belief and this comes across strongly in Carlile's tracts. All of these themes were to be echoed in the variety of temperance societies established throughout the century.

There appears to have been a Ladies' Temperance Society organised in Belfast in 1838, prior to the founding of the Victoria Temperance Society. The women involved organised meetings in their own homes and gave talks on temperance issues.[95] Detailed information on the activities of these societies is difficult to find as such societies were frequently organised and as frequently disbanded. The Ladies' Temperance Union was organised, again in Belfast, in 1862. The meetings were conducted in members' homes and always included a temperance talk and prayer meeting. These women also became involved in practical work by visiting the homes of the poor, engaging a temperance missionary, presumably male, to spread their message, looking after the education of poor children and organising public meetings for the cause.[96] The honorary secretary of this society was Mrs Mayne, wife of Alexander Mayne, the temperance activist. In Dublin a Ladies' Metropolitan Temperance Union was formed in 1866 and the Church of Ireland Total Abstinence Association had a large number of women as executive and council members when it was established in 1862. This latter society had developed from the earlier Dublin Ladies' Total Abstinence Association, formed some years previously.[97]

Women's enthusiasm for this cause waxed and waned and it was not until the 1870s that Irishwomen really took up the issue with any degree of consistency. In 1874, in Belfast, the Women's Temperance Association was launched, and by 1889 there were reported to be

[95] Anon., *Will You Help Us? The Story of the Belfast Women's Temperance Association and Christian Workers' Union* (Belfast, n.d.), p. 2.
[96] Ibid., pp. 2–3.   [97] Malcolm, *Ireland Sober*, p. 286.

forty branches organised around the country.[98] By 1875 the WTA had opened three 'refreshment houses ... where there can be no temptation to drink', in Belfast, one of which offered 'nutritious dinners to girls engaged in factories'.[99] The women of the WTA were also aware of the work being done for the temperance cause in America and in 1876 invited Mrs Stewart, or Mother Stewart as she was known in her homeland, to speak to the association.[100] In one of its leaflets women, as a group, were recognised as suffering most from the evils of intemperance. It was to women, as wives, that this society looked to help remedy the situation. 'Is it not', they asked, 'the duty of women in the spirit of meekness, by the power of a strong personal and womanly influence, to endeavour to help men to overcome the tyrannical drinking customs of society?'[101] It was through her influence in the home that the wife was to stem the intemperance of her husband. One means of doing this, according to the society, was to place a ban on all alcoholic spirits in the home. The domestic authority of women was to be invoked for a moral end. The WTA also saw temperance as God's work, a unification of the moral and religious dimensions of female benevolence. Among the original committee of this association was Isabella Tod, who, as we have seen, was active in a myriad of societies dealing with issues relating to women's social, philanthropic and political interests.

Mrs Byers, founder and headmistress of Victoria College in Belfast and secretary of the WTA, spoke particularly of the need for women in this field: 'She who founds a temperance society at her own hearth, who imbues her sons and daughters with a hatred of intemperance and its kindred vices, and trains her children in habits of self control, is doing good work for the nation.'[102] Temperance was to be inculcated in the home, the 'power' sphere of women. The Dublin Bible Woman Mission organised temperance societies within the city for both men and women. These societies judged their success in terms of making men more responsible for the financial care of their families. In one story, related in an annual report, a father 'who used to spend his wages in a public house is now able to pay for his son's education ... with money saved from

---

98 Anon., *Will You Help Us?*, p. 5; *EWR*, June 1875, p. 272.
99 *EWR*, June 1875, pp. 272–3.
100 *EWR*, May 1876, p. 219; see Epstein, *Domesticity*, for the work of Mrs Stewart.
101 Quoted in *Will You Help Us?*, p. 3.
102 Quoted in ibid., p. 5.

drink'.[103] These temperance societies provided the practical means
for abstainers to benefit from their abstinence by encouraging them
to save regularly. The priority of this type of society was to ensure
the financial well-being of the family by stressing the responsibility
of the breadwinner towards his dependants. All of the stories related
in the annual reports of these organisations concentrate on this
aspect of the benefits of teetotalism. Regular meetings, which
encouraged members to adhere to their temperance resolution, and
visitations to the homes of the members were other methods used to
strengthen them and to influence them for good.[104] The Bible
Woman Missions which operated these societies were branches of
the male run Church of Ireland Temperance Society. But, as we
have previously seen, women were left in full control and their only
obligation to the parent body was to report annually on their
operations.

The Belfast Ladies' Temperance Association branched out from
supporting temperance to initiating schemes for social reform. They
saw temperance as a means to an end, 'if a man lives a sober, he must
also live an honest and righteous life if his sobriety is to be of sterling
value'.[105] This applied to both men and women. In instilling social
values they concentrated on working with women. To this end they
established the Prison Gate Mission and a home for inebriate
women. 'The world is unspeakably harder to a woman who falls
than a man, and [the] doors of escape which stand open to him are
closed to her', wrote Isabella Tod in 1881.[106] The woman drunkard
was also seen as a 'fallen woman', and like her penitent or criminal
sister she needed the protection of an organisation which would
cater specifically to her needs. The Ladies' Temperance Union was
reformed as the WTA in late 1862 and they also opened a home for
inebriate women in Belfast sometime in 1880 or 1881.[107] The women
who entered this home had been encountered by the committee in
their work with the Belfast Prison Gate Mission. Constant employment and attention to religious practices were the methods used to
wean the women from their dependence on alcohol. From this

---

[103] Annual report, Dublin Bible Woman Mission, 1878, p. 11. Another wife is quoted as
    saying 'Thank God we joined the Temperance Society Miss . . . He is not the same man
    since.'
[104] Annual report, Dublin Bible Woman Mission, 1878, p. 12.
[105] *EWR*, 15 April 1882, p. 152.
[106] *EWR*, 15 June 1881, pp. 247–8.   [107] Ibid., p. 250.

inebriate home had gone forth 'wives and mothers, restored to their proper place of affection and direction in their family; and household servants, who can be trusted by their mistresses, and who desire to show their gratitude for the kindness shown to them by a faithful discharge of homely duties'.[108]

As well as providing homes for these women the WTA also gave lectures to the poor, as a major cause of alcohol abuse among the working classes was seen to be 'untidy homes, insufficient diet [and] weak health'. They began classes in cookery and hygiene to combat these problems. The differences in attitude expressed towards the working classes can also be seen in one aspect of the society's work. In 1882 the WTA opened a home for girls. The children of the upper stratum of the 'poor class' were thought to be adequately looked after by their parents, but the children of a 'lower and vagrant class ... where the children cannot possibly grow up sober and industrious', needed looking after. The home was to prevent these children falling into vice.[109] At the end of its first year of operation it catered for twenty-one children and the committee also boarded out infants. In 1887 the home was certified as an industrial school. Overall by the end of the 1880s the WTA had 'established coffee houses, and homes for inebriates and [the] Prison Mission, and perhaps', as Tod hoped, 'this new departure [the home for destitute children] may prove the beginning of a widespread movement among Christian women in battling against corruption and vice'.[110] By 1894 all the branches of the WTA merged into one organisation called the Irish Women's Temperance Union, whose motto was 'United to Win Ireland', and their first annual conference was held in Dublin in May of that year.[111]

Some of the women involved in this work were wary of legislation in this field. Isabella Tod, in a talk she gave on the methods to be used to cure drunkards, felt that government initiatives in this area would lead to interference in the liberty of the individual. She believed in the duty of each individual to practise their own moral judgement and felt that government interference would only coerce people, thus removing them from their duty to practise right. 'To supersede the conscience', she stated, 'is to weaken it.' It was only through example and the concern of individuals in the moral and

---

[108] Ibid., p. 251. [109] *Will You Help Us?*, pp. 7–8; *EWR*, 15 May 1883, pp. 227–30.
[110] *EWR*, 15 April 1882, p. 153. [111] *Will You Help Us?*, pp.12–13.

religious welfare of drunkards that any changes should be brought about. Through these means inebriates would be led to an understanding of their duty and responsibility to themselves and to society. While women did support some changes in legislation, particularly dealing with fines and closing hours, they placed great stress on personal responsibility. They felt that their homes and refuges, their preventive and reformative work were the best means which could be used to initiate change.[112]

It is very difficult to assess the practical implications of the work these temperance women did or indeed how influential they were in changing the social and moral habits of the people they helped. Women in the most active temperance societies had a strong tradition of religious activism. In 1883, for example, the WTA added the Christian Workers' Union to its title.[113] In Dublin the Bible Woman Mission initiated temperance societies after a number of years activity in the poorer parts of the city running mother's meetings and classes for poor children.[114] The majority of women active in the area were Protestant or Presbyterian; Catholic women do not appear to have organised any public temperance societies though temperance was encouraged in the sodalities and confraternities run by nuns. Some general characteristics were common to all the temperance societies organised by women. Temperance, sanitary and health reform were linked together. Alcohol abuse, by both men and women, contravened the moral and social standards held by activists. Through temperance work they hoped to influence the social and moral world of the poor. Women's work in the temperance field was also used by Tod as an argument for the granting of women's suffrage. 'The whole temperance movement', she wrote, 'is based upon the acceptance of social responsibility by the individual for herself ... that acceptance is caused by the conviction of the existence of mighty evils all around her ... and which she has some power to lessen.'[115] The power to reduce evil lay within the woman's practice of her innate goodness and Tod argued that the granting of the franchise would extend this power for good which

---

[112] Isabella Tod, 'On the principles on which plans for the curative treatment of habitual drunkards should be based', *Statistical and Social Inquiry Society of Ireland Journal*, 6:7 (May 1875), pp. 408–10.

[113] *EWR*, 15 May 1883, p. 227.

[114] See the reports of Dublin Bible Woman Mission, 1877, 1878, and the report of the Nurses' Home and Bible Woman Association, 1883.

[115] *EWR*, 15 March 1888, p. 105.

women had. She urged women to seek the vote because 'no vote is a vote, and is a vote inevitably on the side of evil'.[116] Politics were part and parcel of everyone's life and affected not only women's material and intellectual circumstances but, much more importantly for Tod, her moral choices. Women's involvement in charity work, and in this instance in temperance work, had proven women's true value, the 'addition of women to the electorate would mean a far larger proportionate addition to the ranks of good'.[117]

PHILANTHROPY AND THE SUFFRAGE MOVEMENT

In the latter years of the century a small band of women joined societies which can be considered reformist. The Ladies' National Association, the National Society for the Prevention of Cruelty to Children, the Philanthropic Reform Association and the Irish Workhouse Association were the most progressive philanthropic societies operating through the entire century. Each of these organisations, with the exception of the LNA, had mixed executive committees which investigated the conditions in workhouses and actively sought changes in the law regarding abused children and destitute people. The women on these committees developed a new awareness of women's disabilities which encouraged them to attack discriminatory social practices. These reformist women associated the acquisition of the vote with social change. The links between philanthropic women generally and the suffrage campaign have received no attention in the histories of the latter campaign in Ireland.[118] However, if we look at those women of the reformist mould, who were active in the above mentioned societies, we can discern that a sizeable minority of women who supported the suffrage campaign were also social activists and indeed many of them were philanthropic activists before they were suffragists.

From the 1860s debates were taking place in Ireland about issues relating to women's employment, education and political rights. These debates were not formulated in a vacuum and were affected by the experiences many middle-class women had within philanthropic organisations. Through their involvement in such organi-

---

[116] Ibid.   [117] Ibid., pp. 106-7.
[118] See, for example, Rosemary Cullen Owens, *Smashing Times: A History of the Irish Women's Suffrage Movement, 1889–1922* (Dublin, 1984) and Cliona Murphy, *The Women's Suffrage Movement and Irish Society in the Early Twentieth Century* (Brighton, 1989).

sations women believed that the only way in which they could enforce change was through the granting of the local and parliamentary franchises. In many cases Irish women's political activism sprang from a belief in their mission to improve society through their moral influence; that influence would be much more forceful if it were backed by the right to vote.

The involvement of a number of women in the suffrage campaign reveals strong links with various philanthropic organisations. Women like Rosa M. Barrett, Isabella Tod, Margaret Byers and Anna Haslam, all had philanthropic interests. Anna Haslam, for example, was born into a Quaker family in Youghal in 1829 and established a lace-making industry in the town as a means of offering employment to local girls. She married Thomas Haslam in 1854 and established the Dublin Women's Suffrage Association in 1876. She was also, as we have seen, active in the Ladies' National Association and became a member of the English executive committee of that society in 1888. She was also on the council of the National Association for the Repeal of the Contagious Diseases Acts, which co-ordinated the national campaign against the acts from London. She was a committee member of the Philanthropic Reform Association and the Irish Workhouse Association. Both she and her husband actively campaigned to improve the rights of women in Ireland through advocating changes in the educational system and the improvement of the legal position of women.[119]

Isabella Tod, a Presbyterian born in Scotland in 1836, spent most of her life in Belfast. Her initial interest in the economic and political position of women arose through her visitation of poor women. Tod was an activist on a range of issues relating to women. She was the first woman in Ireland to demand that women be admitted to Irish universities and in 1874 published a pamphlet on the need for a practical education for girls.[120] While operating a branch of the LNA from Belfast she was also a member of the executive committee, based in London, of that society. She was active in the Belfast Women's Temperance Association and through this society became involved in the care of female ex-prisoners and destitute children. Again, like so many other philanthropic women, little is known of her personal life. She remained unmarried, was a staunch Unionist

[119] See Cullen Owens, *Smashing Times.*
[120] Isabella M.S. Tod, *On the Education of Girls of the Middle Classes* (London, 1874).

who campaigned vigorously against Gladstone's attempts to grant Home Rule to Ireland, and appears to have suffered much ill-health in the later years of her life.[121]

Those women suffragists involved in reform societies also used women's tradition of charity work as an argument for getting the vote. Whereas benevolent women had attempted to change society through example, reformist women wanted this example to have a political edge. Tod argued in 1884 that the care of the poor had always been women's work and women had a special understanding of that work which men could never have. 'Just as mothers must inculcate on their children, day by day, truth and purity, and the thought of all that is due to others, so also with different machinery but the same end, must women feel it their task to uphold truth, purity and justice to all, in the legislation and administration of the realm.'[122] The vote, she argued was not an end in itself, but a means to an end, and it would allow women to have a new source of authority in society.

The various suffrage societies which existed in the last decades of the century organised a vigorous campaign to achieve the right for women to sit as poor law guardians. They were supported in this campaign by the IWA and the PRA, which had mixed managing committees. One of the stated aims of the IWA was 'the enlistment in the service of the workhouse poor of women, whether as inspectors, poor law guardians, or as members of local visiting committees'.[123] One writer stated in 1901 that

above all, we want women Guardians, for it has now been incontestably proved that women (where the right ones are selected) make the most excellent Guardians. They have more leisure time to devote to visiting the workhouse, and they have, as a rule, more ability than men for the particular work demanded of them.[124]

Tod suggested that Irishwomen should have more influence in administering the poor law since:

the subjects with which the guardians of the poor have to deal are almost all what are acknowledged to be 'women's subjects', some of them emphatically so. The care of the poor generally – and especially of women – the care of children, towards whom pity is in no way mixed with censure; the

---

[121] There are numerous references to her ill health in the annual reports of the Ladies' National Association for the 1880s.

[122] *EWR*, 15 December 1884, p. 550.   [123] Annual report IWA, 1907, p. 2.

[124] Stephens, 'Irish workhouses', p. 105.

prevention, no less than the cure of sickness – these are the principal objects for which the Board of Guardians exist, and they are all women's duties on a large scale no less than a small.[125]

She had, of course, almost one hundred years of women's involvement in philanthropic work to back up this claim and women's charitable endeavours had always dealt primarily with the welfare of women and children. Tod was also upholding the belief that women, by their very nature, were superior in both the moral and spiritual sphere to men and she used this generally held belief to support her claims for a formal, legal and political dimension to women's charity work. She cited the case of the election of women as guardians in England and observed that:

the discoveries which they have made on getting to work, of evils and mistakes, omissions of the greatest sort, even wrongs and dangers – unavoidable for the most part under a purely masculine government of the poor – have been such as very greatly to intensify the conviction of the ladies that not one workhouse in the kingdom ought to be left without womanly supervision.[126]

One of the arguments she used to bolster her claim for the appointment of women as guardians was their ability to detect fraudulent recipients of poor relief, a skill, she claimed, they were better at than men.[127] It was not however until 1896 that a bill was passed which allowed women, with certain property qualifications, to serve as poor law guardians. In that year two women guardians were elected, by 1897 twelve women had been elected and by 1899 eighty-five women sat as guardians.[128] The election of women as poor law guardians was encouraged by the Dublin Women's Suffrage and Local Government Association which, in their annual reports, provided practical guidelines for women seeking election. The DWSLGA also declared that the evident good being done by women as guardians and thus public representatives 'conclusively proves that they will be well qualified worthily to perform their

---

125 *EWR*, 15 November 1881, p. 486. Louisa Twining, who established the Workhouse Visiting Society in London in 1858, had numerous articles on the subject published in the *EWJ*. The charge made against the society that it interfered with the smooth running of the workhouse was refuted by her in an article in 1860 when she stated that women could not interfere as they were doing the 'ordained and proper work of women', *EWJ*, July 1860, pp. 335–40.

126 *EWR*, 15 November 1881, p. 487.   127 Ibid., p. 489.

128 Annual reports, Dublin Women's Suffrage and Local Government Association, 1896, p. 3; 1897, p. 4; 1899, p. 3, appendix to report, pp. 2–3.

duties as intelligent electors when the Parliamentary vote has been conferred on them'.[129]

It is difficult to discern the religious backgrounds of most nineteenth-century suffragists but it appears that few were Catholic. Lay women of religious persuasions other than Catholicism had a long tradition of organising independently in voluntary organisations. By the end of the century that voluntary service had, for some women at least, translated itself into activism for social and political change.

Not all of those women involved in charity work were suffragists; indeed the majority of benevolent women continued their work quietly and do not appear to have been interested in or to have supported the suffrage issue. The rise of the suffrage issue in Ireland, however, owed much to the philanthropic activity of women over the century. This brief discussion of the philanthropic interests of suffragists has more to do with examining the role of philanthropy in changing women's lives than with the rise and philosophy of the suffrage campaign itself. Through their philanthropic work they had proved to be socially aware and responsible, and capable of financial and organisational management. They had catered for the needs of many who would otherwise have been neglected. Membership of a voluntary organisation was a respectable way for women to exercise their social duty and provided them with a legitimate platform from which to voice their social and political concerns. Nineteenth-century suffragists argued that the vote should be given to middle-class women who, through their philanthropic activism, had proved they 'deserved' it.

[129] Annual report, DWSLGA, 1899, p. 3.

Conclusion

Whether it was house visitation, instituting an orphanage or school, working in prisons, refuges or workhouses, raising money or simply giving advice, philanthropy became the principal, if largely unpaid, occupation of a great number of middle-class Irish women in the nineteenth century. Motivated by Christian duty, women, regardless of their denominational status, made a significant contribution to the perception of poverty and the poor in Irish society. Through their charitable work they enhanced and expanded the social role of women and made social work a legitimate occupation for them. Ultimately, some of these women claimed that the importance of their contribution earned them the right to take part in the political process. Voluntaryism not alone allowed women to exercise their religious and moral duty to society, it also gave them the opportunity to shape the provision and direction of philanthropic enterprise and to guide it into those areas which they considered to be of major importance. As a consequence charitable provision for women and children developed on a much broader scale than that provided for men. Women philanthropists believed implicitly in the moral and spiritual superiority of women. It was, many of them believed, principally through work by women, with women, that the social and moral regeneration of society could be attained.

The myriad of philanthropic associations, societies and institutions established by women catered for specific needs and had limited objectives. The narrowness of their operations was determined by practical issues, primarily by their financial solvency. Few of these organisations dispensed charity unconditionally and one of the major concerns of women philanthropists was to channel relief to the 'deserving poor'. In many cases they initiated a system of selection in order to guarantee 'worthiness' and since many of the relief agencies provided work for their inmates they not only justified

214

the existence of the charity by making the inmates 'deserving', in the sense that they worked for their keep, but also at the same time helped to place the charity on a sound financial footing. The majority of women's voluntary organisations not only embraced narrow goals, but remained localised and rarely developed any network of similar societies to extend their function. All of the lay penitent asylums, for example, were separately managed by committees which appear to have had few links regarding membership, nor do the various committees appear to have communicated with each other regarding advice on management or policy. Similarly the myriad of clothing, Bible and refuge organisations were also quite distinct and operated separately.

Many philanthropic societies were also exclusivist. Membership was determined by social background but to a greater extent by religious affiliation. Philanthropic effort was organised on distinct religious grounds and this proved to be both a cohesive and divisive force in regard to those institutions established by women. There is almost no evidence of any interaction between lay Catholic women or female religious with their Protestant sisters. Exceptionally, one author writing in 1875 notes that Catholic women began the visitation of the sick, in an unnamed workhouse, when a Protestant woman who had already initiated a visitation scheme for Protestant inmates, asked them to do so.[1] The elements of evangelicalism and proselytism, which were found in many charitable organisations, caused tensions between various organisations and this was particularly true of those societies which looked after orphaned or destitute children.

The denominational basis of many charitable societies with similar objectives prevented women from uniting to create larger, more extensive and perhaps more efficient organisations. Religious bias inhibited women from pooling their financial resources and also from building upon each other's experiences as charity workers. Some form of network appears evident between organisations which were run by particular denominations. Thus children and 'fallen women' were often referred from one charity to another, but referrals were never made across the religious divide. In the Catholic sphere female religious were separated from lay women by being allowed almost the sole right to provide charitable services. Female

---

[1] Anon., 'Rounds of visits', *The Irish Monthly*, 3 (1887), p. 80.

religious communities controlled a vast network of welfare organisations. They built the infrastructure of social welfare which bound the people to the church and the church to the people. It is obvious that the Catholic hierarchy offered fewer opportunities for lay women to organise and women in lay organisations were at numerous disadvantages when compared to the freedom allowed nuns, especially in gaining entrance to public institutions. It may be that convents, which were so successful in attracting entrants because they allowed for a practical expression of religious commitment, actually damaged the position of women in society by undertaking work based on vocation rather than a committed desire to alter the position of women in society. Nuns, in their work, exemplified the ideal image of women. They devoted themselves, without complaint, to meeting the needs of others. Although they brought many improvements to the institutions they ran, for example by reforming the nursing care provided in workhouse hospitals, it was a reform brought about by example rather than a determination to ensure that public officials or government provide support for such reform.

The religious basis of many charitable societies also hindered the development of a critique of the social origins of poverty and destitution. Religion, while it gave many women the impetus to organise voluntary societies, also in many cases defined the limits of their approach. Those societies concerned with moral reform, the penitent asylums or criminal refuges, sought to change values by example and persuasion and a belief in the possibility of spiritual regeneration. Even though the women who ran these benevolent societies sought the moral reform of their inmates they were in effect remoulding the 'sinner' rather than questioning or eradicating those conditions which gave rise to the 'sin'. Refuges for the destitute and penitent asylums were offering institutional solutions to social problems, as were the reformatories and industrial schools established for delinquent children after mid-century. Within these institutions, lay and religious women attempted to alter the social, moral and often religious behaviour of their charges. The screen of philanthropy gave them the moral authority to control those who sought their aid. For the majority of women philanthropists the perpetuation of class differences was an implicit part of their work. They were primarily serving their own class interests.

Two traditions of philanthropic activity are discernible, a benevolent and a reformist one. The reformist tradition was a continuation of the benevolent tradition and differed from it in the level of public and political action which women were willing to undertake rather than in a radical shift in philosophy or perception of women's role in society. It is also significant that the reformist tradition owed its existence, principally, to Quaker and Non-conformist women. Reformist societies such as the Dublin Aid Committee (later the National Society for the Prevention of Cruelty to Children) and the Philanthropic Reform Association, for example, were organised by committees of men and women. In these organisations women formed alliances with men in attempting to ensure that the state take responsibility in legislating for change, either in workhouse conditions, or with regard to the protection of children. Women in reformist societies were most likely to become involved in the suffrage issue and to fight for the right to sit as poor law guardians. For many of these women the vote, at local or national level, was intended to provide the most direct means to initiate philanthropic and social change. The acquisition of the vote was also essentially the means for middle-class women to extend their own individual rights.

Philanthropic societies offered women a sense of identity and community, whether on a small scale, as in the lay societies, or as reflected in the larger communities of female religious who engaged in charitable activities. Such societies gave women a sense of purpose and achievement and allowed them to play a role in expressing their concern for the less fortunate in society. Altruism certainly played a major role in female philanthropy but women within charitable organisations also exerted considerable power on a personal basis. The multiplicity of voluntary associations established by women reflects a desire on the part of women for autonomy. From the beginnings of voluntary service women were not content to remain as mere auxiliaries to male run societies. Women also gained a number of practical skills from organising charitable societies. Organising committees, raising funds, keeping accounts, writing annual reports, and, in reformist societies, petitioning local and central authorities, proved women to be capable of successful organisation. Philanthropic involvement also allowed some women, like their British and American counterparts, to develop professional careers in social work. It further granted them some political influence, especially in organisations like the Philanthropic Reform Association. Charitable involvement did not always have positive outcomes. In Ireland the nature of nineteenth-century philanthropy was sectarian, reflecting the sectarianism which existed in society itself. Women's work in philanthropy, particularly their work with children, helped to entrench this sectarianism further.

Many changes occurred over the nineteenth century which altered the position of women in society. Some of these changes were due to the changing expectations of women brought about through improved educational and work opportunities. Women had initiated many of these changes themselves, challenging those systems which attempted to control and confine them. Those who benefited most from women's philanthropic activities in this respect were the middle and upper-class women who organised the societies. For the poor they aided, no alteration in the social or class systems was advocated. For a small number of philanthropic women their involvement in charity work had a politicising effect. They became passionate and articulate reformers of a political and social system which they successfully challenged and altered over the century. The last half of the nineteenth century was, arguably, the time of greatest change in the lives of middle and upper-class women. The expansion of female religious congregations altered the expectations of Catholic women who decided to become nuns. Lay Catholic women were also affected by these changes, and while opportunities were expanding for nuns they were, ironically, contracting for lay Catholic women. Women of other religious denominations found their voices to speak against injustice, to demonstrate publicly against the double standard of sexual morality and to confront the inequalities which existed towards women in society. Because of women's action these injustices were gradually altered. Women's involvement in philanthropy brought many of them to an awareness of injustice and also to the belief that only formal political power would enable them to make the changes necessary to create a more just, though not necessarily more equal, society for everyone. Many of these hopes for change were dashed by the political realities of early twentieth-century Ireland, which divided women just as much as religion had in the nineteenth century.

Select bibliography

PRIMARY SOURCES

When the research for this book was carried out the Public Records Office, housed in the Four Courts, Dublin, contained material which has now been removed to the National Archives, Bishop Street, Dublin. I have retained the classification current at the time the research was conducted.

ARCHIVAL SOURCES

Convent of the Good Shepherd, Belfast

MS Register of the Entrants to the Magdalen Asylum, 1851–1900.
Typescript history of the Good Shepherd in Ireland.

Convent of the Good Shepherd, Cork

MS Register of the Magdalen Asylum, 1872–1900.

Convent of the Good Shepherd, Limerick

MS Register of the Asylum of the Good Shepherd, Limerick, 1828–1900 (4 vols.).
MS Book in which are Written the Names of our Benefactors, 19th century.
MS Monthly Accounts, Magdalen Asylum, Limerick, vol. 1, 1866–76; vol. 2, 1888–1901.
MS Statistics of the Province of Ireland from 1848–1896.
MS Accounts of Laundry Receipts and how Placed, 1892–1913.
MS Annals of the Convent, 1826–1909.
MS St Joseph's Reformatory Register Showing all the Circumstances of Each Case Admitted, Limerick, June 1859.
St George's Industrial School, annual returns, complete collection.
Leaflet requesting funds for the Magdalen Asylum, 1879.
Typescript history of the convent taken from the Annals.

Scrapbook containing newspaper clippings, miscellaneous documents etc., relating to the Magdalen Asylum, nineteenth century.

Convent of the Good Shepherd, Waterford

MS Register of St Mary's Magdalen Asylum, 1842–1900.
MS Convent Annals, 1858–1900.
Typescript History of the Convent taken from the Annals.
Typescript History of St Mary's Home taken from the Annals.

Convent of Mercy, Baggot St, Dublin

MS Register of the House of Mercy, 1866–1971.

Convent of Mercy, Limerick

MS Register of the House of Mercy, 2 vols., 1838–58, 1899–1912.
MS Sick Visitation Book, 2 vols., September 1837–April 1847, April 1847–May 1850.
MS Annals of the Convent, 1838–1900.

Convent of Mercy, Tralee

MS Annals of the Convent, 1854–1927.
MS Copy of the will of Mary Anne Coppinger (died 1855).

Convent of Our Lady of Charity of Refuge, High Park, Drumcondra, Dublin

MS Annals of the Convent, vol. 1, 1853–1939.
MS Register of the Magdalen Asylum, 1839–1904.

Convent of the Sisters of Charity, St Vincent's, Cork

MS Register of St Mary's Magdalen Asylum, 1846–99.

Convent of the Sisters of Charity, Donnybrook, Dublin

MS Register of the Magdalen Asylum, 1796–1899.

Convent of the Sisters of Charity, Milltown, Dublin

MS Mother Catherine's Diary, 2 July 1812–29 August 1825.
MS Alphabetical Catalogue of Entrants, 1812–1900.
MS Copy of Sermon of Fr Kenny, 1816.
MS Notebook Income from Sisters and Expenditure to 1834.

MS Book Amount of Sums Received on Account of Dowers from the Members of the Congregation from August 1815, with notes.

Typescript copy of the Annals, vol. 1, 1816–36; vol. 2, 1837–58.

MS Annals, vols. 3–8, 1854–64, 1864–70, 1870–6, 1876–82, 1882–8, 1888–92.

Cork Archives Institute, Cork

Dowden Papers.

Notes on the Industrious Blind Asylum, Cork, 15th Annual Report, 1858, Day 66/32.

Circular of Cork Central Ragged School Association, 1851, Day 80/145.

Governesses of the Lying-in Hospital, Day 82/11.

Cork Wesleyan Dorcas Society, 13th Annual Report, 1844, Day 80/102.

An Appeal from the Dublin Ladies' Association, Day 77/29.

Cork Ladies' Anti-Slavery Society, Day 80/39.

Printed letter appealing for funds for the Magdalen Asylum, Day 80/87.

Sixth Report of the Committee of the Night Asylum for the Houseless Poor, Dublin, 1843, Day 77/47.

Printed Prospectus for Seminary for Governesses, n.d., Day 81/58.

Printed Statement of the Sick Poor Society, North Parish for 1844, Day 80/113; Day 80/78.

Cottage Home for Little Children, Dun Laoghaire

MS Admissions Book, 1882–1912.

Annual Reports, printed, 1879–1914.

MS Crèche Book, 1879–80.

MS Minute Books, 5 vols., 1882–1901.

Deed of Constitution of the Cottage Home, printed, 1887.

Denny House, Dublin

MS Magdalen Asylum Register, Leeson St Magdalen Asylum, vol. 3, 1809–28.

MS Board of Guardians Minute Book, November 1841–January 1853.

Dublin Diocesan Archives, Clonliffe College, Drumcondra

These archives provide a wide range of material relating to charitable work in nineteenth-century Ireland. There are numerous letters detailing the condition of the poor, the financial affairs of charitable societies and it is a prime source for the work carried out by female religious in the country. There are also many copies of published pamphlets and annual reports of lay charitable societies.

Cullen Papers
Papers of Cardinal Paul Cullen, archbishop of Dublin. These papers deal
with the period after 1852.
Hamilton Papers
These papers cover the correspondence of John Hamilton, archdeacon of
Dublin, from 1820–60.
Murray Papers
The correspondence of Daniel Murray, archbishop of Dublin, for the
period 1809–52.

Fawcett Library, London

MS Letter Book of the Executive of the National Association for the Repeal
of the Contagious Diseases Acts, August 1883–June 1886.
MS Minutes of the National Association for the Repeal of the Contagious
Diseases Acts, 2 vols., 1870–86. Josephine Butler Collection. Contains
annual reports of the Ladies' National Association, leaflets, pamphlets
and miscellaneous documents relating to the Contagious Diseases Acts
campaign.

Girls' Friendly Society, Leeson St, Dublin

Printed Annual Reports, 1879–1900.
MS Minute Books 1877–1904.
Scrapbooks with various pamphlets, circulars etc. published for the society,
1877–1914.
Minutes and Annual Reports of the Protestant Servants' Home, 1873–
1911. (This society was given over to the GFS in 1911.)

Harcourt Home, Harcourt Tce., Dublin

Home for Aged Governesses and Other Unmarried Ladies, Annual
Reports, 1838–1900 (with exceptions).
MS Minute Books, 1838–44; 1856–1923; 1885–1901; 1838–58.
MS Admissions Book, 1 vol., 1838–59.
Typescript, History of the Home taken from the minutes.

Irish Church Missions, Bachelor's Walk, Dublin

Annual Reports of the Society for Irish Church Missions to the Roman
Catholics, 1889–1900.
Annual Reports of the Irish Society, 1819–31, 1839–44, 1892–4.
Scrapbooks of the Irish Society containing newspaper cuttings, annual
reports, communications, leaflets, advertisements etc. relating to the
society c.1822–1900, 2 vols.

Irish Society for the Prevention of Cruelty to Children, Dublin

Typescript copy of the first report of the Dublin Aid Committee, 1898.

Lilly Library, Earlham College, Richmond, Indiana, USA

MS Notes on prisons, reformatories, gaols etc. through Ireland and Great Britain taken by Charles A. Coffin.

Mageough Home, Cowper Rd., Rathmines, Dublin

MS Minute Books, 3 vols., 1871–1913.

MS Register of the Inmates of the Charity, 1878–1928. Scrapbook with various printed documents relating to the Home, nineteenth and twentieth centuries.

National Library of Ireland

MS 640 Account of Catholic Orphanages in Dublin including statistics of numbers therein, 1789–1832, compiled by Thomas Osler, 1834.

MS 3,288 Report by P.F. Johnston and E. Moylan on Charity in Waterford, 1834.

MS 14,280 Accounts of annuities and subscriptions to charity paid by members of the Drake (later DrakeDeane?) family, 1849–70.

MS 12,941 Account of personal expenditure, mainly on charity, presented by Ellen Paul to Mrs Paul, 1854.

MSS 1066, 1054, 1069 Kilmainham papers.

Old Ladies' Asylum, New St, Dublin

MS Minute Book of the Asylum, 1838–present, 1 vol.

Public Records Office, Four Courts, Dublin

M 1133 Deed 1835 and notes on the history of the Penitent Relief Society, 1830–5.

M 1194 Trustees' Minute Books of Baggot St Asylum and church, 1835–1909; 1909–24.

MSS Registers of Grangegorman Female Prison, January 1851–December 1897, Prisons 1/9/13, V16–4–2 to 1/9/39, V 16–4–28.

MS Census records, 1901.

Public Records Office, Northern Ireland

Annual Report of the Belfast Ladies' Temperance Union, 1865, D3606/3/1.

Annual Report of the Belfast Female Prisoners' Aid Society, 1876, D 905/2/179B.

Annual Report of the Larne District Nursing Society, 1897–8.

Antrim Presbytery Widows' Fund Minutes, 1783–1860, T 1053.

Belfast Association for the Employment of the Industrious Blind, D 3563. Includes minute books, printed annual reports and correspondence of the ladies' committee, 1871–1905.

Fisherwick Place Presbyterian Church, Belfast, FIN 1/23.

Jane Brownlow's Charity, FIN 1/12.

Jane Lee's Charity, FIN 1/19.

Letter from John Campbell to Miss H. Kiernan, Dublin discussing the feminine anti-slavery movement, 16 May 1828, D1728/2/6.

Letters from the Rev. Mark Cassidy re Ulster Female Penitentiary c.1816, D1088/22; D1088/26.

Prison Gate Mission for Men, FIN 1/2/5.

Records of the Clogher Diocesan Widows' Fund Society, 1859–84, T 1562 and MIC 42.

Records of the Society for Providing Nurses for the Sick Poor, Belfast, D 1630. Includes minutes and annual reports from 1877–1904.

Victoria Home, printed leaflet, n.d., D3603/3/2.

Women's Temperance Association, booklet, n.d., D3606/3/3.

Presentation Convent, Ballingarry, Co Tipperary

MS Annals, 1871–1926, 1 vol.

MS Annals and Accounts, 1878–1955.

MS Profession List 1871–1913.

Miscellaneous collection of newspaper cuttings and letters relating to the convent.

Presentation Convent, Carrick-on-Suir, Co Tipperary

MS Annals, 1813–90, 1 vol.

Presentation Convent, Cashel, Co Tipperary

MS Register of Elections and Annals of the Convent, 1830– , 1 vol.

Presentation Convent, Clonmel, Co Tipperary

MS Annals, 1813–1970, 1 vol.

MS Profession Book, 1813–1938, 1 vol.

Typescript copy of the annals.

Presentation Convent, Fethard, Co Tipperary

MS Annals, 1862–1990, 1 vol.

Presentation Convent, Thurles, Co Tipperary

MS Annals, 1817–, 1 vol.

Protestant Aid, Upper Leeson Street, Dublin

Annual Reports of the Association for the Relief of Distressed Protestants, 1837–1921 (with exceptions).
Annual Report of the Albert Retreat for Aged Protestant Females, 1921.

Representative Church Body Library, Braemore Park, Churchtown, Dublin

Prison Gate Mission, Dublin, minute books, 2 vols., 1883–9, 1900–15.
Female Penitentiary, Dublin, box 140. Loose papers, 1840–1907 referring mainly to the appointment of a chaplain.
Mageough Home, 1869–1958, Loose papers, box 139.
Mountjoy Female Prison, box 140. Loose papers, 1850–64 referring mainly to the appointment of a chaplain.
Hibernian auxiliary to the Society for the Extinction of the Slave Trade and for the Civilisation of Africa, minute book, letter book and two pamphlets for the years 1841–3. MS 316.

Royal College of Physicians, Kildare Street, Dublin

Dublin Sanitary Association, minute book, 1 vol., 1883–94.
Records of the Westmoreland Lock Hospital: MSS General registers of patients, 4 vols.: 1816–27, 1827–41, 1841–57, 1857–68.
MS Visitor's Book, 1825–89. This contains many notes on the state and condition of the hospital.
MS Chaplains' Visiting Book, 1861–64. This volume notes the attendance of the Protestant and Catholic chaplains to the hospital.
MSS House Committee Books, 2 vols., 1862–71, 1871–5.
MS Registrar's Report Book, 1872–7.
MSS Board Minute Books, 2 vols., 1885–99.

Society of Friends Library, Swanbrook House, Dublin

MS Committee minute book of the Liberty Crèche, 92 Meath St, December 1892–January 1896. (Unfortunately due to removal to new premises access to material in this library was limited and undoubtedly much more can be revealed about the Quaker influence on charity once the material becomes available.)

St John's House of Rest, Merrion, Dublin

Annual Reports, 1872–1900.
Committee Minute Book, 1881–1911.
MS Register of Inmates, 3 vols., 1870–7, 1877–85, 1885–91.

Young Women's Christian Association, Sandymount, Dublin
Annual Reports, 1887–1900, printed.

OFFICIAL PUBLICATIONS

Dublin Metropolitan Police: Statistical Tables, 1838–1853.
Criminal and Judicial Statistics (Ireland), 1870–1900.
*Report of the Commissioners of Enquiry on State Prisons and Gaols in Ireland, May
     1809*, HC 1809 (265), vii.
*Report of the Select Committee on Gaols and Other Places of Confinement and to Whom
     Several Reports, Returns and Petitions were Referred with Minutes of Evidence
     and Appendix*, HC 1819 (425), vii.
First Report of the General Board of Health in the City of Dublin (Dublin, 1822).
Second Report of the Commissioners of Education Inquiry, HC 1826–7 (12), xii.
*Report of Commissioners Appointed by the Lord Lieutenant of Ireland to Report on
     Certain Charitable Institutions in Dublin*, HC 1830 (176), xxvi.
Reports and Summary, Select Committee on the State of the Poor in Ireland 1830, HC
     1830 (589, 654, 665, 667), vii.
*Returns Relating to the Number of Sturdy Beggars, Foundlings etc., in Cork,
     Waterford and Limerick Cities*, HC 1831–2 (565), xliv.
*Reports of the Commissioners for Inquiring into the Conditions of the Poorer Classes in
     Ireland: First Report*, HC 1835 (369) xxxii, pts. 1&2; *Second Report*, HC
     1837 (68), xxxi; *Third Report*, HC 1836 (43), xxx.
*Report of Commissioners Appointed by the Lord Lieutenant of Ireland to Inspect
     Charitable Institutions in Dublin 1842*, HC 1842 (337), xxxviii.
*Return in Provinces, of the Number of Children sent out to Service from the Union
     Workhouses in Ireland, in the years 1842, 1843 and 1844*, HC 1845 (351),
     xxxviii.
*Number of Persons under the Age of Eighteen Years in the Workhouses in Ireland on
     the 3rd May 1849*, HC 1849 (609), xlvii.
*Report from the Select Committee on Criminal and Destitute Children Together with
     the Proceedings of the Committee, Minutes of Evidence, Appendix and Index*,
     HC 1852 (515), vii.
Report of the Inspectors General on the General State of the Prisons in Ireland, HC
     1852–53 (167), liii.
*Report from the Select Committee on Criminal and Destitute Children Together with
     the Proceedings of the Committee, Minutes of Evidence and Appendix*, HC
     1852–53 (674), xxiii.
*Return of the Number of Females with their Illegitimate Children in the Workhouses
     of Ireland on 1 January 1854*, HC 1854 (183), iv.
Report from the Select Committee on Dublin Hospitals, HC 1854 (338), xii.
*Annual Reports of the Directors of Convict Prisons in Ireland, with appendices:
     First Report* – 1854 (1958), HC 1854–6, xxxvi, 609.
     Second Report – 1855 (2068), HC 1856, xxxiv, 1.

Fourth Report – 1857 (2376), HC 1857–8, xxx, 389.

Sixth Report – 1859 (2655), HC 1860 xxxvi, 95.

Seventh Report – 1860 (2844), HC 1861 xxx, 145.

Tenth Report – 1863 (3367), HC 1864 xxvii, 481.

Fifteenth Report – 1868 (4171), HC 1868–9 xxx, 413

Twenty-first Report – 1874 [1220], HC 1875 xxxix, 613.

Twenty-fourth Report – 1877 [2161], HC 1878 xliii, 641.

The Census of Ireland for the Year 1851, pt vi: General Report, with Appendix, County Tables, Miscellaneous Tables, and Index to Names of Places [2134], HC 1856, xxxi.

Report from the Select Committee on Poor Relief (Ireland), HC 1861 (408), xx.

The Census of Ireland for the Year 1861, pt v: General Report, with Appendix, County Tables, Summary of Ireland and Index to Names of Places [3204–IV], HC 1863 lxi.

Report of the House of Commons Select Committee on the Contagious Diseases Act, HC 1868–9 (306), vii.

Report from the Royal Commission on the Administration and Operation of the Contagious Diseases Acts 1866–9 [C.408–1], HC 1871, xix.

Report of the House of Commons Select Committee on the Administration, Operation, and Effects of the Contagious Disease Acts of 1866–9, HC 1878–9 (323), viii; HC 1880 (114), viii; HC 1880 (301), viii; HC 1881 (351), viii; HC 1882 (340), ix.

Return of the Number of Nuns Employed as Nurses in Workhouses, HC 1873 (246) lv.

Census of Ireland, 1871, pt. iii: General Report, with Illustrative Maps and Diagrams, Summary Tables and Appendix [C.1377], HC 1876, lxxxi.

19th Report of the Board of Superintendence of Dublin Hospitals with Appendices, [C.1936], HC 1878, xl.

Twenty-First Report of the Board of Superintendence of Dublin Hospitals with Appendices [C.2565], HC 1880, xxiii.

Census of Ireland, 1881, pt ii: General Report, with Illustrative Maps and Diagrams, Tables, and Appendix [C.3365], HC 1882, lxxvi.

Twenty-Fifth Report of the Board of Superintendence of Dublin Hospitals with Appendices [C.3739], HC 1883 xxvii.

Reports of the Royal commission on Prisons in Ireland 1884 [C.4233–1], HC 1884–5, xxxviii.

Third Report of her Majesty's Commissioners for Inquiring into the Housing of the Working Classes (Ireland) [C.4547–1], HC 1884–5, xxxi.

Twenty-Ninth Report of the Board of Superintendence of Dublin Hospitals with Appendices [C.5141], HC 1887, xxxv.

Dublin Hospitals Commission. Report of the Inquiry, 1887, Together with Minutes of Evidence and Appendices [C.5042], HC 1887, xxxv.

Census of Ireland, 1891, pt ii: General Report, with Illustrative Maps and Diagrams, Tables and Appendix [C.6780], 1892, xc.

Seventeenth Report of the General Prisons Board, Ireland 1894–5 [C.7806], HC 1895, liii.

Reports from the Inspectors of Prisons (Ireland), HC 1898, xlvii.
Workhouse Infirmaries in Ireland in which Nuns were Employed in any Capacity in 1903 [C.1694], HC 1903, lix.

ANNUAL REPORTS OF CHARITABLE SOCIETIES

Annual Report of the House of Refuge, Baggot Street, 1803.
Annual Report of the Night Asylum for the Homeless Poor, 1874.
Association for Bettering the Condition of the Prisoners in the County Gaol of Wicklow, 1820.
Association for the Improvement of Prisons and Prison Discipline in Ireland, 1819–25.
Association for the Relief of Ladies in Distress through Non-Payment of Rent in Ireland.
Asylum for Aged and Infirm Female Servants, 1818.
Asylum for Penitent Females, 1831.
Belfast Nurses' Home and Training School, 1872, 1873, 1889.
Belfast Ladies' Clothing Society, 1836, 1850, 1852, 1860.
Belfast Ladies' Industrial National School, 1856–1910 (with exceptions).
Bird's Nest and Mission Ragged Schools, 1882, 1883, 1887, 1888, 1890, 1892, 1893, 1894.
British and Irish Ladies' Society for Improving the Condition and Promoting the Industry and Welfare of the Female Peasantry in Ireland, 1823, 1824, 1825, 1826, 1828.
British Society for Promoting the Reformation of Female Prisoners, 1823.
Catholic Institution for the Deaf and Dumb, 1st–9th annual reports, 1847–55.
Charitable Repository and School of Industry, Bandon, 1814.
Christian Work among Soldiers and Police, 1881–2.
Coombe Ragged Schools, 1864–70.
Coombe Boys' Home, 1874.
Coombe Ragged Schools and Boys' Home, 1888.
Cork Ladies' Society in Association with the British and Irish Ladies' Society . . ., 1825, 1828.
Cork Merciful Society, 1825.
County Kildare Auxiliary Bible Society and Naas Ladies' Association, 1829.
Crèche or Day Nursery, Lower Gardiner Street, 1889–90.
Crèche or Day Nursery, Holles Street, 1888.
Dorset Institution for Industrious Females, 1816.
Dublin Auxiliary Bible Society, 1839.
Dublin Bible Woman Mission, 1877, 1878, 1883.
Dublin Discharged Female Roman Catholic Prisoners' Aid Society, 1886–8, 1890–3, 1905–7, 1909.
Dublin Female Association, 1815.

Dublin Female Penitentiary, 1814–17, 1819–20, 1823–4.

Dublin Ladies' Anti-Slavery Society, 1856.

Dublin Ladies' Church Missionary Association n.d.

Dublin Ladies' Clothing Society, 1849, 1852, 1854–5.

Dublin by Lamplight, 1856–8, 1867, 1879.

Dublin Midnight Mission and Home, 1876.

Dublin Mission Visiting Branch of the Society for Irish Church Missions to the Roman Catholics, 1861, 1871, 1885, 1888, 1889, 1894.

Dublin Providence Home, 1839–42, 1854, 1872.

Dublin Sailors' Home, 1884–5.

Dublin White Cross Association, 1898.

Female Orphan House, 1851, 1875.

Fresh Air Association, 1908–9.

General Irish Reformation Society for the Restoration in Ireland of her Primitive Religion and the Necessary Protection of Converts, 1886, 1889.

Grand Canal Street School for Little Ragged Children, 1892.

Helping Hand, A Mission Home for Lads, 1892.

Hibernian Auxiliary to the Society for the Extinction of the Slave Trade, 1842.

Hibernian Bible Society, County Cavan Auxiliary, 1841.

Hibernian Bible Society, 1831, 1887.

Hibernian Ladies' Negroes' Friend Society, 1833.

Hibernian Society for Aiding the Translation of the Holy Scriptures into Foreign Languages, 1824.

Hibernian Sunday School Society, 1811.

Homes for Destitute Boys and Girls, Belfast, 1884.

Irish Auxiliary to the London Society for Promoting Christianity among the Jews, 1886–7.

Irish Branch of the Society for Irish Church Missions, 1884, 1889.

Irish Women's Suffrage and Local Government Association, 1896–1918.

Irish Workhouse Association: Report of the Provisional Committee, 1897.

Irish Workhouse Association, 1906, 1907.

Ladies' Association for Bettering the Condition of the Female Peasantry, Carlow and Graigue Branch, 1830.

Ladies' Association of Charity of St Vincent de Paul, 1852–62.

Ladies' Auxiliary of the Hibernian Church Missionary Society, 1816, 1825.

Ladies' Bible Association for the 7th District of the City of Dublin, 1819.

Ladies' British Society for the Reformation of Female Prisoners, 1828.

Ladies' Hibernian Female School Society, 1824.

Ladies' Industrial Society for Ireland, 1852.

Ladies' Irish Association, 1887, 1897.

Ladies' National Association for the Repeal of the Contagious Diseases Acts, 1870–86.

Liberty Infant School, 1889.

Luke Street Girls' Home n.d.

Male and Female Ragged and Sunday Schools, 1857.

Marchioness Wellesley Female Tontine Society, n.d.

Meath Charitable Loan, 1908.

Mill Street Schools and Mission, 1885–7.

Mission to the Liberties, 1887.

Mission Ragged Schools n.d.

Mullabrack Clothing Society, 1836.

National Association for the Repeal of the Contagious Diseases Acts, 1870–86.

National Institution for the Education of Deaf and Dumb Children of the Poor in Ireland, 1817.

National Society for the Prevention of Cruelty to Children, 1889–1909.

Olive Mount Institution of the Good Samaritan, 1843, 1845.

Philanthropic Reform Association, 1896–1914.

Presbyterian Church Missions, 1890–6.

Queen's Institute of Female Professional Schools, 1871.

Ragged Boys' Home, Grand Canal St, 1884–5, 1888–9.

Ragged School Shoe-Black, Broomer and Messenger Society, 1852.

Report of the British Association for the Relief of Extreme Distress in Ireland and Scotland, 1849.

Report of the Committee of St Thomas's Infants School, 1830.

Report of the Managing Committee of the House of Recovery and Fever Hospital in Cork St, Dublin, 1837.

Report of the Trustees for Bettering the Condition of the Poor in Ireland, 1825.

Report of the Committee Appointed to Distribute Relief to the Poor of Dublin during the Severe Winter in the Months of January, February and March, 1814.

Report of the Committee for the Relief of the Industrious Poor, 1818–20.

Report of the Managing Committee of the Whitworth Hospital, Drumcondra, 1825.

Richmond National Institution for the Instruction of the Industrious Blind, 1856.

Rosevale Home, Lisburn, 1873.

Rotunda Girls' Aid Society, 1887–8, 1892.

School for Little Ragged Children, 1875.

Schools for Little Ragged Children and Women's Sewing Class, 1885.

Shelter for Females Discharged from Prison, 1823, 1829–34, 1837–8, 1839, 1842.

Society for Promoting the Education of the Poor in Ireland, 1817.

Society for the Relief of the Industrious Poor, 1818, 1820.

Spiddal Orphan Home, 1893.

St Joseph's Asylum for Aged and Destitute Females, 1838.

St Patrick's Nurses' Home and Bible Woman Association,1882–3.
Townsend Street Ragged Schools and Girls' Home, 1874, 1875, 1885, 1888, 1892.
Training School for Female Servants, 1857.
Ulster Female Penitentiary, 1828, 1834.
Ulster Magdalene Asylum, 1904–5.
Wicklow St (late Fishamble St) Sunday Ragged School, 1862.
William Henry Elliott Home for Waifs and Strays, 1875.
Working Boys' Home, Dublin, 1876.

SECONDARY SOURCES

NEWSPAPERS AND PERIODICALS

The Banner of Truth.
Belfast Newsletter.
British Medical Journal.
Cork Chronicle.
Echoes of Erin, The Journal of the Irish Women's Temperance Association.
Englishwoman's Journal.
Englishwoman's Review.
Erin's Hope.
Freeman's Journal.
Irish Church Directory.
Irish Ecclesiastical Gazette.
Irish Times.
Northern Whig.
Pall Mall Gazette.
The Lady of the House.
The Medical Enquirer.
The Philanthropist.
The Sentinel.
The Shield.
The Vigilance Record.
Transactions of the National Association for the Promotion of Social Science

DIRECTORIES

Bassett, George Henry, *The Book of County Antrim* (Dublin, 1888).
Belfast and Ulster Directory for 1892.
Belfast and Province of Ulster Directory for 1858–9 (Belfast, 1858).
Burdett's Hospitals and Charities 1899. The Year Book of Philanthropy and Hospital Annual (London, 1899).
Catholic Directory 1845–1868.

Egan, P.M., *The Illustrated Guide to the City and County of Kilkenny* (Kilkenny, 1905?).
English Woman's Yearbook and Directory 1888, 1894, 1897.
Finny's Royal Cork Almanac for 1831 (Cork, 1832).
Guy's Munster Directory (Cork, 1886).
Guy's City and County Cork Almanac and Directory for 1889 (Cork, 1889).
Irish Catholic Directory 1869–1900.
Pettigrew and Oulton, *Dublin Almanac and General Register of Ireland* 1834–1849.
Reformatory and Refuge Union: Classified List of Child Saving Institutions (London, 1915, 21st edn).
Religious Orders and Congregations in Ireland (Dublin, 1933).
Thom's Irish Almanac and Official Directory 1844–1900.
Wilson and Watson, *The Treble Almanack* 1800–1837.

ARTICLES, BOOKS AND PAMPHLETS PUBLISHED TO 1900

Abstract Report and Statistical Sketch of the Magdalen Asylum, High Park, Drumcondra, June 1881 (Dublin, 1881).
Address from the Dublin Ladies' Association, Auxiliary to the Hibernian Church Missionary Society, to the Female Friends of the Missions (n.p., n.d. c.1820).
Alcorn, James G., 'Discharged prisoners' aid societies', *Journal of the Statistical and Social Inquiry Society of Ireland*, 8 (December 1881).
An Appeal to the Public from the Committee of the Intended New Dublin Female Penitentiary (Dublin, 1812).
Anon., *An Address to the Ladies forming the Committee of the Intended New Dublin Female Penitentiary in Consequence of their Appeal to the Public* (Dublin, 1813).
An Appeal to the Public on Behalf of the Ulster Female Penitentiary (Belfast, 1834).
Anderson, Rev. William, 'Workhouse hospitals in the west of Ireland', *Transactions of the National Association for the Promotion of Social Science* (1867).
Anon., *A Letter to the Public on an Important Subject* (Dublin, 1768).
Anon., *Rules and Regulations for the Asylum of Penitent Females* (Dublin, 1785).
Anon., *New Edition of the Tract which gave Rise to the Institution of the Lock Penitentiary with an Account of its Progress and Present Circumstances Earnestly Recommended to the Attention of the Humane and Affluent* (Dublin, 1805).
Anon., *Four Letters in Answer to an Address to the Committee of the Dublin Female Penitentiary* (Dublin, 1813).
Anon., *Address to Ladies of Bible Associations* (Dublin, 1825).
Anon., *The Life and Transactions of a Female Prostitute* (Belfast, c.1826).
Anon., *The Young Believer or Memoir of Eleanor D——* (London, 1852).
Anon., 'Convict systems – past and present: a review on prison reports etc. including annual report of the inspectors of government prisons in Ireland', *Irish Quarterly Review*, 4 (December 1854).

Anon., 'Women's work; a review of the Sisters of Charity', *Irish Quarterly Review*, 6 (December 1856).

Anon., 'Benevolent apprenticing society', *Irish Quarterly Review*, 8 (April 1858), appendix.

Anon., 'A glance at Irish charitable institutions', *Irish Quarterly Review*, 8 (January 1859).

Anon., 'Begin at the beginning', *Irish Quarterly Review*, 8 (January 1859).

Anon., 'Quarterly review of the progress of reformatory and ragged schools, and of the improvement of prison discipline', *Irish Quarterly Review*, 8 (January 1859).

Anon., 'St Joseph's Industrial Institute with special reference to its intern class of workhouse orphans', *Irish Quarterly Review*, 8 (January 1859).

Anon., 'Cork industrial ragged school', *Irish Quarterly Review*, 8 (October 1859).

Anon., 'St Joseph's industrial institute and the workhouse orphans', *Irish Quarterly Review*, 8 (January 1859).

Anon., 'Protestant asylum for females discharged from the convict prisons', *Irish Quarterly Review*, 9 (January 1860).

Anon., 'Second report of the Order of Our Lady of Charity and Refuge', *Irish Quarterly Review*, 9 (January 1860).

Anon., 'Convict systems in England and Ireland', *Edinburgh Review*, 117 (January 1863).

Anon., 'Proposed improvements at Grangegorman penitentiary', *The Dublin Builder*, 5: 87 (August 1863).

Anon., 'Grangegorman new female prison', *The Dublin Builder*, 6 (August 1864).

Anon., 'Female convicts', *Victoria Magazine* (March 1864).

Anon., 'The service of the poor', *Fraser's Magazine* (September 1871).

Anon., 'Sisters and sisterhoods', *Fraser's Magazine* (November 1871).

Anon., 'Women and work', *Dublin University Magazine*, 80 (December 1872).

Anon., 'Rounds of visits', *The Irish Monthly*, 3 (1875).

Anon., *Records of the Connemara Orphan's Nursery* (Glasgow, 1877).

Anon., *Immoral Legislation: A Few Facts for the Irish Clergy* (Dublin, 1880).

Anon., 'Save the Child' (reprinted from the *Freeman's Journal* of 1 March 1883).

Anon., 'Two Dublin hospitals – St Vincent's and St Joseph's', *The Irish Monthly*, 12 (1884).

Anon., 'The association for visiting hospitals', *The Irish Monthly*, 15 (1887).

Anon., 'Woman's mission', *The Irish Monthly*, 21 (September 1893).

Anon., 'The Magdalens of High Park', *The Irish Rosary*, 1 (1897).

Anon., *The Domestic Mission to the Poor of Belfast* (n.p., n.d.).

Anon., *The Order of Our Lady of Charity of Refuge* (n.p., n.d.).

Anon., *A Century of Proselytism* (reprinted from the *National Review*, n.d.).

Archer, Hannah, *To the Rescue* (London, 1869).

Atkinson, Sarah, *Mary Aikenhead: Her Life, Her Work and Her Friends* (Dublin, 1879).

Bardin, Rev. Charles, *A Sermon Preached in St Peter's Church, Dublin in Aid of the Shelter for Females Discharged from Prison . . . January 4th 1824* (Dublin, 1824).

Barrett, Rosa M., *Guide to Dublin Charities* (Dublin, 1884).

Foreign Legislation on Behalf of Destitute and Neglected Children: a paper read before the Statistical and Social Inquiry Society of Ireland (Dublin, 1896).

The Rescue of the Young (n.p., 1899).

Ellice Hopkins: A Memoir (London, 1908).

Barry, K.M., *Catherine McAuley and the Sisters of Mercy* (Dublin, 1894).

Bellingham, Henry, *Protestant Missions in Ireland* (London, 1880).

Belloc, Bessie R., 'My acquaintance with Ireland and Mrs Atkinson', *The Irish Monthly*, 23 (1895).

Bishop, M.C., 'The K— Dorcas society', *The Irish Monthly*, 7 (1879).

Blackburn, Helen, *A Handy Book of Reference for Irishwomen* (London, 1888).

Women's Suffrage: A Record of the Women's Suffrage Movement in the British Isles, with Biographical Sketches of Miss Becker (London, 1902).

Bradshaw, Myrrha (ed.), *Open Doors for Irishwomen* (Dublin, 1907).

Brady, Chayne, *History of the Hospital for Incurables* (Dublin, 1865).

Burke, Rev. Thomas, *Ireland's Vindication: Refutation of Froude and Other Lectures, Historical and Religious* (London, n.d.).

Byers, M., 'Reforming the habitual drunkard', *New Ireland Review*, 13 (1900).

Cappe, Catherine, *Extracts from Observations on Charity Schools and Other Subjects Connected with the Views of the Ladies' Committee* (Dublin, 1807).

Carpenter, Mary, *Reformatory Prison Discipline as Developed by the Rt. Hon. Sir Walter Crofton in the Irish Convict Prisons* (London, 1872).

'On the treatment of female convicts', *Transactions of the National Association for the Promotion of Social Science* (1863).

Our Convicts, 2 vols. (London, 1864).

Charity Organisation Committee of the Statistical and Social Inquiry Society of Ireland as to the Houseless Poor (Dublin, 1876).

Charlotte Elizabeth, *Letters from Ireland* (London, 1837).

Clay, Walter Lowe, *The Prison Chaplain, a Memoir of the Rev. John Clay* (London, 1861).

Coleridge, Henry J., *The Life of Mother Frances Mary Teresa Ball* (Dublin, 1881).

Crofton, Sir Walter, 'Female convicts, and our efforts to amend them', *Transactions of the National Association for the Promotion of Social Science* (1866).

Dallas, Rev. Alexander, *The Story of the Irish Church Missions*, part 1 (London, n.d.); part 2 (London, 1875).

Daly, E.D., 'Our industrial and reformatory school systems in relation to the poor', *Journal of the Statistical and Social Inquiry Society of Ireland*, 9 (1896).

'Neglected children and neglectful parents', *Journal of the Statistical and Social Inquiry Society of Ireland*, 10 (February, 1898).

Davies, Sarah, *"Them Also": The Story of the Dublin Mission* (London, 1846).
Wanderers Brought Home: The Story of the Ragged Boys' Home (London, 1871).
St Patrick's Armour: The Story of the Coombe Ragged School (Dublin, 1880).
Other Cities Also: The Story of Mission Work in Dublin (Dublin, 1881).

Dickens, Charles, 'Stoning the desolate', *All the Year Round* (London, 1864).

Dock, Lavinia, *A History of Nursing*, 4 vols. (London, 1912).

Dowling, Jeremiah, *The Irish Poor Laws and Poor Houses* (Dublin, 1872).

Dublin International Exhibition of Arts and Manufactures, 1865 (Dublin, 1865).

Dublin Exhibition of Arts, Industries and Manufactures, 1872 (Dublin, 1872).

Dyer, Charles, *A Lecture on the State of Some of the Charities of Belfast* (Belfast, 1860).

Eccles-O'Connor, Charlotte, 'The girls of today and their education', *The Irish Monthly*, 25 (1897).
'A plea for the modern woman', *The Irish Monthly*, 32 (May 1904).

Edgar, John, *The Women of the West: Ireland Helped to Help Herself* (Belfast, 1849).

Extract from a Letter by Lord Monteagle, dated the 20th February, 1898, to the Most Rev. Dr Clancy, Bishop of Elphin (Dublin?, 1898).

Forbes, John, *Memorandums Made in Ireland in the Autumn of 1852*, 2 vols. (London, 1853).

Francis, M.E., *Miss Erin* (London, 1898).

Frazer, Catherine, 'The origin and progress of "The British Ladies' Society for Promoting the Reformation of Female Prisoners", established by Mrs. Fry in 1821', *Transactions of the National Association for the Promotion of Social Science* (1862).

Fry, Elizabeth and Gurney, J.J., *Report Addressed to the Marquess Wellesley, Lord Lieutenant of Ireland, by E.F. and J.J.G. Respecting their Late Visit to that Country* (London, 1827).

Gibson, Edward, 'Employment of women in Ireland', *Journal of the Statistical and Social Inquiry Society of Ireland* (April 1862).

Glynn, J.A., 'Irish convent industries', *New Ireland Review*, 1 (1894).

Great Industrial Exhibition, Official Catalogue, 1853 (Dublin, 1853).

Greenwood, James, *The Wren of the Curragh* (London, 1867).
The Seven Curses of London (London, 1869).

Gregg, Rev. John, *Women: A Lecture Delivered by the Rev. John Gregg, 28th February 1856* (Dublin, 1856).

Hall, Mr and Mrs S.C., *Ireland: Its Scenery and Character*, 3 vols. (London, 1841–43).

Hancock, W.N., 'The workhouse as a mode of relief for widows and orphans', *Journal of the Dublin Statistical Society* (April 1855).
'On the statistics of crime arising from or connected with drunkenness', *Statistical and Social Inquiry Society of Ireland Journal*, 7 (July 1878).

Harvey, Edmund, *The Position of Irishwomen in Local Government* (London, 1895).

Haslam, T.J., *A Few Words on Prostitution and the Contagious Diseases Acts* (Dublin, 1870).

Higgin, Rev. William, *A Sermon Preached . . . in Aid of the Shelter for Females Discharged from Prison* (Dublin, 1825).

Hill, Berkeley, 'Illustrations of the working of the Contagious Diseases Acts', *British Medical Journal* (December 1867).

Hill, Octavia, 'A few words to fresh workers', *The Nineteenth Century*, 26 (September 1889).

'Trained workers for the poor', *The Nineteenth Century*, 33 (January 1893).

Hime, M.C., *The Moral Utility of a Lock Hospital* (Dublin, 1872).

Letters Received on His Essay on Morality (Dublin, 1877).

Hinds, Rev. Samuel, *A Sermon Preached . . . on Behalf of the Parochial Visitors Society* (Dublin, 1852).

Hinks, Rev. Thomas D., *Short Account of the Different Charitable Institutions of the City of Cork* (Cork?, 1802).

Holtzendorff-Vietmansdorf, Franz Von, *The Irish Convict System* (Dublin, 1860).

Reflections and Observations on the Present System of the Irish Convict System (Dublin, 1863).

Hutch, William, *Nano Nagle: Her Life and Labour* (Dublin, 1875).

Mrs. Ball (Dublin, 1879).

Irish Homestead Special: Some Irish Industries (Dublin, 1897).

Jellicoe, Anne, 'A visit to the female convict prison at Mountjoy, Dublin', *Transactions of the National Association for the Promotion of Social Science* (1862).

Kirby, Rev. Bernard, *General House of Refuge for Unprotected Females* (Dublin, 1843).

Knott, Mary J., *Two Months at Kilkee* (Dublin, 1836).

Knox, Kathleen S. 'A visit to an industrial school', *The Irish Monthly*, 22 (1894).

Lady, A, 'About visiting the poor', *The Irish Monthly*, 6 (1878).

Lewis, Samuel, *Topographical Dictionary of Ireland*, 2 vols. (London, 1839).

Logan, William, *The Great Social Evil: Its Causes, Extent, Results and Remedies* (London, 1871).

Lowndes, Fredrick W., *Lock Hospitals and Lock Wards in General Hospitals* (London, 1882).

Magee, Rev. Hamilton, *Fifty Years in 'The Irish Mission'* (Belfast, n.d.).

Martin, Mrs Charles, 'St Martha's home', *The Irish Monthly*, 10 (1882).

Martineau, Harriet, *Ireland: A Tale* (London, 1832).

'Convict systems in England and Ireland', *Edinburgh Review*, 117 (1863).

'Life in the criminal class', *Edinburgh Review*, 122 (1865).

Mason, W.S., *A Statistical Account or Parochial Survey of Ireland*, 3 vols. (Dublin, 1814, 1816, 1819).

Mathieson, G.F.G., *Journal of a Tour in Ireland in 1835* (London, 1836).

Member of the Order, *Leaves from the Annals of the Sisters of Mercy, vol.1, Ireland* (New York, 1881).

Member of the Order of Mercy, *The Life of Catherine McAuley* (New York, 1866).

Meredith, Mrs, *The Lace Makers, Sketches of Irish Character With Some Account of the Effort to Establish Lacemaking in Ireland* (London, 1865).

Monck Mason, H.J., *History of the Origin and Progress of the Irish Society* (Dublin, 1844).

Monteagle, Lord, 'The Irish workhouse system', *New Ireland Review*, 6 (November 1896).

Extract from a letter by Lord Monteagle . . . to the Most Rev. Dr Clancy, Bishop of Elphin (Dublin, 1898).

Mulhall, Marion, 'Boarding-out workhouse children', *New Ireland Review* (November 1896).

Mulholland, Rosa, *A Mother of Emigrants* (Dublin, n.d.).

Giannetta: A Girl's Story of Herself (London, 1889).

'Linen-weaving in Skibbereen', *The Irish Monthly*, 18 (1890).

M[ulholland], R[osa], 'The founder of St Joseph's asylum, Dublin', *The Irish Monthly*, 25 (1897).

Murphy, Rev. Dominick, *Sketches of Irish Nunneries* (Dublin, 1865).

Murphy, J.N., *Terra Incognita or the Convents of the United Kingdom* (London, 1876).

Nicholson, Asenath, *Ireland's Welcome to the Stranger or Excursions Through Ireland in 1844 and 1845* (London, 1847).

Lights and Shades of Ireland (London, 1850).

Noel, Felicia, 'Why so many women cannot find work', *The Irish Monthly*, 32 (July 1904).

O'Brien, Rev., *Sermon Preached . . . on Behalf of the Female Penitent's Retreat . . . 15th October 1818* (Dublin, 1819).

Observations on the treatment of convicts in Ireland (London, 1862).

O'Connell, Mrs Morgan John, 'Poor law administration as it affects women and children in workhouses', *Journal of the Statistical and Social Inquiry Society of Ireland*, 8 (April 1880).

O'Connor, Mrs Charles, 'Our young work girls', *The Irish Monthly*, 7 (1879).

O'Hanlon, Rev. W.M., *Walks Among the Poor of Belfast and Suggestions for their Improvement* (Belfast, 1853).

O'Reilly, Rev. Bernard, *The Mirror of True Womanhood* (Dublin, n.d.).

Orsmby, Francis B., *Homes for Working Boys* (Dublin, 1878).

O'Shaughnessy, Mark, 'Some remarks on Mrs. Hannah Archer's scheme for befriending orphan girls', *Journal of the Statistical and Social Inquiry Society of Ireland*, 3 (1862).

Pim, W.H., 'On the importance of reformatory establishments for juvenile delinquents', *Journal of the Statistical and Social Inquiry Society of Ireland*, 1 (1854).

Report Showing the Foundation and Progress of the Monastery and Order of Our Lady of Charity of Refuge (Dublin, 1857).

Rules and Regulations for the Asylum of Penitent Females with an account of receipts and disbursments, hymns, and an account of all the women who have been admitted (Dublin, 1785, 1796).

Russell, Rev. Matthew, 'St Brigid's orphans', *The Irish Monthly*, 4 (1876).

'In memory of a noble Irishwoman', *The Irish Monthly*, 21 (1893).

'Mrs Sarah Atkinson, a few notes in remembrance', *The Irish Monthly*, 21 (1893).

'A few more notes on Mrs Atkinson', *The Irish Monthly*, 22 (1894).

'Mrs Ellen Woodlock, an admirable Irishwoman of the last century', *The Irish Monthly*, 36 (1908).

Secretaries of the Belfast Ladies' Committee, *To the Members of the Belfast Committee for the Repeal of the Contagious Diseases Acts* (Belfast, 1878).

Shaw, Edith M., 'How poor ladies might live. An answer from the workhouse', *Nineteenth Century*, 41 (April 1897).

Sherlock, Fredrick, *Ann Jane Carlile: A Temperance Pioneer* (London, 1897).

Sister of Mercy, *The Life of Reverend Mother Catherine McAuley* (Dublin, 1864).

Smedley, Menella, 'Comparison between boarding-out and pauper schools', *Journal of the Statistical and Social Inquiry Society of Ireland*, 8 (April 1880).

Stephens, Laura, 'An Irish workhouse', *New Ireland Review*, 13 (May 1900).

Taylor, Fanny, *Irish Homes and Irish Hearts* (London, 1867).

Timpson, Rev. Thomas, *Memoirs of Mrs. Elizabeth Fry* (London, 1849).

Tod, Isabella M.S., 'Advanced education for girls of the upper and middle classes', *Transactions of the National Association for the Promotion of Social Science* (1867).

'On the principles on which plans for the curative treatment of habitual drunkards should be based', *Statistical and Social Inquiry Society of Ireland Journal*, 6:7 (May 1875).

'Boarding out of pauper children', *Statistical and Social Inquiry Society of Ireland Journal*, 7:5 (August 1878).

'The new crusade and woman's suffrage' (Reprinted from the *Pall Mall Gazette*, 1885).

'On the education of girls of the middle classes', in Dale Spender (ed.), *The Education Papers: Women's Quest for Equality in Britain 1850–1912* (London, 1987).

Trench, Maria, 'Sick nurses', *Macmillan's Magazine*, 34 (September 1876).

Tynan, Katharine, *A Nun, Her Friends and Her Order, Being a Life of Mother Mary Xaviera Fallon* (London, 1892).

Warburton, J.W., Whitelaw, J. and Walshe, R., *History of the City of Dublin*, 2 vols. (London, 1818).

Woodward, Rev. Henry, *A Charity Sermon Preached at the Magdalen Asylum on the 20th February 1825* (Dublin, 1825).

Wright, G.W., *An Historical Guide to the City of Dublin* (London, 1825).

Young, Margaret Ferrier (ed.), *The Letters of a Noble Woman* (London, 1908).

ARTICLES, BOOKS AND PAMPHLETS PUBLISHED SINCE 1900

Abel-Smith, Brian, *A History of the Nursing Profession* (London, 1960).

Aberdeen, Lord and Lady, *We Twa* (London, 1925).

More Cracks with We Twa (London, 1929).

Anon., *The Providence Home; Its Origin, Object and Work* (Dublin, 1900).

Anon., *Records and Memories of One Hundred Years, 1817–1917, Presentation Convent, Thurles* (Thurles, 1917).

Anon., *A Century of Service, 1834–1934, St Vincent's Hospital* (Dublin, 1934?).

Banner, Lois W., 'Religious benevolence as social control: a critique of and interpretation', *The Journal of American History*, 60 (1973).

Barkley, J.M., *The Sabbath School Society for Ireland, 1862–1962* (Belfast, 1961).

The Presbyterian Orphan Society, 1866–1966 (Belfast, 1966?).

Barnes, Jane, *Irish Industrial Schools 1868–1908* (Dublin, 1989).

Bauman, Sr M. Beata, *A Way of Mercy: Catherine McAuley's Contribution to Nursing* (n.p., 1958).

Bayley Butler, Beatrice 'Lady Arbella Denny, 1707–1792', *Dublin Historical Record*, 9 (1946).

Bayley Butler, Margery, *A Candle was Lit: The Life of Mother Mary Aikenhead* (Dublin, 1953).

Berg, Barbara J., *The Remembered Gate: Origins of American Feminism, The Woman and the City 1800–1860* (New York, 1981).

Bolster, Sr M. Angela, *Catherine McAuley in her Own Words* (Dublin, 1978).

Mercy in Cork, 1837–1987 (Cork, 1987).

(ed.), *The Correspondence of Catherine McAuley, 1827–1841* (Cork, 1989).

Catherine McAuley: Venerable for Mercy (Dublin, 1990).

Breathnach, Eibhlín, 'Women and higher education in Ireland, 1879–1914', *The Crane Bag*, 4:1 (1978).

Bristow, Edward J., *Vice and Vigilance: Purity Movements in Britain Since 1700* (Dublin, 1977).

Burke, Helen, *The People and the Poor Law in 19th Century Ireland* (Dublin, 1987).

Butler, Sr Katherine, *"We Help Them Home": The Story of Our Lady's Hospice, Harold's Cross, 1879–1979* (Dublin?, 1979?).

Centenary Celebration 1887–1987: Sisters of Our Lady of Charity, Sean McDermott St. (privately printed, 1987).

Centenary Celebrations 1861–1961, Poor Clare Convent, Kenmare (Tralee, 1961?).
Centenary Record 1857–1957. Sisters of Charity of St Vincent de Paul (Dublin, 1957).
Century of Service 1834–1934: St Vincent's Hospital (Dublin, 1934?).
Clayton, Helen R., *'To School Without Shoes', History of the Sunday School Society of Ireland* (Dublin, 1979).
Clear, Caitriona, *Nuns in Nineteenth-Century Ireland* (Dublin, 1987).
   'Walls within walls, nuns in ninteenth-century Ireland', in Chris Curtin et al. (eds.), *Gender in Irish Society* (Galway, 1987).
Concannon, Helena, *The Poor Clares in Ireland* (Dublin, 1929).
Crofton, D.H., *The Children of Edmondstown Park* (Portlaw, 1980).
Cullen, Mary, 'How radical was Irish feminism between 1860 and 1920' in P. Corish (ed.), *Radicals, Rebels and Establishments, Historical Studies* XV (Dublin, 1985).
Cullen-Owens, Rosemary, *Smashing Times: A History of the Irish Women's Suffrage Movement, 1889–1922* (Dublin, 1984).
   '"Votes for ladies, votes for women" organised labour and the suffrage movement, 1876–1922', *Saothar*, 9 (1983).
Curtayne, Alice, *The Servant of God: Mother Mary Aikenhead, 1787–1858* (Dublin, 1935).
Daly, Mary E., 'Women in the Irish workforce from preindustrial to modern times', *Saothar*, 7 (1981).
   A Social and Economic History of Ireland Since 1800 (Dublin, 1981).
   Dublin: The Deposed Capital, A Social and Economic History (Cork, 1984).
   The Famine in Ireland (Dublin, 1986).
Day, Susanne R., *Women in the New Ireland* (Cork, n.d.).
   'The crime called out-door relief', *The Irish Review* (April 1912).
   'The workhouse child', *The Irish Review* (June 1912).
Dock, Lavinia, *A History of Nursing*, 4 vols. (London, 1912).
Duff, Frank, *Miracles on Tap* (Dublin, 1981).
Egan, Rev. P.K., *The Parish of Ballinasloe* (Dublin,1960).
Epstein, Barbara Leslie, *The Politics of Domesticity: Women, Evangelism and Temperance in 19th Century America* (Wesleyan University Press, 1981).
Evans, Richard J., *The Feminists: Women's Emancipation Movements in Europe, America and Australasia, 1840–1920* (London, 1977).
Fagan, Patrick, *The Second City: Portrait of Dublin 1700–1760* (Dublin, 1986).
Fahey, Tony, 'Nuns in the Catholic church in Ireland in the nineteenth century' in Mary Cullen (ed.), *Girls Don't Do Honours: Irish Women in Education in the 19th and 20th Centuries* (Dublin,1987).
Ffrench-Eagar, Irene, *Margaret Anna Cusack: A Biography* (Dublin, 1979).
Finegan, John, *The Story of Monto: An Account of Dublin's Notorious Red Light District* (Cork, 1978).
Finnegan, Frances, *Poverty and Prostitution: A Study of Victorian Prostitutes in York* (Cambridge, 1979).
Fitzpatrick, David, *Irish Emigration 1801–1921* (Dundalk, 1984).

'Marriage in post-Famine Ireland' in Art Cosgrove (ed.), *Marriage in Ireland* (Dublin, 1985).

'The modernisation of the Irish female' in P. O'Flanagan et al. (eds.), *Rural Ireland: Modernisation and Change, 1600–1900* (Cork, 1987).

Freedman, Estelle B., *Their Sisters' Keepers: Women's Prison Reform in America, 1830–1930* (Ann Arbor, 1984).

Gahan, Robert, 'Old almshouses in Dublin', *Dublin Historical Record*, 5:1 (1942).

Gallagher, Eric, *At Points of Need: The Story of the Belfast Central Mission, 1889–1989* (Belfast, 1989).

Gibbons, Margaret, *Life of Margaret Aylward* (London, 1928).

Gildea, Rev. Denis, *Mother Mary Arsenius of Foxford* (Dublin, 1936).

Goodbody, Olive C., *One Hundred Years A-Growing, 1879–1979, The Cottage Home for Little Children* (Dublin, 1979).

Graham, B.J. and L.J. Proudfoot (eds.), *An Historical Geography of Ireland* (London, 1993).

Grant, Elizabeth, *The Highland Lady in Ireland: Elizabeth Grant of Rothiemurchus*, P. Kelly and Andrew Todd (eds.) (Edinburgh, 1991).

Grubb, Isabel, *Quakers in Ireland, 1654–1900* (London, 1927).

Hallack, Cecily, *The Servant of God: Mother Mary Aikenhead* (Dublin, 1937).

Harrison, Brian, 'Philanthropy and the Victorians', *Victorian Studies*, 9 (June, 1966).

Drink and the Victorians: The Temperance Question in England, 1815–72 (London, 1971).

'For church, Queen and family: the Girl's Friendly Society, 1874–1920', *Past and Present*, 61 (1973).

'State intervention and moral reform in nineteenth-century England' in Patricia Hollis (ed.), *Pressure from Without in Early Victorian England* (London, 1974).

Harrison, Richard S., *Irish Anti-War Movements, 1824–1974* (Dublin, 1986).

Cork City Quakers, 1655–1939: A Brief History (n.p., 1991).

'Irish Quaker perspectives on the anti-slavery movement', *Journal of the Friends Historical Society*, 56:2 (1991).

Heath-Stubbs, Mary, *Friendship's Highway* (London, 1935).

Hempton, David and Myrtle Hill, *Evangelical Protestantism in Ulster Society, 1740–1890* (London, 1992).

Hewitt, Nancy A., *Women's Activism and Social Change: Rochester, New York, 1822–1872* (Ithaca, 1984).

Holcombe, Lee, *Wives and Property: Reform of the Married Women's Property Law in Nineteenth Century England* (Oxford, 1983).

Hughes, A.E., *Lift Up a Standard: One Hundred Years With the Irish Church Missions* (London, 1948).

Jeffreys, Sheila (ed.), *The Sexuality Debates* (London, 1987).

Jordan, Alison, *Margaret Byers* (Belfast, 1990?).

Who Cares? Charity in Victorian and Edwardian Belfast (Belfast, 1992).

Kerr, Donal A., *Peel, Priests and Politics* (Oxford, 1982).

Larmour, Paul, 'The Donegal industrial fund and its cottage industries', *Irish Arts Review Yearbook, 1990–1991* (Dun Laoghaire, 1990).

Lee, Joseph, 'Women and the church since the Famine' in M. MacCurtain and D. O'Corrain (eds.), *Women in Irish Society: The Historical Dimension* (Dublin, 1978).

Lennon, Sr M. Isidore, *Mother Catherine McAuley, A Great Social Worker* (n.p., 1954).

Lindsay, Deirdre, *Dublin's Oldest Charity* (Dublin 1990).

Loreto Sister, A, *Joyful Mother of Children: Mother Frances Mary Teresa Ball* (Dublin, 1961).

Lovibond, M.F., 'Women and hygiene in modern life', *New Ireland Review*, 21 (1904).

Luddy, Maria, 'Women and charitable organisations in nineteenth-century Ireland', *Women's Studies International Forum* 11:4 (1988).
  'An outcast community: the wrens of the Curragh', *Women's History Review*, 1:3 (1992).
  'Presentation convents in county Tipperary, 1806–1900', *Tipperary Historical Journal* (1992).

Luddy, Maria and Cliona Murphy (eds.), *Women Surviving: Studies in Irishwomen's History in the 19th and 20th Centuries* (Dublin, 1990).

Lyons, J.B., *The Quality of Mercer's: the Story of Mercer's Hospital 1734–1991* (Dublin, 1991).

McCarthy, Michael J.F., *Priests and People in Ireland* (London, 1912).

McConville, Sean, *A History of English Prison Administration* (London, 1981).

McCrone, Kathleen, 'Feminism and philanthropy in Victorian England: the case of Lousia Twining', *Canadian Historical Association, Historical Papers* (1976).

MacCurtain, Margaret, 'Towards an appraisal of the religious image of women', *The Crane Bag*, 4:1 (1980).

McFarlan, D.M., *Lift Thy Banner: Church of Ireland Scenes 1870–1900* (Dundalk, 1990).

McHugh, Paul, *Prostitution and Victorian Social Reform* (London, 1980).

McNeill, Mary, *Vere Forster, 1819–1900: An Irish Benefactor* (Plymouth, 1971).
  The Life and Times of Mary Ann McCracken, 1770–1866 (Belfast, 1988).

MacSweeney, P.H. (ed.), *Letters of Mary Aikenhead* (Dublin, 1914).

Malcolm, Elizabeth, *'Ireland Sober, Ireland Free' Drink and Temperance in Nineteenth-Century Ireland* (Dublin, 1986).

Marnane, D.G., *Land and Violence: A History of West Tipperary from 1660* (Tipperary, 1985).

Member of the Congregation, *The Life and Work of Mary Aikenhead* (Dublin, 1925).

Murphy, Cliona, *The Women's Suffrage Movement and Irish Society in the Early Twentieth Century* (Hemel Hempstead, 1989).

Murray, S.W., *The City Mission Story* (Belfast, 1977).

Neumann, Sr M. Ignatia (ed.), *Letters of Catherine McAuley* (n.p., 1965).

O'Brien, Joseph V., *'Dear Dirty Dublin': A City in Distress, 1899–1916* (London, 1982).

O'Cleirigh, Nellie, 'Lady Aberdeen and the Irish connection', *Dublin Historical Record*, 39 (December 1985–September 1986).

Carrickmacross Lace (Dublin, 1985).

'Limerick lace', *Irish Arts Review Yearbook* (Dublin, 1988).

O'Connor, Anne V., 'Influences affecting girls' secondary education in Ireland, 1860–1910', *Archivium Hibernicum*, 41 (1986).

'The revolution in girls' secondary education in Ireland, 1860–1910' in Mary Cullen (ed.), *Girls Don't Do Honours: Irish Women in Education in the 19th and 20th Centuries* (Dublin, 1987).

Ó Gráda, Cormac, *The Great Irish Famine* (London, 1989).

O'Malley, Mary Pat, *Lios an Uisce: The History of a House and its Occupants from 1753 to the Present Day* (privately published, 1981).

O'Neill, Marie, 'The Dublin Women's Suffrage Society and its successors', *Dublin Historical Record*, 38 (December 1984– September 1985).

O'Neill, T.P., 'Clare and Irish poverty', *Studia Hibernica*, 14 (1974).

Order of Our Lady of Charity of Refuge 1853–1953: A Centenary Record of High Park Convent, Drumcondra, Dublin (Dublin, 1953).

Pauline, Sr Mary, *God Wills It! The Centenary Story of the Sisters of St Louis* (Dublin, 1959).

Pope, Barbara Corrado, 'Angels in the devil's workshop: leisured and charitable women in nineteenth-century England and France' in R. Bridennthal and C. Koonz (eds.), *Becoming Visible: Women in European History* (Boston, 1977).

Problems of a Growing City: Belfast 1780–1870 (Belfast, 1973).

Prochaska, F.K., 'Women in English philanthropy, 1790–1830', *International Review of Social History*, 19 (1974).

Women and Philanthropy in Nineteenth-Century England (Oxford, 1980).

Reed, Sir Andrew, *The Irish Constable's Guide* (4th edn, Dublin, 1901).

The Children's Charter (Dublin, 1908).

Rendall, Jane, *The Origins of Modern Feminism: Women in Britain, France and the United States, 1780–1860* (London, 1985).

Robins, Joseph, *The Lost Children: A Study of Charity Children in Ireland, 1700–1900* (Dublin, 1980).

Rules of the Religious Sisters of Charity (Dublin, 1941).

Rules and Constitutions of the Congregation of the Sisters of Charity (Rome, 1912).

Ryan, Mary P., 'The power of women's networks' in J.L. Newton et al. (eds.), *Sex and Class in Women's History* (London, 1985).

Savage, Roland Burke, *A Valiant Dublin Woman, The Story of George's Hill, 1766–1940* (Dublin, 1940).

Catherine McAuley, The First Sister of Mercy (Dublin, 1949).

Schupf, Harriet Warm, 'Single women and social reform in mid-nineteenth century England: the case of Mary Carpenter', *Victorian Studies*, 17 (March 1974).

Sibbett, R.M., *The Revival in Ulster* (Belfast, 1909).

For Christ and Crown: The Story of the Belfast Mission (Belfast, 1926).

Smyly, Vivienne, *The Early History of Mrs. Smyly's Homes and Schools* (privately printed, 1976).

Smyth, J.P. (ed.), *Social Service Handbook* (Dublin, 1901).

Steele, Francesca M., *The Convents of Great Britain* (London, 1902).

Summers, Anne, 'A home from home – women's philanthropic work in the nineteenth century' in Sandra Burman (ed.), *Fit Work for Women* (London, 1979).

Townend, Kathleen, *Some Memories of Mrs. Townsend* (London, 1923).

Tynan O'Mahony, Nora, *Una's Enterprise* (Dublin, 1907).

Vaughan, W.E., and Fitzpatrick, A.J. (eds.), *Irish Historical Statistics: Population, 1821–1971* (Dublin, 1978).

Vicinus, Martha, *Independent Women: Work and Community for Single Women, 1850–1920* (London, 1985).

Vicinus, Martha (ed.), *Suffer and Be Still: Women in the Victorian Age* (London, 1973).

A Widening Sphere: Changing Roles of Victorian Women (London, 1977).

Walkowitz, Judith R., *Prostitution and Victorian Society: Women, Class and the State* (Cambridge, 1980).

'Male vice and female virtue; feminism and the politics of prostitution in nineteenth-century Britain', in Ann Snitow et al. (eds.), *Desire: The Politics of Sexuality* (London, 1984).

Walkowitz, Judith R. and D.J. Walkowitz, 'We are not beasts of the field: prostitution and the poor in Plymouth and Southampton under the Contagious Diseases Acts' in M.S. Hartman and Lois Banner (eds.), *Clio's Consciousness Raised: New Perspectives on the History of Women* (New York, 1974).

Walsh, T.J., *Nano Nagle and the Presentation Sisters* (Dublin, 1959).

Ward, Margaret, '"Suffrage first above all else!" an account of the Irish suffrage movement', *Feminist Review*, 10 (February 1982).

Unmanageable Revolutionaries: Women and Irish Nationalism (Dingle, 1983).

'The Ladies' Land League', *Irish History Workshop*, 1 (1981).

Widdess, J.D.H., *The Magdalen Asylum, Leeson Street, 1766–1966* (Dublin, 1966).

The Charitable Infirmary, Jervis Street, Dublin 1718–1968 (Dublin, 1968).

Williams, G.D. (ed.), *Dublin Charities, A Handbook* (Dublin, 1902).

Woodnutt, Mrs K., 'Sarah Atkinson as a social worker', *Dublin Historical Record*, 21:4 (1967).

Young, Margaret Ferrier, *The Letters of a Noblewoman* (London, 1908).

Zedner, Lucia, *Women, Crime and Custody in Victorian England* (Oxford, 1991).

UNPUBLISHED THESES AND PAPERS

Breathnach, Eibhlín, 'A history of the movement for women's higher education in Dublin, 1860–1912' (MA, University College Dublin, 1981).

Butler, Sr Katherine, 'Rosa Solomons', unpublished typescript.

Clayton, Helen Ruth, 'Societies formed to educate the poor in Ireland in the late 18th and early 19th centuries' (M.Litt., Trinity College Dublin, 1981).

Gabriel, Sr, 'History of the Good Shepherd Convents in Ireland', unpublished typescript.

Heard, Ruth, 'Public works in Ireland, 1800–1831' (M.Litt., Trinity College Dublin, 1977).

Hearn, Mona, 'Domestic servants in Dublin, 1880–1920' (Ph.D., Trinity College Dublin, 1985).

Jordan, Alison, 'Voluntary societies in Victorian and Edwardian Belfast' (Ph.D., Queen's University Belfast, 1989).

Kelly, Sr Patricia, 'From workhouse to hospital: the role of the workhouse in medical relief to 1921' (MA, University College Galway, 1972). .

Lohan, Rena, 'The treatment of women sentenced to transportation and penal servitude, 1790–1898' (M.Litt., Trinity College Dublin, 1989).

Luddy, Maria, 'Women and philanthropy in nineteenth-century Ireland' (Ph.D., University College Cork, 1989).

O'Neill, T. P., 'The state, poverty and distress in Ireland, 1815–1845' (Ph.D., University College Dublin, 1971).

O'Shea, Sr Marian, 'Social work with prostitutes from a religious sister's perspective', unpublished typescript.

Prunty, Jacinta, 'Margaret Louisa Aylward, 1810–1889', unpublished typescript.

Slator, P.M., 'The Brabazon Trust', unpublished typescript.

Wolfe, William, 'Short note on the Methodist Widows' Home', typescript, private communication.

Various authors, 'Mary Aikenhead: her faith flowering in works', printed for private circulation by the Sisters of Charity, Milltown, Dublin.

Index